SUCCESSFUL SPORT
FUND-RAISING

WILLIAM F. STIER, JR.
State University of New York, Brockport

WCB Brown &
Benchmark
PUBLISHERS

Madison, Wisconsin•Dubuque, Iowa•Indianapolis, Indiana
Melbourne, Australia•Oxford, England

To my wife, Veronica
and our five children—
Mark
Missy
Michael
Patrick
Will III
for loving encouragement
and unselfish support.

Book Team
Executive Editor *Ed Bartell*
Editor *Chris Rogers*
Developmental Editor *Scott Spoolman*
Production Editor *Diane Clemens*
Photo Editor *Shirley Lanners*
Visuals/Design Developmental Consultant *Marilyn A. Phelps*
Visuals/Design Freelance Specialist *Mary L. Christianson*
Publishing Service Specialist *Sherry Padden*
Marketing Manager *Pamela S. Cooper*
Advertising Manager *Jodi Rymer*

**Brown &
Benchmark**
A Division of Wm. C. Brown Communications, Inc.

Executive Vice President/General Manager *Thomas E. Doran*
Vice President/Editor in Chief *Edgar J. Laube*
Vice President/Sales and Marketing *Eric Ziegler*
Director of Production *Vickie Putman Caughron*
Director of Custom and Electronic Publishing *Chris Rogers*

Wm. C. Brown Communications, Inc.

President and Chief Executive Officer *G. Franklin Lewis*
Corporate Senior Vice President and Chief Financial Officer *Robert Chesterman*
Corporate Senior Vice President and President of Manufacturing *Roger Meyer*

Cover design and illustration by Kim Schreacke, Rokusek Design

Interior design by Rokusek Design

A Times Mirror Company

Library of Congress Catalog Card Number: 92–85121

ISBN 0-697–17196–5

Printed in the United States of America by Wm. C. Brown Communications, Inc.,
2460 Kerper Boulevard, Dubuque, IA 52001

10 9 8 7 6 5 4 3

Contents

3
Contributors to the Athletic Program, 30

4
Staffing—Personnel and Working with Others, 48

5
Publicity and Public Relations—Working with the Media, 74

6
Public Relations and Promotional Activities Working with Various Constituencies, 94

7
Promotional Activities and Fund-Raising Techniques—The Art and Science of Raising Money, 108

8
Pragmatic Approaches to the Raising of Resources, 132

9
Techniques and Tactics of Fund-Raising, 156

10
Special Fund-Raising Projects, Promotional Tactics, and Ideas, 194

11
Putting Ideas and Concepts to Work in the Real World — Specific Fund-Raising Techniques, 224

Appendices, 237

Acknowledgments

This book is dedicated to my wife, Veronica, and our five children—Mark, Missy, Michael, Patrick, and Will III—who not only put up with me during the 24 months that it took to prepare the manuscript but provided real encouragement during the long, late hours spent researching and compiling the materials for this publication. For their loving encouragement and unselfish support this book is dedicated.

Thanks is also given to countless coaches and athletic administrators who have been so kind in sharing their ideas and success stories of raising money for sport programs at all levels. Without their significant help and willing assistance this book could not have been possible.

I am also grateful to these reviewers for their efforts:

Richard L. Irwin
Dept. of Physical Education
Kent State University
Kent, OH 44242

Robert D. McBee
Dept. of Intercollegiate Athletics
Robert Morris College
Narrows Run Road
Coraopolis, PA 15108-1189

Tom H. Regan
Dept. of Sports Administration
Carolina Coliseum, Rm 2012C
University of South Carolina
Columbia, SC 29208

Special appreciation is also expressed to Ms. Gale Player who served as my secretary during my tenure as Athletic Director at the State University of New York and who not only played a key role in proofing the early versions of the manuscript but also offered many significant suggestions for inclusion within the text.

SUCCESSFUL SPORT
FUND-RAISING

Kellogg's paid $32,500 to Oregon State University for the use of former player and All American Gary Payton. Payton was one of twelve players featured on the trading card in Kellogg's Raisin Bran. The man wearing the Oregon State University sweater is athletic director Dutch Baughman. (Courtesy of Oregon State University Sports Information Office/photo by Mike Shields)

Introduction to Successful Sport Fund-Raising

1

The goal of this book is to provide the reader with insight into the ways and means by which greater support (financial and otherwise) may be obtained and sustained for the athletic arena, at any level. However, one does not deal exclusively with the topic of FUND-RAISING without also examining, to some extent, other aspects of sport organization, management, and administration.

Thus, the topics of *Fund-raising* as well as *Promotions* and *Public Relations* will be examined from the perspectives of the coach *and* the athletic administrator or manager, as well as members of booster organizations. The emphasis, however, will be on (1) strategies, (2) planning methods and (3) the implementation techniques associated with FUND-RAISING efforts. For without adequate funding of one's athletic program, whatever its intrinsic value, the program is doomed to failure.

This publication will enable the reader to understand, interpret, and master the general fund-raising PRINCIPLES, as well as promotional GUIDELINES, which are applicable to almost any sports situation in which one might find oneself. Such PRINCIPLES are provided strategically throughout this publication in an effort to enhance and reinforce the basic tenets of fund-raising as applied to sports. These principles have been developed and refined over a period of 20+ years by the author in his role as athletic director on the junior high, high school, and collegiate levels. Additionally, in chapter 11, specific real-life examples of successful fund-raising tactics and strategies are provided.

With a thorough understanding and appreciation of fundamental fund-raising principles, guidelines, and examples, the basis of a realistic and significant body of knowledge in the area of sport fund-raising can be formulated. This body of knowledge will, in turn, facilitate (1) the development of a minimum level of competency and technical skills, and (2) the decision making process itself. Possession of appropriate knowledge and the ability to make correct and timely decisions and interpretations are absolutely necessary in sport promotion, public relations, and fund-raising. By observing these fundamental principles of fund-raising, readers should be able, in a variety of situations, to make appropriate decisions and judgments in the real world of sport fund-raising, out there on the so-called "firing line."

Figure 1.1 Relationships:
Fund-raising, promotion,
and public relations.

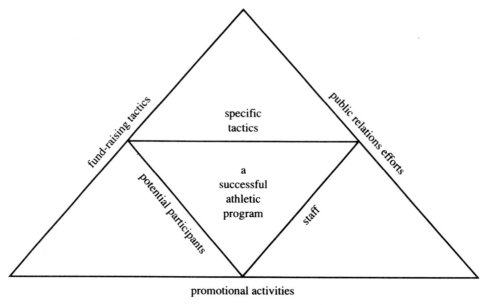

Relationships between Fund-Raising, Promotions, and Public Relations

Individuals who are involved with competitive athletics, whether at the youth sport, scholastic, collegiate, or professional levels, find themselves involved, at least to some degree, with what is commonly referred to as *fund-raising, promotions, and public relations*. This is true whether or not one is an athlete, a coach, or one associated with the managerial or administrative aspect of sport.

Fund-raising **tactics,** promotional **activities,** and public relations **efforts** are closely intertwined and all have a direct impact upon the success or failure of a sport program. As such, there needs to be successful coordination and integration of all three areas within the total administrative structure of the entity, be it a school, a college, a university, a recreational organization, a sports program within industry or business, a youth sports program, or a semiprofessional or professional team. One also needs to think in terms of staff, specific tactics and the potential participants when contemplating or planning a fund-raising, promotional, or public relations effort. The relationships between these areas are visually depicted by figure 1.1.

Whenever fund-raising strategies in sports are implemented, those involved in the athletic program, by definition, MUST be heavily involved with the public relations aspect of sports *and* in promotional activities. Fund-raising *cannot* be undertaken without involving public relations and the promotion of the so-called "product"—the sports activities, the participants, and the staff.

However, promotional activities can be undertaken without attempting to raise monies. Similarly, public relations may involve activities that have nothing to do with the raising of funds. *It is the area of generation of financial support, that is,*

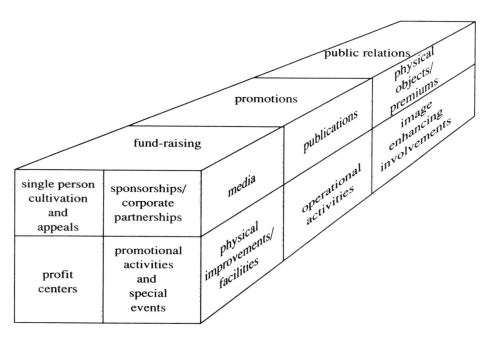

Figure 1.2 Promotional, public relations activities, and fund-raising tactics.

fund-raising, which by definition involves both promotional activities and public relations. Similarly, the ART and SCIENCE of fund-raising serves as the foundation of many sports programs and is the focal point of this publication.

Promotional, Public Relations, and Fund-Raising Perspectives of Sport

Figure 1.2 illustrates the interrelationships of the essential ingredients for generating funds, conducting promotional activities, and implementing a positive public relations effort. In terms of promoting the sports program, promotional and public relations activities may be classified under the following six categories, each of which will be addressed within this book.

1. *Involving* the media (radio, television, print)
2. *Creating* publications, photos, and printed materials for advertisement purposes (programs, schedule cards, posters, pens, displays, calendars, billboards, etc.)
3. *Instituting* physical improvements (facilities, equipment, supplies) and image enhancing efforts
4. *Utilizing* image enhancing activities and involvements (association with other organizations and/or projects that lend respectability)
5. *Implementing* operational and home event activities (policies, procedures, practices, and priorities)
6. *Selecting* of physical objects (premiums)—to distribute, sell, give, exchange, etc.

Figure 1.3 Components of a successful athletics program.

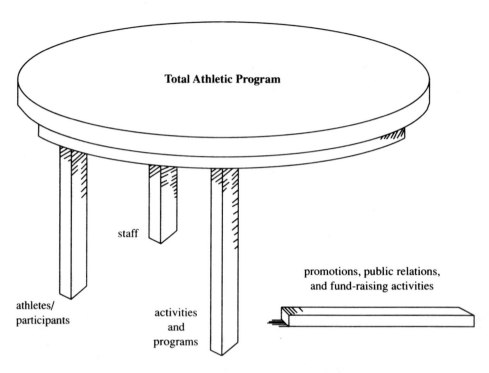

Similarly, efforts in raising money, as well as promoting aspects of sports, are arbitrarily classified under the following four categories and will, in turn, be topics for review as well.

1. *Single person cultivation and appeals*—seeking money, services and products; person to person, or door-to-door, or via telephone
2. *Sponsorships/corporate partnerships*
3. *Profit centers*—concessions, parking, store sales, tickets, clinics, camps, and sales of merchandise
4. *Use of promotional type activities and special events*—designed to raise money, increase attendance, improve image, and provide recognition for team members, coaches, boosters, and sponsors

Ingredients of Successful Athletic Programs

A successful athletic program, regardless of the level of its sophistication, is supported by four essential ingredients. Schematically, such a program might be likened to a table with four legs (fig. 1.3).

The tabletop represents the total success of the athletic program, supported as it is by four strong legs. The four legs, the essential supporting ingredients that form the foundation of the successful athletic program, are (1) the athletes; (2) the coaching and administrative staff; (3) the actual athletic programs, experiences and opportunities; and (4) the promotional, public relations, and fund-raising activities. If any of these supporting ingredients are absent or not at full strength, the tabletop begins to tip and may fall completely. The consequences can indeed be significant and far reaching. That is, the total athletic program suffers and fails to reach its actual potential.

Importance of Developing Competencies in Fund-Raising

Expertise within the realm of fund-raising, public relations, and promotional activities remains essential for the sustained and successful operation of any worthwhile athletic program (Sabock & Bortner, 1986). Since it is important for coaches, administrators, and boosters to develop such managerial skills, it behooves those involved in sport programs to make good-faith efforts to master a basic working knowledge and maintain at least a minimal level of competency in terms of fund-raising strategies, promotional activities, and public relations efforts.

The world of sports within the United States at the present time continues to be in a constant state of flux (Fox, 1990). As such, it becomes obvious that in terms of fund-raising, there exists a need to continue to learn and to be able to adapt to the changes and innovations taking place within this area of sport management. It is absolutely necessary for the coach, athletic administrator, and the athletic booster to maintain a posture of openness and of receptivity, especially when it comes to self-improvement and grasping the body of knowledge supporting the generation of fiscal support for sports.

This acquisition of knowledge, enrichment of ideas, and enhancement of skills may be realized through both formal and informal in-service education efforts, as well as from actual practical experience. Such in-service education activities might include attendance at formal clinics, conferences, and workshops, as well as the reading of professional literature—such as this publication.

The ultimate objective, insofar as fund-raising is concerned for the individual involved in a sports program, is to maintain a correct perspective, to develop an up-to-date knowledge base, and an awareness of tactics and strategies that may be utilized in:

1. The expansion of the financial support of sports programs
2. The promotion of sports activities themselves
3. The increase in public exposure of specific sports programs and the sponsoring organization

Keeping Things in Perspective

It is important for those involved in fund-raising to keep their efforts in the proper perspective. Too often it seems those in sports are enamored by the prospect of involvement with fund-raising activities. They perceive themselves, whether they are on the youth sport level, the secondary level, or the collegiate level, as being another Don Canham, former athletic director at the University of Michigan, who is known for being a leader in sport fund-raising and promotional activities. They see themselves raising BIG DOLLARS (millions, billions, if not trillions) for their own athletic programs. They are too frequently quixotical in nature with respect to fund-raising and promotion involvement for their sport program.

A fund-raiser needs to keep both feet on the ground. There is a constant danger of becoming infatuated with the "activities" themselves, with the supposed glamour

▬ Principle 1 ▬

Fund-raising is a means to an end, not an end in itself.

and excitement associated with such fund-raising and promotional activities. *Fund-raising is not an end in itself.* Such efforts are simply a means to an end, the gaining of the wherewithal with which to have a meaningful learning and satisfying experience for those participating in the sport program.

■ **Principle 2** ■

Take care of the home front before branching out.

A common fault of athletic staff members, both coaches and athletic directors, is the failure to take care of the so-called home front, that is, the primary responsibilities for which one is hired. The athletic director or coach should not spend so much time and effort on fund-raising activities and promotional efforts that other administrative or coaching responsibilities suffer. This is especially true in those situations in which fund-raising is not a high or official priority on the athletic director's or coach's list of job responsibilities.

Granted, on the NCAA Division I level, the direct involvement of both athletic directors and coaches in fund-raising is often expected and frequently required. However, in many high schools and small to medium-size colleges, the prime responsibility of the staff may not be fund-raising. There may be other tasks and responsibilities associated with the internal operation of the athletic program that are deemed to be of a higher priority by one's superiors. In the above scenario, the athletic administrators and coaches may be placing their respective positions in jeopardy if too much time and effort are devoted to fund-raising and promotional activities to the obvious detriment of the more essential duties associated with their positions. This is especially true for those duties assigned a higher priority in the minds of their superiors.

■ **Principle 3** ■

There are few things that are really new in fund-raising.

There really aren't many new things in the world of promotions and fund-raising—only adaptations. An athletic director was once complimented on the numerous "new" ideas he was instrumental in bringing to the athletic department since he had arrived a few years earlier from another university. The response to this statement was that "it isn't that I am doing anything *NEW,* it is just that I am doing things that are *new here* or *different here.*"

The point is that although fund-raising techniques, public relations activities, and promotional ideas or tactics may be new in a specific setting or circumstance, these same activities, tactics, techniques, and ideas have probably been implemented elsewhere, in some form, innumerable times. Frequently, the only things different are the circumstances in which the fund-raising and promotional activities take place and the actual people who are involved in the implementation *and* evaluation process.

It is important to determine what has previously been tried and accomplished—successfully as well as unsuccessfully—within one's own organization and community. It is equally important to examine what has been attempted elsewhere—everywhere and anywhere! The challenge is not to originate activities but to be creative in the implementation of those things that have produced results elsewhere (Canham, 1986).

There need be no embarrassment for attempting to adapt a fund-raising effort or idea, proven to be successful and productive elsewhere, to one's own specific situation or circumstances. In fact, it is often the sincerest form of flattery. The crux of the matter is simple. Will the fund-raising project or tactic be successful? The proof of the pudding, so to speak, is whether the end result is successful. Success itself is often determined by the circumstances in which one finds oneself.

The individual fund-raiser, whether relatively new to the exciting world of promotions and fund-raising or a tried-and-true veteran, can always learn from the successes and failures of others. Of course, you must be able to determine which fund-raising programs, activities, and projects are suitable and are appropriate to use in one's own project. This borrowing and adapting of strategies, ideas, and methods from others is a most productive method of examining what is feasible in one's own situation.

The ability to recognize reality is important. It is necessary to take stock of the particular situation in which one finds oneself and recognize where one's program sits within the pecking order of worthy causes. For example, there are inherent differences, in terms of what can be accomplished in youth sport programs, in high school programs, in small college programs, and in the so-called big-time university programs. A small liberal arts college cannot attempt to successfully emulate exactly the fund-raising activities of UCLA, the University of North Carolina, or Syracuse University with all of their resources and inherent advantages (image, history, alumni support, etc.). Similarly, a small, rural high school in Iowa cannot attempt to mimic exactly what a large secondary school, located in a large metropolitan city, such as New York City, attempts in terms of fund-raising and promotional activities.

This does not mean that there is not room for following general fund-raising principles. Time-proven and successful tactics and techniques used elsewhere can be adapted and adjusted to fit in with one's own situation. For example, there are various types of raffles, as well as golf outings, which have been successfully utilized through the years to generate various amounts of financial support for different types of athletic programs. The key to the successful implementation of these traditional fund-raising activities is the ability to ADAPT the actual activity (in this case the raffle or golf outing) to fit with the local circumstances and environment. *This adaptation is the key to the success.*

The ability to follow general fund-raising principles is one of the more important factors in determining the success or failure of any fund-raising effort. Similarly, the likelihood for success in generating monies can be enhanced by adapting the planning, implementing, and evaluating aspects of any fund-raising effort to be compatible with the sports organization's particular situation and circumstances.

In all that one does, but especially within the areas of promotional activities and fund-raising, one must remain an optimist. In the promotion of any sports activity and in the raising of financial support, one is in constant danger of rejection and failure. The difference between an *optimist* and a *pessimist* lies in how one views the circumstances that exist. Two people, an optimist and a pessimist, viewing a bottle with cola up to the halfway mark will respond differently. The pessimist taking the viewpoint that the bottle is half empty while the optimist finds the same bottle, with the same amount of cola, to be half full. It is all in the way things are viewed. For the promotional and fund-raising practitioner, being an optimist is a decided advantage (fig. 1.4).

Principle 4

Do not attempt to be something you are not.

Principle 5

Be the eternal optimist.

Figure 1.4 Optimist or pessimist.

Definitions

Although the terms **fund-raising, promotions,** and **public relations** are quite freely bantered about within athletic circles, there is often a lack of clear understanding of what is meant by each. Additionally, there are other terms to be understood which have a significant impact upon the successful management of the athletic program and its fund-raising and promotional efforts. These include:

Fund-Raising Activities. Fund-raising activities are those efforts aimed at generating additional financial support (money, services, and tangible goods) for a charitable or worthy cause. Generating such support is both a science and an art. It is a *science* in that there is a systematic application of generally accepted principles, guidelines, and knowledge that support these efforts.

Fund-raising can also be viewed as an *art* due to the positive results emanating from the *creative* application of these same principles, guidelines, and knowledge associated with the fund-raising efforts. This creative application involves adapting ideas to suit one's own particular circumstances.

Promotional Activities. Sport promotion involves activities associated with the marketing and selling of ideas, services, and products to the public for either purchase or acceptance. Promotional activities help create and reinforce opinions as well as motivate changes in behavior regarding the sports program and those involved with the program.

Sport promotion includes the associated activities of marketing, fund-raising, and merchandising. An essential ingredient for successful promotional activities in sports is adequate communication with publics, constituencies, and potential consumers.

Public Relations. The task of public relations is to gain support or a favorable impression from various constituencies (Bucher, 1987). Public relations are the sum product of on-going, multifaceted, never-ending activities in which an organization engages. It is these activities that may create awareness and a positive, favorable image in the eyes of target constituencies and publics toward specific personnel, a particular activity, an event, an organization, or a program. Public relations activities and promotional efforts are different and distinct in that the organizational activities or products in promotions are explicitly planned or stated, while in public relations they are not.

Publicity. As a segment of public relations, publicity has more immediacy in terms of objectives and goals through public relations (Mason and Paul, 1988). It has a specific, short-term message about a certain activity or event and has as its primary purpose to inform and create a general awareness of a particular program with segments of the community. The primary objective of publicity is to draw attention to a specific person, program, sport, institution, or function. It is important to note that the effectiveness of publicity tends to remain with effective and continuous public relations efforts.

Advertising. The communication to various segments of the public and various constituencies through the mass media, that is, the printed word, radio, and television, is what is commonly understood to be advertising. Advertising can be obtained on a paid basis or on a free basis.

Human Relations. Personal relationships between individuals can be thought of as human relations (Voltmer, Esslinger, McCurs, and Tillman, 1979). Human relations can be considered to be public relations on an individual basis and involves use of various methods to disseminate information. In addition, human relations can influence others in the direction of intelligent group action and support.

Personal Selling or Salesmanship. The art and science of convincing others, usually in a face-to-face setting, to accept a belief, an opinion, a product, or a service is what is called personal selling (Railey and Railey, 1988). The focus is centered on the needs (real or perceived) of the potential buyer or purchaser.

Public Opinion. How the sport program is viewed by various segments of the general public or various constituencies is deemed to be public opinion. Public opinion is an ever-changing phenomenon, and it may be significantly swayed by the magnitude and frequency of events as well as by the quality of happenings.

Opinions and Attitudes. An opinion can be thought of as an expression of an attitude. An attitude, on the other hand, is a tendency or inclination to react in a specific way to any given situation (Bronzan, 1986). Attitudes are the product of all conscious experiences such as family, religion, educational experiences, economic class, and social class. Attitudes can be the result of unconscious feelings and prejudices.

Attitudes and opinions form the foundation for actions by individuals and groups. This is why it is so important to instill appropriate attitudes and opinions among members of the general public. The desired end result is a specific action and such action depends, for the most part, on the possession of attitudes and the expression of opinions.

Marketing. More than promotion, marketing is the key to the entire process of securing and satisfying various constituencies by meeting their *needs* in a specific area. Marketing is all of the activity used in moving or promoting services, ideas, or goods from the producer to the consumer (Cutlip, Center, and Broom, 1985).

Marketing identifies needs and wants, helps marshall the organization's resources to produce desired products or services, and persuades potential customers to buy because its offerings will satisfy them. Intangible concepts and images as well as tangible products and benefits (tickets, clothing, etc.) may be marketed. In fact, anything is capable of being marketed to a potential consumer or constituency (Buell, 1984).

Market Segmentation. The use of marketing strategy to identify specific target populations, based upon knowledge of the populations, their characteristics, and background, is referred to as market segmentation (Horine, 1991). Specifically, it involves dividing the total market into several smaller, homogeneous subsets of people or markets, each differing in terms of individual needs and *characteristics*.

Marketing Mix. There are five essential ingredients that may be utilized in attempting to market any product or service (Railey and Railey, 1988; Yiannakis, 1989). These ingredients are commonly referred to as the five Ps and include:

1. the **product** or service identified
2. the **place** or niche for the product or service which needs to be identified
3. the **price** (reasonable) to be established within the marketplace
4. the **public(s)** which must be identified as potential consumers
5. the **promotional plan** or strategy to be identified and implemented

Constituencies. Constituencies are those individuals, groups, and organizations having some association or potential for some type of association with the athletic program. Additionally, constituencies can refer to those individuals or groups *within* the athletic program itself as well as *outside* the confines of the sport program.

Public(s). A public is a group of individuals drawn together by some common factor, such as, a common interest, being from a specific geographic area, or possessing a common feature such as age, religion, sex, occupation, race, nationality, politics, income, social status, affiliation, or educational background. An individual can be categorized as belonging, simultaneously, to more than one public (Jensen, 1992).

References

Bronzan, R. T. (1986). *Public relations, promotions, and fund-raising for athletic and physical education programs*. Daphne, Alabama: United States Sports Academy Publishing House. Copyright 1977, by John Wiley & Sons, Inc., reprinted by permission of the author, 1986.

Bucher, C. (1987). *Management of physical education & athletic programs* (9th ed.). St. Louis: Times Mirror/Mosby College Publishing.

Buell, V. P. (1984). *Marketing management: A strategic planning approach.* New York: McGraw-Hill Book Co.

Canham, D. (1986). Fund-raising. *Athletic Director & Coach, 4* (3), 4–6.

Cutlip, S. M., Center, A. H., & Broom, G. M. (1985). *Effective public relations* (6th ed.). Englewood Cliffs, N.J.: Prentice-Hall.

Fox, E. D. (1990). A time to sow, a time to reap—Marketing & promotions. *Journal of Physical Education, Recreation and Dance, 61* (3), 65–70.

Horine, L. (1991). *Administration of physical education and sports programs* (2nd ed.). Dubuque, Iowa: Wm. C. Brown Publishers.

Jensen, C. R. (1992). *Administrative management of physical education and athletic programs.* (3rd ed.). Philadelphia: Lea & Febiger.

Mason, J. G. & Paul, P. (1988). *Modern sports administration.* Englewood Cliffs, New Jersey: Prentice-Hall.

Railey, J. H. & Railey, P. A. (1988). *Managing physical education, fitness, and sports programs.* Mountain View, California: Mayfield Publishing Company.

Sabock, R. J. & Bortner, J. E. (1986, September). Fund-raising: High priority in Division I-A. *Athletic Business,* p. 82.

Voltmer, E., Esslinger, A., McCurs, B., & Tillman, K. (1979). *The organization and administration of physical education* (5th ed.). Englewood Cliffs, New Jersey: Prentice-Hall, Inc.

Yiannakis, A. (1989). Some contributions of sport sociology to the marketing of sports and leisure organizations. *Journal of Sport Management, 3* (2), 105–115.

Meet the Team Night following a gymnastics meet. (Courtesy of University of Georgia Athletic Association/photo by Jim Metcalf)

Organizational and Administrative Ingredients of Sport Promotions, Public Relations, and Fund-Raising

2

There is a real need for quality organization, management, and administration in the support of activities under the umbrella of what is commonly referred to as sport fund-raising, promotion, and public relations. There is also a need for both a systematic approach to whatever one attempts to do, as well as a need for consistency and continuity, both in terms of quality and quantity of one's efforts and actions. A common criticism leveled at those in athletics is that there is generally a lack of consistency in the quality of promotional and fund-raising efforts. Those individuals are often looked upon as being a ''flash in the pan'' with no real staying power, lacking credibility, and having no real substance in the arena of promotions, fund-raising, and public relations.

What are the components of good sport management, of competent administration, and of successful fund-raising efforts? As early as 1937, seven essential or basic tasks comprising administration and management were delineated by Gulick and Urwick (1937). These essential tasks were represented by the acronym POSDCORB representing (1) planning, (2) organizing, (3) staffing, (4) directing, (5) coordinating, (6) reporting, and (7) budgeting.

In an effort to be more specific within the umbrella of fund-raising, promotions, and public relations, the author has added the competencies of *recording, evaluating, supporting* or *facilitating* to the seven tasks enumerated by Gulick and Urwick. Thus, the new acronym becomes **POSDCoRRFEB,** shown in figure 2.1.

Essential Administrative Ingredients—POSDCoRRFEB

1. Planning
2. Organizing
3. Staffing
4. Directing
5. Coordinating
6. Reporting
7. Recording
8. Facilitating
9. Evaluating
10. Budgeting

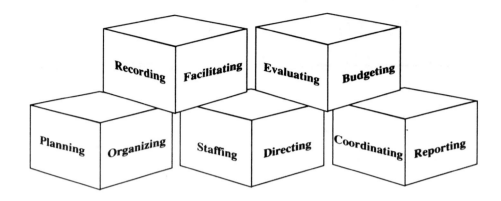

Planning. Planning is THE ESSENTIAL INGREDIENT—the foundation—that determines whether future actions will be meaningful or merely examples of aimless activity. The components of planning consist of (1) deciding on what is to be accomplished, (2) when the activities should be completed, (3) under what conditions they are to be done, and (4) how they are to be achieved. Planning implies determination of special needs, as well as goals and objectives. It is the creation of a road map (Ensor, 1988).

In the absence of planning, one is caught in the perpetual trap of aimlessly wandering around. Planning helps delineate not only what the realistic objectives might be but aids in the establishment of priorities. Planning also helps identify and utilize the available resources within specific time restraints.

Similarly, planning takes into consideration the tools or resources available to those involved in fund-raising. Planning is the anticipatory phase of the process and involves activities undertaken prior to the actual fund-raising efforts. Of course, once actual fund-raising activities are initiated, continual monitoring of the plans remains necessary for the successful completion of those activities that comprise the overall fund-raising project(s).

Organizing. To be able to organize is to successfully allocate resources and place in proper perspective all of the components essential to the overall success of one's efforts. To place onto the top of the table, so to speak, all of the ingredients or factors one must take into consideration, in the proper sequence in which they are to be utilized, symbolizes the epitome of organization. ''The first fundraising rule is to get ORGANIZED'' (Palmisano, 1984).

Staffing. Human resources, *people,* are at the core of any effort to achieve meaningful success in gaining funds for athletic programs. Working with a wide variety of staff personnel on an individual basis, as well as in small and large groups, is an ever looming challenge to the fund-raiser. Proper staffing is absolutely essential. Without adequate staffing, both paid and volunteer, one's efforts at fund-raising are necessarily severely limited. However, mere numbers are not the answer. The key in terms of staffing is securing the services of highly motivated, dedicated, and trained individuals. Staffing also includes the appropriate training and retraining of staff members who need such assistance.

Finally, the staffing task involves recognition of the skills and capabilities (as well as the limitations) of individual staff (individually and collectively) and the proper placement or matching of such staff with appropriate areas of responsibilities. One of the worst sins a fund-raising administrator can commit is to assign an otherwise-motivated, professional, and qualified staff member to a task for which the individual is not suited, either by temperament, training, or experience.

Directing. Directing refers to the task of providing guidance and direction to personnel within the organization, as well as to so-called outsiders, whether they be groups, organizations, or individuals. Directing qualified staff members as well as ''outsiders'' to appropriate tasks is a highly desired trait.

Coordinating. Matching the tools and resources available to the fund-raiser with the challenges and tasks at hand is an important coordinating challenge. **To successfully juggle all of the essential components of a fund-raising operation requires skillful coordination.** To be able to coordinate all of these components or essentials is frequently the determining factor for the success or failure of a fund-raiser.

Frequently one needs to coordinate dates, deadlines, needs of others, available tools, resources, etc. Without such coordination, there is confusion, and the successful generation of meaningful funds for the athletic program is as much a result of good luck as anything.

Juggling many things at once seems to be a prerequisite of many fund-raisers. While this can seem to be unproductive, the very nature of fund-raising often necessitates the doing of many things at once. Thus, coordinating these often separate, distinct activities on behalf of many individuals and groups calls for skillful coordination. The fund-raising process has been likened, with some accuracy, to a puzzle with many individuals attempting to put the puzzle parts together. It remains the responsibility of the fund-raising administrator to coordinate everyone's actions and activity so that, eventually, the pieces start to fall into place and what emerges is the completed and coherent picture puzzle (fig. 2.2).

Reporting. Accountability is of prime importance in the fund-raising arena. The basic component of accountability is *reporting*, which refers to keeping others, various constituencies, and one's own staff fully informed and abreast of all developments. Additionally, it is important to follow the administrative Golden Rule, always follow the chain of command when working with individuals within a hierarchical organization.

Recording. The keeping of meticulous records facilitates the accountability challenge facing all fund-raisers. One needs to accurately record what transpires so that an accurate perception is obtained of exactly what has taken place. This recording process also enables one to more accurately assess whether what took place was positive or negative and further assists in the planning process for future activities.

Facilitating—Supporting. The task of facilitating, within the fund-raising umbrella, refers to being able and willing to assist others in their tasks and to making the tasks ''doable'' by providing assistance in any way feasible and appropriate. To facilitate means to operate in the HELP MODE, providing adequate support mechanisms to the entire fund-raising operation, as well as to those individuals involved in the process. There must be a *willingness* to provide meaningful support—moral, personnel, financial—to the program, to the process itself, and to the staff associated with the fund-raising activity or effort.

Figure 2.2 Completing the parts of the fund-raising puzzle.

Evaluating. Assessing effectiveness and efficiency of one's efforts is essential in any organization. To know where one has been, where one is currently, and where one is going is the objective. This cannot be accomplished without an evaluation. It is important to think of evaluation as an on-going activity, program, or process.

Thus, determining criteria by which success and failure can be judged or determined is essential to the assessment or evaluation process. Evaluation aids in the determination of what should be done next and what should be changed, if anything. Evaluation is an approved form of hindsight—with a purpose.

Budgeting. Providing proper financial support and the allocation of monies to specific areas are tasks that have significant impact on the ultimate success of the fund-raising operation. Since it often does take money to earn or raise money, one of the cardinal sins of fund-raisers is to waste or not properly use what resources are available for the task at hand, that is, to generate additional monies. An appropriate budgeting process assists in the proper allocation of resources (dollars) in ways that would be most productive.

Resources, Tools, and Assets Available to Support Fund-Raising and Promotional Activities

Exactly what tools, resources, or assets are available to support the fund-raising and promotional activities of an athletic program? Generally speaking, they may be classified into one or more of the following categories:

1. Time
2. Personnel (internal/external and paid/volunteer)
3. Equipment
4. Supplies
5. Facilities
6. Reputation (what people think/feel without seeing firsthand)

7. Image (what people think/feel in reaction to what they see)
8. Accomplishments and achievements
9. Status—level of competition
10. Money
11. Climate, atmosphere, and environment
12. Services
13. Associates (people)
14. Other (anything that facilitates the fund-raising process)

It behooves the sport administrator to recognize that the above list may be viewed both as objectives (desirable to be obtained) as well as resources, tools, or assets that can be used (when available) to generate additional resources and/or to realize objectives and goals.

Resources Available to the Sport Fund-Raiser

Available Time (to work). Attempting to do too much in too little a period of time is an open invitation for failure. There must be made available an appropriate amount of *quality* time to carry out the fund-raising activity or project. Time is a tool just as much as money, facilities, and staff.

Time management skills are essential for the sport promoter and fund-raiser. Time, being finite, is one resource that must be guarded most carefully lest it slip through one's fingers. Wasting time is an act that can easily take place even without our consciously realizing it. An important factor to keep in mind is the amount of *quality time spent on task(s)*. It is the amount of *quality time* spent that determines the effectiveness and efficiency of one's efforts, which in turn has a direct effect upon the realization of the objectives and goals of the mission (fig. 2.3).

Time is one of the greatest assets an individual or organization can possess. Since there are only 24 hours in a day, it is how the available hours are actually utilized that matters. Let's face it—most people waste far too much time. Hence, their efforts are diluted and their effectiveness diminished. Coaches, athletic administrators, and sport boosters are no exception. Through efficient time management and the recognition and setting (and following) of priorities, the athletic fund-raiser and promoter is able to increase the effectiveness and efficiency of the efforts initiated. Time is indeed a valuable tool for the athletic fund-raiser. Lack of time or failure to utilize time appropriately most assuredly invites failure.

Personnel (internal/external and paid/volunteer). Having adequate personnel, both in terms of the number of individuals and in terms of their capabilities and competencies, is an additional requirement for any successful fund-raising effort. Lacking adequate personnel within the athletic staff to support and sustain a successful fund-raising project, the athletic administrator is faced with the task of looking elsewhere to obtain the services of skilled, trained, and experienced personnel. The key to success is to be able to draw upon sufficient personnel, individuals who are motivated, trained, hopefully experienced, capable, and interested in being involved in the world of fund-raising.

▧ **Principle 6** ▧

Hours in a day are like bullets in a six shooter—there are a limited number of bullets; hence they must be used carefully, wisely, and sparingly.

Figure 2.3   Managing
time efficiently.

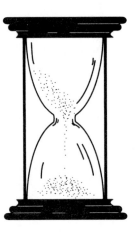

Equipment and Supplies. Under this category falls the multitude of items essential for any business or organization—both hardware and software. Included are such items as typewriters, computers, copiers, fax machines, phones, paper, merchandise, premiums, tickets, automobiles, etc.

Facilities. The facilities available for fund-raising and promotional activities will vary as much as individual booster organizations or sport programs vary. Under this category would fall office space, indoor and outdoor athletic sporting facilities (gymnasia, natatoria, weight rooms, dining halls, conference rooms, ball diamonds, etc.), as well as other facilities that may be rented or borrowed by the athletic program.

Reputation (what people think/feel without experiencing firsthand). The reputation (from a distance) of an athletic program is what others think or feel about that athletic entity and what it stands for; that is, its worth. A reputation is a perception gained without actually having a firsthand experience with the athletic program. Possessing a general positive reputation can enhance fund-raising, as well as promotional activities and public relations efforts. Members of the general public, as well as internal or external constituencies, are more likely to support an athletic program with a sound reputation thought of in a positive light.

The reputation of an athletic program can be determined by a host of factors, such as the quality of the teams and how the coaching staff is viewed by the news media. However, the reputation of any organization or program *is usually not determined by one single factor.* Rather, a whole host of factors go into creating a reputation. Finally, reputations are usually gained over a period of time rather than resulting from a single experience or instance.

Image (what people think/feel in reaction to what they see). A program's image is the impressions or views created when an athletic program is viewed up close, firsthand, by others. Although reputation and image are closely associated, the difference between the two is that an athletic reputation can have an affect upon individuals who have had no personal contact with the athletic program. On the other hand, an image is usually created by firsthand, personal association or dealings with the athletic program or staff.

Like reputation, the image (real or perceived) that others have of the athletic program can have a profound effect upon whether individuals and groups will support the fund-raising and promotional activities of the athletic program. An image may be created deliberately or accidentally. That is, an image of a team, athletic program, or specific sport program can be determined or shaped by the way the staff is dressed, by the manner in which home event activities are organized, by the way the athletes behave (on and off the field or court), etc. An image is more immediate. It can be created by a single experience, episode, or a series of experiences or happenings.

Accomplishments and Achievements. Accomplishments and achievements in sports can have a positive and long-lasting impact upon segments of the public and various constituencies. Past achievements can be utilized as a tool in that such accomplishments make others more receptive to being in a "help" mode. Everyone wants to be associated with a winner. Witness the number of people wearing the sweatshirts and hats and other paraphernalia of successful sport teams. A wise fundraiser will utilize a team's accomplishments as a tool with which to open doors of potential contributors or untapped constituencies.

Status—Level of Competition. The **status** held within the athletic arena can be a decisive and helpful tool. Notre Dame, with its status as one of the major educational and athletic institutions in the United States and a member of the NCAA Division I, enjoys a certain status by virtue of its membership in the most competitive division of the NCAA. It also enjoys a certain status because of its historical past within both the academic and athletic arenas. The institution enjoys this status by virtue of its involvements and associations (past and current) in sport, its successes in sport, its tradition, its reputation, its image, its facilities, its staff, etc.

Utilizing this status as a tool only enhances the likelihood of additional gains in terms of fund-raising, promotional activities, and public relations. Such efforts will tend to be more successful, with less effort expended, merely because the focus of the fund-raising and promotional activity is Notre Dame itself. The same can be said of certain secondary schools and smaller colleges and universities, as well as many youth sport organizations and teams. The status of a sport entity is often self perpetuating. In other words, the status of an athletic program enables that program to maintain the level of success or even achieve greater successes because of its status. As a result of such successes, the status is further enhanced—and the cycle is perpetuated again and again and again. The challenge for any sports organization or program is to do what it takes to achieve relatively high status, which in turn facilitates further enhancement activities and leads to further improvement or reinforcement of the high status.

Money. The old adage, "It takes money to make money" (Palmisano, 1988), still holds true today. Money itself is a very important tool; however, the absence of money should not be a deterrent to successful fund-raising or promotional activities. Other techniques, strategies, and tools can be used in lieu of actual dollars. For example, "trade-outs" are an effective means of securing products and services from others without having to pay cash for these products and services. The end result is that the sport program obtains the needed products and services without exchanging money.

Nevertheless, hard, cold cash remains a most valuable tool or resource. Adequate cash flow provides much needed flexibility. It enables an organization to secure services and products on an almost immediate basis. The crux of the matter is to use this valuable resource in a timely and effective fashion. Nothing is more disheartening and discouraging than to misuse such a valuable tool as cash. After all, the objective is to raise monies for the athletic program. When monies used in fund-raising efforts are not used in the most productive manner, the result is a double whammy—money already on hand is wasted *and* anticipated monies are not generated to the extent expected. This is an unforgivable situation in which to find oneself as a fund-raiser.

Climate, Atmosphere, and Environment. There are intangible aspects of a sports program, such as the climate, atmosphere, and environment surrounding either the total sports operation or some segment of the total, which can serve as powerful tools or assets. In some instances, they can be equally powerful hindrances. The atmosphere or climate affecting sports programs can be viewed as either internal or external.

An **internal climate** or **atmosphere** is exemplified by the **working conditions** in which the athletic staff and those involved in fund-raising efforts find themselves. A friendly, open atmosphere and climate can contribute to the overall progress of the fund-raising project, as well as facilitate the interpersonal relationships of those involved with the project. The absence of a positive work environment creates a needless hindrance to the successful completion of any fund-raising attempt by destroying morale and lessening the motivation of those involved.

One type of **external atmosphere** is the **financial climate** or environment in which the fund-raisers find themselves at the time when the fund-raising activity is to take place. For example, in a healthy economy when there is a healthy financial growth within the community, it is certainly easier to have funds contributed to worthy athletic causes. However, the converse is true when the economy is on a downturn, is faulty, when there are high interest rates, when a major employer is leaving the community, when the stock market is on the decline, and when money is generally "tight" in the community. During these times of financial hardship, the task facing the fund-raiser is much more difficult due to the lack of a healthy economic climate or environment.

Another type of **external environment** is the **political climate** existing within the community. When the head football coach has just been named "man of the year" by the local service club, the climate or environment is conducive for the generation of financial support for the football program. When the basketball team at the local high school wins the state championship or when the wrestling team at the area college/university returns home with the national NCAA championship trophy, the atmosphere, the setting, the climate, the timing is *ripe* for positive consequences to result from a fund-raising effort, either on behalf of an individual team and/or on behalf of the total athletic program.

Conversely, it is not advisable to kick off a major fund-raising effort for the football program when the head coach and the head of the football boosters are being officially and publicly charged with fiscal mismanagement. Such a negative political climate will only impede the fund-raising efforts.

Services. Services that are available to a sport organization may be categorized in two areas: first, those that are available from within the organization itself; and, second, those available from outside, from other sources or organizations. There is a wide range of services (both external and internal) that may be made available to the fund-raiser or promoter. Some examples are printing services, duplicating services, tax services, legal services, and cleaning services—just to mention a few. These services become significant tools that the sport administrator or manager may exploit even if they are not free or at a reduced cost.

Associates. People with whom the sport administrator or coach is acquainted can function as significant resources or assets. This is nowhere more evident than in the areas of fund-raising, promotions, and public relations. **Associates,** especially those people who are held in high esteem by other individuals and constituencies, can serve as "tools" or assets by lending their presence or prestige (becoming centers of influence) to the fund-raising efforts or projects. These people whom the fund-raiser knows may be tapped for their experience and areas of expertise. Thus, the cultivation of associates becomes of paramount importance in establishing a firm base of support and creating resources that may be turned into real assets to be used in the fund-raising and/or promotional project.

Other Assets and Resources. Generally speaking, anything that can assist the fund-raising process may be considered a tool, an asset, or a resource (McKenzie, 1988). Undoubtedly, there are many other resources which, from time to time, might prove to be of significant help to those interested in generating monies and support for sports programs or segments thereof. It is up to the personnel involved in the fund-raising scheme to look around and ascertain whether there exists sufficient tools and resources, as well as potential for success, prior to embarking upon a specific fund-raising program or project.

The ultimate goal, in terms of sports administration and management, is to obtain as broad a base of internal and external support as possible, both financial and moral, given the resources, limitations, and circumstances in which one finds oneself. Hopefully, through good strategic planning, possession of a high level of competency, and the implementation of realistic promotional tactics and fund-raising efforts, this goal can become a reality.

Essential Qualifications of Athletic Fund-Raisers

In the not too distant past, almost anyone and everyone "associated" with sports considered themselves to be "expert" in the areas of promotions, fund-raising and public relations. This is rapidly changing. The definition of an expert is not "an individual who travels 50 miles with a briefcase and a slide show." Today, there is greater recognition that truly successful efforts in these areas require more than merely an interest, a desire, or even an honest effort.

There is a need for a significant degree of professionalism and a rather high standard of excellence in the area of fund-raising. This need has never been greater in sport than today. Gone are the days, if they ever existed, when any well-meaning individual (a "good old boy" or a "good old girl") could step onto the "firing line" and experience meaningful and sustained success in the areas of sport fund-raising, promotions, and public relations. Presently, there is an urgent demand for greater sophistication, more extensive knowledge, better planning, more accurate

Figure 2.4 Maneuvering the tightrope as a fund-raiser.

assessment, more effective implementation, and honest follow-up than ever before. The age of **Accountability** is upon us in the world of sports promotion and fund-raising.

Both the coaches and administrators are being judged, as never before, by higher standards. Standards have been set by successful athletic coaches and managers as well as by professionals outside of sport and those within the general field of public relations, fund-raising (development), and promotion. The result is that there now exists greater expectations placed upon those individuals attempting to promote sports and attempting to increase the funding base of athletic activities and programs.

Athletic fund-raisers walk the proverbial tightrope between being an obnoxious prima donna and being a well-meaning, dedicated, skilled professional expending efforts to achieve specific goals within an overall plan of attack (see fig. 2.4).

Today, involvement in fund-raising, sport promotions, and public relations has become, by necessity, a professional task to be completed by those who are knowledgeable in using *generally accepted* **principles** or **guidelines,** adapted to fit one's own particular situation or circumstance. It is this ability to adapt facts, information, ideas, principles, and guidelines to fit one's own individual circumstances, resources, and needs, which distinguish the successful sport fund-raiser or development officer from the imposter.

In the examination of the promotional, fund-raising, and public relations activities of any sports program, there are six essential areas in which minimal skills or competencies are necessary for the successful administrator or coach. These competencies are a MUST for the personnel involved, if the stated objectives and goals are to be realized in a timely fashion and at an acceptable quality level. They include (1) basic skills, (2) technical skills, (3) interpersonal skills, (4) conceptual skills, (5) dedication or commitment skills, and (6) imagery skills (see fig. 2.5).

Basic Skills

Basic skills are those competencies that any reasonably educated, trained, and experienced professional should possess. Included within this initial category of skills are those used in writing, speaking, listening, reading, understanding or comprehending, which distinguish the educated individual from the uneducated in our society.

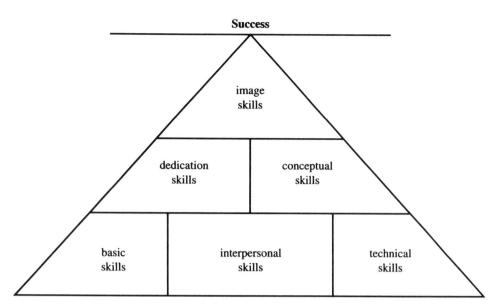

Figure 2.5 Essential skills and competencies of an effective administrator and fund-raiser.

Technical Skills

Technical skills may be viewed as " . . . an understanding of, and proficiency in, a specific kind of activity . . . involves specialized knowledge, analytical ability within that specialty, and facility in the use of the tools and techniques of the specific discipline'' (Katz, 1955, p. 34). Technical skills are those involving technological or semi-high tech areas that form the foundation of promotional activities, fund-raising tactics, and strategies, and public relations efforts.

These skills include, but are not limited to, competency in typing, graphics, printing, photography, computer literacy, selling, accounting, phone usage, etc. Mastering these technical skills of fund-raising is similar to the basketball coach mastering the Xs and the Os, the technical tactics and strategies, of the sport of basketball.

Interpersonal Skills

''No man is an island.'' In our society we are quite literally forced, for our daily survival, to be able to work in a variety of circumstances and for a multitude of purposes with other human beings. This is certainly a maxim within the sport arena. To understand others and to be able to work effectively with them is a highly prized competency (Katz, 1955). Perhaps in no other area of sport is the need to work with people more essential than in fund-raising, promotions, and public relations.

It is essential that the fund-raiser be able to work effectively and efficiently with other people (positive human relations), on a one-to-one basis, as well as within a group setting. In reality, this competency is too frequently lacking in individuals working within the umbrella of fund-raising, promotions, and public relations, even at a minimally acceptable level. The result is that failure is frequently experienced in what is a ''person to person'' or ''people'' business because of a lack of expertise in working with human beings, that is, with people.

Conceptual Skills

How one views the total picture of one's athletic program is very important. Having an appropriate and accurate perception of the mission, the available resources and limitations, as well as specific objectives and global goals of the sports program or activity, is highly desirable. One must be able to understand the needs of the total sports program, as well as the role of each of its components, and be able to make decisions accordingly. In terms of a school athletic program, the football coach must be able to have a realistic picture of exactly where all of the sports (not just the sport of football) fit within the total athletic program in respect to the school's goals and objectives *and* in terms of both resource allocation and priorities.

Similarly, in terms of promotions, public relations, and fund-raising, those individuals involved in such activities, under the umbrella of the sports program, must understand the role of the total sports program, as well as each of the components of the total (school) program, *in respect to priorities, resources, limitations, missions and goals.* Failure to have such a firm, clear grasp leads one to aimlessly struggle, to "spin one's wheels," to go off on tangents, and to inadequately utilize resources in an ineffectual and inefficient manner. People need direction and guidance, without which the coach, administrator, or booster member flounders, wastes valuable energies, time and resources, and, eventually experiences failure.

Dedication and Commitment Skills

The ability to demonstrate dedication and commitment to the task at hand is an invaluable skill. A sports person must, by the very nature of one's involvement in sports and by the very nature of the beast (sport), be willing to expend an exceptional (even, at times, extraordinary) amount of energy, effort, and time in the performance of one's job in promoting, raising monies, and creating positive public relations for a sports program or activity (Stier, 1986). Being able and willing to make a significant time commitment is certainly an asset. However, merely spending time and effort at a task is only part of the challenge. There must, in addition, be quality work accomplished during the time spent on task. *Effort alone will not suffice.* Practice alone will not make perfect. *Perfect practice makes perfect.* It is the bottom line, the end results, that are all too frequently the measure of one's success.

Paying attention to details is vital. Mackay (1988) stated that while managers need to delegate they also need to pay strict attention to detail—a fact not necessarily in conflict with the idea of time management. Everyone has the same amount of time. It is what we do with it that makes one person different from another. It is the quality of our work (time spent on task) that differentiates the successful fund-raiser from the average person.

Quality work coupled with an adequate quantity of time spent at a task *may* equal a meaningful outcome in terms of goals and objectives sought. Nothing guarantees success; however, without being dedicated and willing to make a commitment in terms of the amount and quality of time one spends working for goals, one is doomed to failure.

It is also most helpful to have an understanding spouse (and children) when it comes to committing oneself to a series of tasks or to a goal. Being able to truly be committed and dedicated and to spend the necessary time on task—without having to face undue criticism at home—is a significant asset. Having an understanding family willing to support the coach or athletic administrator's efforts to achieve success in sport promotion and fund-raising is invaluable.

Image Skills

How one is perceived by others, whether that perception is accurate or not, is of the upmost importance. Sometimes the perceived perception is more important than the reality of the situation. What an individual is can be termed *reality*. What others think of the same individual are *perceptions*.

Perceptions held by others may have no resemblance to reality. In another instance, perceptions may have some resemblance or a great deal of resemblance to what is real. Nevertheless, the perceptions are formed by a variety of factors, some within one's control and others outside a person's control. It is the task of the sports person to work within such a climate and conduct oneself so that the perception closely resembles reality in terms of the quality of the program or activity itself *and* the quality of the effort supporting this program or activity.

It is essential for sports personnel, at any level, to present the most positive image or picture possible to as many individuals and groups or publics as possible, on a consistent basis. Through this effort, which is what public relations is really all about, the correct and positive image of the program can be effectively disseminated to and successfully received and internalized by the numerous publics and constituencies.

The image we project as professionals within a sports organization is created and reinforced by a multitude of factors. These include, but are not limited, to the following:

1. Clothing worn
2. Physical appearance
3. Speech
4. Communication skills
5. Mannerisms
6. Work ethic
7. Habits
8. Attention to detail
9. Associates—organizations, groups, and/or individuals
10. Other

There is an old saying which is appropriate in the discussion of imagery skills. It says: "What you are speaks so loudly I cannot hear what you are attempting to say." It is necessary that coaches and managers, as well as boosters, pay more attention to their personal and professional image, to the quality of their activities, and to the perception others have of them. For, in reality, such an image plays a significant role in creating perceptions that are held by members of various constituencies. It is these perceptions that have an effect, either positive or negative, on how the sports person is viewed, treated, and supported by others.

■ **Principle 7** ■

The perception of what is real, in terms of a person or program, is as important as the reality of the situation itself.

References

Ensor, R. (1988, September). Writing strategic sports marketing plan. *Athletic Business,* pp. 48–52.

Gulick, L. & Urwick, L. (Editors) (1937). Papers on the science of administration. New York: Institute of Public Administration.

Katz, R. (1955). Skills of an effective administrator. *Harvard Business Review, 33* (1), pp. 34–35.

Mackay, H. (1988). *Swim with the sharks without being eaten alive.* Ivy Books, New York: Ballantine Books.

McKenzie, B. (1988, August). Mastering the art of fund-raising. *Athletic Business,* pp. 54–58.

Palmisano, M. (1984, May). Fund-raising's first rule: Get organized. *Athletic Business,* pp. 20–23.

Palmisano, M. (1988, October). Michigan raises funds for new swimming facility. *Athletic Administration,* pp. AA15–AA17.

Stier, W. (1986). Athletic administrators expect qualities, competencies in coaches. *Interscholastic Athletic Administration, 12* (3), 7–9.

Executive Director Grants/In/Aid Dike Eddleman (left) with John Southwood, Chicago-area director, before press conference announcing name change to Fighting Illini Scholarship Fund. (Courtesy of University of Illinois Sports Information Office/photo by Mark Jones)

Contributors to the Athletic Program

Only through a concerted effort on behalf of a number of individuals will specific sports programs be deemed worthy of support. Who are these people? What roles do these individuals or groups play in the support of a sports program?

There are a number of "role players" or groups of individuals who may play an essential role in the support of any athletic program, as shown in figure 3.1. They may be classified as internal (students, student-athletes, coaches, administrators, teachers, staff) as well as external in nature (parents, fans, businesses, booster club members, etc.). These individuals and groups have the potential to perform one of three functions insofar as any sports program are concerned: first, to help or assist the athletic program; second, to remain neutral to the program; and third, to assume an adversarial posture.

The exact role that these groups and/or individuals actually play in any given situation is dependent upon a multitude of factors. The important points to remain cognizant of are that there are potential contributors to any athletic program and the degree to which these individuals and groups actually assist in a meaningful manner is dependent upon a wide range of factors. Some of these factors can be controlled, or at least affected, by the professional fund-raiser and promoter. There are other factors, however, that are outside of any single person's control or power.

First and foremost, it is critical that there be a *quality* sports program to promote, to show off, and to expose to the various publics. It is important to recognize that without a sound athletic program or activity, all of the promotional, public relations, and fund-raising activities will be to no avail. There must actually be "something of value" to promote, to sell, to highlight, and to point to as being worthy of support—monetarily and otherwise. There must be actual substance within the sports program or activity if one is to successfully promote and solicit meaningful and sustaining support.

Principle 8

There must be substance to that which is to be promoted.

To do otherwise, by attempting to promote and generate support for something of little value, is not only a waste of time and effort, but also self-defeating for the sports person who wishes to operate on a long-term basis within a specific environment or geographical area.

Human beings have long memories. People may forgive but they infrequently forget. This is especially true when it comes to credibility and integrity of an individual or a program. Attempting to pull the "wool over the eyes" of constituencies in terms

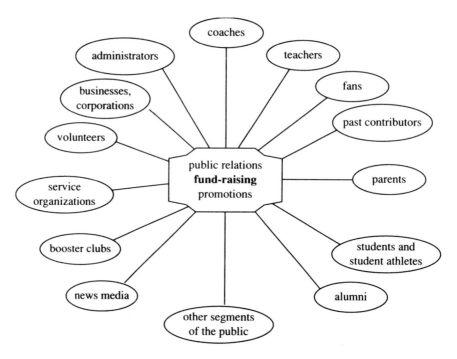

of promoting "what is not" (a falsehood) leads eventually to a reduction, if not complete loss, of credibility and effectiveness. In the business of sports fund-raising, the most important quality one can possess is integrity. Without it, one's effectiveness is questionable, if not nonexistent. *The cornerstone of any good sports fund-raising activity, promotional involvement, and public relations effort is a sound athletic program.*

Athletic Support Groups (ASG)

One of the first things that comes to mind when one considers obtaining outside assistance for the sports program is the viability of athletic booster clubs or support groups. Generally speaking, booster-type organizations have the potential to assist athletic programs by providing fiscal support and moral backing as well as assistance in communicating a positive message about the sports program to the various constituencies.

Certainly there are differing opinions as to the advantages and disadvantages of such organizations. One position is represented by the athletic director who, when asked why there was not a booster club associated with the school's athletic program, reportedly indicated, "Why would I want to organize my own lynch mob?"

The opposite position is reflected by the athletic director at the State University of New York College at Brockport, who in 1988 stated, "The support group (Friends of Brockport Athletics—FOBA) at this University has played a major role in rejuvenating the intercollegiate athletic program—both in terms of generating moral support, fan interest, and in thousands and thousands of dollars in fiscal assistance. Without the meaningful support of the Friends of Brockport Athletics our total athletic program, involving some 27 teams, would not be the quality program that it is today'' (Stier, 1990).

A major factor when it comes to considering the organizational structure and purpose of potential booster-type organizations is whether there should be one single booster club or support group for the entire athletic program or multiple support (booster) groups organized around different sports. For example, should the football program have its own football booster organization (Touchdown Club)? Should there exist a Tip Off Club supporting the basketball program? Should there be a separate booster club for women's sports and another for men's sports?

To the question of whether or not a booster or club or support group should be organized, **there is no single answer.** Likewise, to the question of whether there should be a single booster club or multiple support groups, there is no single answer.

Rather, the answers to both questions posed above depend, to a great extent, upon the individual circumstances in which the sports staff and supporters find themselves. The answers depend on (1) the tradition and history of support and financial assistance with that particular sports program, (2) the background and experiences of the people involved, (3) the prejudices, opinions, expectations, and power of administrators, athletic staff, and potential boosters, (4) the level of financial and other forms of support needed or desired for various segments of the athletic program, (5) the philosophy and persuasiveness of the sport administration and staff, and, (6) the political climate in which all of the planning, discussing, questioning, and consulting takes place.

People are resistant to change. When they have worked in an organization for a period of time they are even more resistant to changes, especially when the changes are being proposed by a person new to the position or to the organization. As a result, sport administrators and promoters need to be cognizant of this tendency to react to proposed changes with hesitancy and reluctance.

A good rule of thumb to follow is not to make any major changes for at least 2–3 months after assuming a new administrative position unless absolutely necessary. The rationale behind this tactic is threefold. *First,* it takes that long frequently to learn about the organization and its inner workings and its personnel. *Second,* there is a tendency for a new administrator to any organization, office, or position to be bombarded with information and input from a number of individuals all attempting to influence the decision-making ability of the new manager or administrator. Unless one is very careful, the decisions the new administrator makes may not be those of the administrator but those of people who were able to influence the new person. It is best to wait until one is familiar with the organization, its staff, and its operation before making major decisions.

The *third* reason why some time should elapse before significant changes are made is to lessen the possibility of bruised feelings among those individuals who remain on staff and who feel that the previous way of conducting business was just fine. Of course, there might still be some people on staff who had a role in instituting the present policies, procedures, and practices, and who might still be in positions to serve as obstructionists if not handled in a diplomatic fashion.

▒ **Principle 9** ▒

There is always more than one way to reach any objective.

▒ **Principle 10** ▒

It is frequently difficult to make changes in established policies, procedures, and practices—therefore, be cautious in instituting major changes quickly.

History of Booster Clubs Within the United States

Booster clubs have had a long history in the review of amateur sports in this country. Some booster clubs were originally created through a cooperative effort between school administrators and civic-minded sports leaders for the purpose of meeting specific financial needs of an athletic program. Others were established through efforts of parents of athletes desiring to provide a more beneficial and safe learning experience for their youngsters. But not all schools have so-called booster clubs, for a variety of reasons. The University of Notre Dame has no athletic booster clubs as such (May, 1990).

Just as sports programs have expanded and evolved throughout the years, booster clubs have similarly grown in number, degree of sophistication, and impact. Sport support programs have been developed throughout the country and at all levels, from youth sports to the intercollegiate level. The result in many instances have been increased financial support for the sports programs and an enhanced positive image for both the sports programs and the booster clubs.

Two of the challenges facing booster clubs in the years ahead are (1) maintaining continuity in general membership, as well as in the officer corp, and (2) the consistent generation of essential resources on an annual basis, to insure that the vital elements (money, equipment, supplies, facilities, staff, etc.) are available for the sports programs in this country.

Membership by both women and men within such booster-type organizations has continued to grow as the booster clubs themselves have expanded and matured in scope and significance. Officers of booster clubs have provided excellent leadership and guidance for the clubs themselves, as well as for the members therein. Officers have been trained through experiential means, as well as through formal educational programs. The end result is the availability of more qualified and highly sophisticated men and women who find themselves involved in either a leadership or "followship" role within the sports booster club organization.

While booster clubs, in the past, have been involved in obtaining so-called "extras" for the sport programs, many of the booster clubs of today are getting involved more and more in generating essential support (money, goods, and/or services) for the sport teams, programs, and individual athletes. Thus, the *importance of such support organizations or booster clubs* and the *significance of their involvement and contributions* have quadrupled within recent years. The end result is that booster clubs have in many respects become essential elements within the sports scene in the last part of the twentieth century.

It behooves every athletic administrator, coach, booster, and fan to seriously examine the advantages of being involved with such a support organization as a booster club. These advantages can take the form of providing both tangible and intangible (moral) support in the areas of resources, as well as providing a foundation of an excellent public relations component so necessary for any sports program. A booster club should be considered as another *tool* that may be utilized to help meet the needs, objectives, and goals of the total sport program. If viewed in this manner, booster clubs can indeed be an invaluable asset to the sports program and to the participants, the athletes, and to themselves. In the final analysis, the justification of athletics is whether or not the participants actually benefit from the experience. The ultimate justification of booster clubs is whether or not these support organizations truly facilitate the sporting experience so that the athletes, the youngsters, can experience these benefits.

Justification for the Existence of Booster Clubs—Athletic Support Groups

The number of sports programs (at all levels) having problems or challenges in securing sufficient funding for their existing or desired level of competition and sport offerings is very high. There are many reasons why there is a real need for additional sources of financial support for sports programs at all levels. Some of these reasons include, but are not limited, to the following factors (Briggs & Duffy, 1987; Yiannakis & Braunstein, 1983).

Why Athletic Programs Need Additional Financial Support.

1. *General inflation*

   Doing business today—that is, providing a meaningful learning experience for the athletes—costs more than it did in the past and will undoubtedly cost more in the future. Such is life as we know it.

   During 1988 and 1989 the cost of operating major collegiate athletic programs with football programs rose some 13.5 percent. This outpaced earned income, which saw an increase of 9 percent. There was a 35 percent increase during the three year period 1985–86 through 1988–89. In fact, at the Division-I college and university level, the median costs exceeded $9.75 million. The maximum and minimum costs during the 1988–89 academic year was $19.57 million and $4.24 million respectively (Operating Costs, 1990).

   More and more universities are showing sizeable deficits in their athletic programs. In fact, the average deficit in 1988–89 was $112,000.00. In the CFA Financial Survey conducted by the College Football Association (Operating Costs, 1990), it was revealed that more than 75 percent of those responding cited low gate and postseason receipts, fewer cash gifts, and a decline in radio and television broadcast licensing fees as the major reasons for the decline of income for intercollegiate athletics.

   Hence, it is necessary to plan for greater expenditures in almost every category associated with the administration of sports. For example, transportation, officials, maintenance, utilities, crowd control measures, medical costs, equipment, supplies, repairs, refurbishments, etc. The list goes on and on.

2. *Increase in the cost of liability insurance*

   Spiraling costs within the liability insurance industry is a well-known fact within our society. Sports programs are not immune from this plight. The alarming increase in the successful lawsuits by sport consumers and participants, coupled with landmark cash settlements awarded plaintiffs, are legitimate causes of concern for the sports administrator. In fact, increases in insurance costs have become one of the major challenges facing those responsible for financing sports at all levels. Some expenses must just be absorbed, period. Unfortunately, liability insurance is all too frequently just one such expense.

3. *Increase in the cost of medical insurance and medical services*
The entire area of health care continues to expand in terms of capabilities and in terms of cost to the consumer. The sports participant is better cared for than at any time in the history of sports. But the cost of such protection and treatment or rehabilitation is high and must necessarily be passed onto either the participants or to the sports program itself. The end result is an even greater portion of many athletic budgets being absorbed by medical related expenditures. With seemingly ever increasing annual premiums being charged to athletic programs insurance coverage for their athletes, more and more colleges and universities are facing a financial crunch in their efforts to come up with the funds to cover such premiums. Some athletic departments have chosen to eliminate their responsibility for securing and paying for medical insurance for their athletes because of the seemingly ever increasing cost of such insurance policies. In fact, in the late 1980s several institutions belonging to the State University of New York Athletic Conference (SUNYAC), including SUNY Brockport, SUNY Cortland, the State University of New York at Binghamton, elected to eliminate athletic insurance coverage paid for by their athletic departments and instead required individual athletes to provide insurance themselves.

4. *Increase in the cost of obtaining and training qualified athletic staff*
Never has there been more emphasis on, and recognition of, the need for qualified staff associated with sport programs than at the present time. When such staff members are on salary or stipend, the cost of financing the staff's salaries can rapidly become a weighty burden on the already tight financial picture of the sports program. Even in those instances where the athletic staff consists of volunteers (youth sport coaches, etc.), there is still the cost involved in their continual in-service training or education. It is inevitable that there be escalating expenses associated with the athletic staff of any sports program.

5. *More opportunities for sports participation by more people*
There are more participants, at every level, than at any other time in our country's history. Programs in amateur sports in this country have steadily increased since the beginning of the twentieth century. This expansion is evident from the lower elementary levels through high school and extending into colleges and universities. There has been a dramatic increase in the number of females, as well as in the number of males, participating in amateur athletics in recent years. There has also been a corresponding increase in the number of sports available, for males and females, particularly in secondary schools and colleges.

Certainly, **Title IX** (1972) has had a significant impact in the area of increased athletic participation by women. Likewise, the **Civil Rights Restoration Act of 1987,** passed by Congress on March 22, 1988, has served as a significant boost to the original intent of Title IX (Kramer et al., 1988). The surprising vote by the U.S. Supreme Court, February 26, 1992, really put the teeth back into the 1972 law. It was on that date that the court, with an unanimous 9–0 vote, decided in the Franklin v. Gwinnett County (GA) Public

Schools that Title IX plaintiffs of intentional sexual discrimination and bias under the statute in schools may sue for unlimited money damages instead of just pursuing a promise to end the bias or the discrimination (Mauro, 1992, February 27).

It must be noted, however, that the increase in sports participation and availability of opportunity are not limited only to women. Greater participation by both males and females has been evident in the past and will continue well into the twenty-first century—and in a wider range of sports activities. To put it plainly, more teams are being sponsored today by various youth sports organizations, junior high schools, and high schools. In high schools alone, during the 1987–88 school year, over 5 million (5,275,461) boys and girls were involved in sports, an increase of 75,023 from the previous year (*Sunday Democrat and Chronicle*, 1988).

The college and university level has not been immune to this ever-increasing participation by men and women. Even the professional level has had increases in participation due to the fact that there are more professional teams in every sport than only a decade ago. A complete list of professional sports organizations and teams may be found in the publication Sports Market Place (Lipsey, 1992).

6. *Insufficient gate receipts*
There is only so much funding available from gate receipts, which are dependent to a certain degree on seating capacity, attractiveness, and competitive level of a particular sport activity in competing for the consumers' time, interest, and disposable income dollars. Anything that reduces or limits the income from gate receipts can have a significant impact on the financial support base of the athletic program. One such factor that has had a devastating effect on the gate receipts of a sizable number of sports programs is the proliferation of the number of options open to the viewing public.

The seemingly never-ending growth, expansion, and availability of collegiate and professional sports programs are constantly competing for the consumer's dollar when it comes to gate receipts. Never before has the sports viewing consumer had greater opportunities and more options available to spend their sports entertainment dollar and their valuable time.

Additionally, the opportunity, almost on a 24-hour basis, to watch major college, national, and international sporting events on television tends to erode the income traditionally generated from gate receipts for many sports programs. Witness Ted Turner's Sports channel WTBS and ESPN's programming in this respect. This phenomenon is pervasive and has a debilitating effect at all levels from youth sports to high school athletics to the college and university level and even extends to the professional ranks. The over-saturation of sporting opportunities for the consumer is already upon us. In a sizable number of athletic programs at all levels, this over-saturation is currently affecting gate receipts in a negative fashion.

7. *Decrease in funding from traditional institutional resources*
In the summer of 1990, the Slayton (Oregon) High School board of education eliminated all interscholastic sports. This was due to the failure of two property

tax levies that went down to defeat. The board had to cancel the school paper, band concerts, and the school play in addition to the high school sports program (Oregon High School, 1990). Slayton High School is not alone in having to look at other sources of income to support school sports.

Athletic programs, in general, are getting a smaller piece of the institutional financial pie at both the secondary and the collegiate levels. More and more athletic programs are being expected to assume a greater responsibility for their own financial well being. With a lessening of financial support from central administrative budgets, it falls upon the athletic administrators and coaches of these programs to examine and pursue other avenues for *replacing lost revenue,* as well as generating new sources of income for enhancement purposes.

In light of the seven factors cited here, it becomes obvious that there is a real need for assistance in the generation of much-needed financial resources for sports programs. *This assistance can be realized through a well-organized and administered sports booster club.* A booster club that has a clear overall goal, excellent leadership, specific organizational guidelines, and a receptive atmosphere in which to work for specific objectives for the betterment of the student-athletes is what is needed in many cases.

The rationale for the existence of an athletic booster-type organization essentially centers around *one major question*. The question is simply this: **Is the support organization able and willing to facilitate the realization of specific objectives and general goals that might have been beyond the reach of the athletic program without the existence and work of the athletic support group (ASG)?** If the athletic support group can actually help the athletic program in a real and material fashion without getting in the way of or interfering with the operation of the athletic program, there may indeed be real, tangible advantages to establishing such a support organization for the sports program.

Working with Athletic Booster Clubs and Support Groups in a Wholesome, Productive Atmosphere

The failure, in a minority of cases, to control booster groups from excesses is well known and frequently publicized. However, the failure of the few should not dictate to the vast majority whether or not such organizations should be created and utilized. The failure of athletic administrators, central administrators, and booster club members to adequately take advantage of the inherent advantages that booster clubs offer is tragic. This failure, however, is often the result of the lack of planning, foresight, organization, safeguards, policies, and procedures, coupled with the administration's inability to be decisive in critical situations.

The ultimate purpose of booster clubs or similar athletic support groups (ASG) is to serve in the role of a facilitator and supporter of the athletic program, not to dictate policy, to manipulate the decision-making process, or to be involved in day-to-day operations of the athletic program. The words "to facilitate" best describe the role of the booster club and its members. The organization exists and the members belong so that there might be significant assistance, in a wide variety of ways, provided to the athletic program, athletic staff, and the athletes. The booster club should indeed facilitate the athletic operation. When the booster club fails to assume this role, the justification for its very existence ceases to exist.

Organizing a Booster Club or Athletic Support Group (ASG)

Athletic support groups (ASG), whether they are called booster clubs or are identified by some other designation, do not come into being by themselves. *It takes a great deal of work* to plan and organize a sound athletic support group or booster club. Once such an organization has come into existence, its mere presence does not automatically guarantee that the organization will have any positive, long-term impact in terms of the support of the athletic program. *It takes work* to make such an organization a workable force in providing meaningful and consistent support to a sports program.

The key to creating a successful support group rests in adequate *advanced* planning coupled with skilled leadership—external and internal leadership. When it comes right down to it, the success of such an organization is dependent upon the quality of those individuals who make up the organization. Appendix A outlines a success story in the creation of an ASG.

Seven Steps in the Establishment of Athletic Support Groups.

1. *Recognition of the need for such an organization*
    It is important that the awareness of the need for an athletic support group be shared with a large number of individuals, groups, or constituencies. If the only person who believes that the organization should exist is the athletic director, the likelihood that the support group will come to fruition is extremely limited.
2. *Communication with school officials*
    The appropriate school administrators and staff must understand the purposes of such an organization. Similarly, they should become familiar with the administrative structure of the entity and its objectives and goals.
3. *Consultation with representatives of various internal and external constituencies*
    Various segments of the community or representatives of the numerous publics should be consulted in terms of the feasibility and advisability of such an organization, in light of the existing circumstances in which the athletic program finds itself. Likewise, input should be sought from within the school and/or athletic program—from coaches, teachers, staff, etc.
4. *Establishment of general principles and guidelines of the support group*
    There is a need to delineate the purposes and goals of the organization in clear, concise language so that all will readily understand the function and purpose of the athletic support group.
5. *Recognition of potential pitfalls that should be avoided*
    Being cognizant of the problems and pitfalls to be avoided is half the battle. Some of these potential challenges are:

    a. Dealing with the potential challenges of overzealous ''boosters'' who may want to exert inappropriate influence over the athletic program

▨ **Principle 11** ▨

Anticipate challenges, problems, and pitfalls.

Tent gathering at the State University of New York-College at Brockport. (Courtesy of State University of New York-College at Brockport/photo by James Dusen)

b. Selecting the proper accounting method for all fiscal transactions
c. Establishing priorities of support-group activities
d. Determining the appropriateness of special projects sponsored by the organization
e. Establishing the proper relationship between the booster group and the athletic program
f. Planning for continuity in members, officers, and board members while also insuring opportunities for "new blood"
g. Creating the proper relationships between the members of the support group and the coaching and administrative staff

Doubtless, there are numerous additional potential challenges to be addressed in the planning stage of the establishment of such an organization as an ASG. How these challenges will be addressed will depend upon the circumstances surrounding the athletic program and the quality of both the paid and volunteer athletic staff. The goal remains the same—to establish appropriate guidelines to enable the support group to fulfill its mission of helping the athletic program, the staff, and the athletes.

6. *Dissemination of information about the organization and its purpose(s)*
One of the initial steps to take, once an ASG has been established, is to extensively publicize both its existence and the reasons for its existence to all constituencies. The creation of such a group might call for a special "kick-off" activity (luncheon, dinner, breakfast, wine & cheese gathering, etc.). This presents an opportunity for past, present, and potential supporters, contributors, and members to gather together to talk and learn about the athletic program *and* the newly organized booster group. Such a situation also provides an excellent opportunity to actually make a commitment to support the athletic program via the booster organization.

7. *Determination of the organizational structure of the group*

The specific organizational structure (the bylaws) of the athletic support group need to be clearly established and well-defined. The organizational structure will provide the framework for all future activities of the club or group and, hence, one way to help insure that a booster club assumes its proper role (facilitating, supporting) is to have the structure of the club or support group properly organized with an appropriate set of bylaws. The bylaws are key ingredients for insuring that the support group or booster club fulfills its appropriate mission.

Bylaws provide the framework as to how the organization is to be organized and run by addressing each of the following issues: (1) organization structure, (2) purposes, (3) membership, (4) officer elections, (5) duties of officers, (6) executive committee, (7) executive board, (8) meetings, (9) standing and special committees, (10) property rights, (11) constitutional amendments, (12) dues structure, and, (13) relationship with the principal and the athletic department. A generic example of booster club bylaws, adapted from the *Official Handbook* (1981) of the Booster Clubs of America, is provided in Appendix B.

Organizational Structure of Athletic Support Groups. Although the exact organizational structure of booster clubs may vary, there are many common elements applicable for any ASG. Some of the major components of the organizational structure of such an organization include:

1. Officers of the booster club
   a. President
   b. Vice president (or president-elect)
   c. Treasurer
   d. Secretary
   e. Board members
2. Makeup of the membership of the board of directors
   a. "Inside" versus "outside" members
   b. Ad hoc members of the board (athletic administrator)
3. Orientation and training sessions for new officers and board members
4. Limitations or specific ratio of members, officers, and board members, in terms of:
   a. School personnel
   b. Athletic personnel
   c. Community personnel
   d. Staggered terms of board members
   e. Right to succeed oneself
5. Establishment of minimum expectations of officers and board members
   a. Provision for recall of officers
   b. Provision for recall of board members
6. Committees
   a. Standing committees
   b. Ad hoc committees

7. Newsletters and other forms of communication to keep general membership informed
8. Membership criteria and membership levels
9. Number of meetings each year and the determination of the annual business meeting where elections take place
10. Determination of to whom the booster club is answerable in the final analysis
    a. To whom or what body is the annual report presented? To itself? To the athletic director? To a particular administrator?
    b. Creation of an organizational chart coupled with a job description of all officers and board members

▒ Principle 12 ▒

Provide for a balance between continuity and new blood in terms of leadership within the board of directors and officers of the athletic support group.

Membership Terms of the Board of Directors and the Corps of Officers. One of the challenges facing any organization, and especially support groups, is keeping a balance between insuring continuity in staff positions, as well as board memberships, and insuring that there is sufficient so-called "new blood" for the good of the organization.

There are two schools of thought regarding limiting the number of terms individuals may consecutively serve on the board of directors or as officers. One viewpoint holds that board members (or officers) should be limited to one or two such terms (whatever the regular term of office might be). The rationale behind this line of thinking is two-fold. *First,* an individual board member should not monopolize a slot on the board or become such a so-called permanent fixture that the individual becomes so powerful a force within the organiztion that the effectiveness and efficiency of the overall board is diminished.

The *second* justification for mandating such a limit on board members' and officers' length of membership beyond a specified number of years is that there really is a need for new blood from the various constituencies the booster club serves. Without vacancies periodically occurring, the likelihood of new members being able to join the organization at the board level or as officers is remote, if not nonexistent.

There are others, however, who recommend that there should be no limit on consecutive membership as a board member or as an officer. These advocates hold that it is advisable, if not necessary, to have significant longevity in leadership at the board level and in terms of the officers. This point of view holds that members of boards and officers function better when board members and/or officers have had significant experience in their respective posts.

The basic concept remains. One must constantly be on the lookout for those with self-serving interests becoming permanent fixtures on self-perpetuating boards or as officers. Stipulations within the bylaws, as to length of consecutive terms and the inclusion of staggered terms of office for both officers and board members, can alleviate many potential problems.

Additionally, in terms of officers, the bylaw might call for a position of president-elect to exist. An individual elected to this position would become president when the term of president-elect expires. This concept can also work with other officers such as the position of secretary-elect and the post of treasurer-elect. The advantage of organizing the officer corps in this manner is the time available for an understudy to learn the "ropes" for the position the person will assume within a year.

It is essential, for continuity purposes, as well as for effectiveness and efficiency of the organization, to provide orientation sessions and training sessions for booster club officers and board members. This is an effort to:

1. Create awareness and appreciation of past, current, and future activities, programs, goals, procedures, policies, and practices of the booster club, the athletic program, and the school or sponsoring organization itself
2. Instill insight into the support role of the booster club insofar as the athletic program is concerned
3. Contribute ideas for current and future activities of the organization
4. Actively play a role in the planning and implementation of activities sponsored by the organization and the athletic program
5. Motivate others within the organization and under the umbrella of athletics toward action in support of the athletic program

Financial Considerations of Athletic Support Groups

The establishment of a booster club or support organization involves work not only in the raising of funds but in the proper managment of the monies gathered. Thus, there are several key financial considerations that should be thoroughly understood by those involved with the raising of funds for sports. These are:

1. To determine whether or not the athletic support group should elect to incorporate as a nonprofit organization and operate as a tax exempt organization (under the eyes of the Internal Revenue Service).
2. To secure an attorney or other qualified individual to prepare and oversee incorporation process, if incorporation is desired, and to complete required annual reports.
3. To establish procedures, if the group is not incorporated, whereby all contributions are made directly to the institution's tax deductible entity (alumni office, development office, foundation, etc.), thus retaining the tax deductibility of contributions.
4. To secure an outside auditor to conduct the annual audit of all financial records (all transactions and records must be available for inspection and be beyond reproach).

Whether to Incorporate or Not

There are advantages and disadvantages of incorporating as a booster club. Being an unincorporated association only necessitates a simple set of by-laws that define membership, provide for the election of officers, the holding of meetings, and include a statement of purposes. Usually it is not even necessary to file any documents in a public office.

A recognized (by the IRS) nonprofit corporation may make it possible to secure a tax-exempt status. While being a nonprofit corporation has specific advantages relating to possible tax deductibility of contributions, there are rather strict federal and state income tax laws that must be complied with in an exact manner. In this instance, the organization's documents, bylaws, and constitution must clearly stipulate that it exists for a nonprofit and charitable purpose, that is, is established to promote educational and sports activities.

It is not necessary, however, for the booster organization to be incorporated as a nonprofit entity in order to play an integral and significant role in generating tax-deductible contributions for the school's athletic program. This may be accomplished by having such contributions and donations made directly to the school's development or alumni office, which, in many instances, will qualify the contributions as tax deductible. Of course, in the final analysis, it is appropriate for peace of mind to confirm the actual interpretation of the federal and state laws with an accountant, attorney, or a representative of the Internal Revenue Service.

Benefits to Booster Club Members

Why do people belong to athletic support groups? There is no single answer to this question. Many people like to be associated with sports, with athletes, and with staff members who make up the sports scene. Others like to have a role in making significant contributions to a worthy cause. Parents of current, future, or former athletes join because of their children. Some individuals desire to pay back to the sporting world some of the benefits which they or their family received as athletes. Still others do it for the pure enjoyment they receive through such association and efforts. Whatever the reasons, and they are both numerous and varied, there are both tangible and intangible benefits that booster club members enjoy.

In many situations, people who join or sustain their membership in support organizations often qualify to receive any number of tangible benefits. Frequently, there is a sliding scale of benefits accruing to those members who join the booster organization at varying levels or within specific categories. This is especially true at the larger colleges and universities, although it need not be the exclusive property of such programs.

Specific Gifts Accruing To Donors

The larger the program, naturally the more options are available in terms of benefits that might be made available to contributors to the sports program and to the athletic support group's membership. Generally speaking, the range of benefits may include, but not be limited to the following list. Benefits the sports promoter might provide for contributors include: (Briggs & Duffy, 1987; Bronzan, 1986; Yiannakis & Branstein, 1983):

1. Preferred parking
2. Complimentary or reduced price tickets
3. Special events ticket priority
4. Dinner and banquet seating priority
5. Plaque or other gift items (premiums) to recognize donor
6. Invitation to social events
7. VIP lounge privilege membership card
8. Periodic newsletters
9. Press guide(s) and other publications
10. Ticket and seating priority (purchase)—various sports

11. Mention and recognition in game programs
12. Away game ticket priority
13. Travel with specific teams
14. Access to press box or other special areas for special teams and/or events
15. Specific apparel to identify donors and contributors
16. Private booth for home contests
17. Auto decal(s)
18. Free golf at university course
19. Free or reduced membership in college health/wellness center
20. Scholarship named after donor
21. Building named after donor
22. Dinner to honor donor
23. Perpetual award given in donor's name
24. Others . . .

One such membership plan, with corresponding tangible benefits accruing to members at varying membership levels, is included in Appendix C. This plan has numerous levels of memberships (including one for corporate sponsorship) with each level possessing different benefits that accrue to the purchaser of the booster club membership.

Controlling Potential Negative "Outside" Influences. The fear of the potential abuse of power and negative influences that booster groups might wield are the principle arguments generally expressed in opposition to such sports organizations. This abuse of power and exertion of negative influence is exemplified in the situation in which donors to the athletic program feel that they have an automatic right, or even an obligation, to exert extreme pressure in terms of how the athletic program is managed or administered.

Challenges Associated with Booster Clubs or Support Groups

While solicitation of outside input is healthy and often advisable, when such input hinders the normal operation of the athletic program, it becomes interference rather than meaningful assistance. On the other hand, a tax-paying citizen should not lose rights just because an individual elects to become a member of a sports support group, such as a booster club. One of the solutions is to have a very clear delineation as to what is acceptable and unacceptable behavior of the booster club itself, as well as its members. With the proper organizational document *coupled* with skilled and dedicated leadership, the so-called booster organization can become an invaluable ally to the total sports program, the staff, and the school itself.

Handling the "Three O'Clock Booster Wonders." Another real concern to athletic administrators and coaches is the "three o'clock booster wonder." It is imperative that the administrators in charge of the fund-raising effort be aware of this category of would-be helpers and be able to identify and deal with them.

The "three o'clock wonders" are those individuals who talk about doing great things but rarely, if ever, actually produce. Often, these individuals are honest, well-meaning persons who would like to be able to do what they say they want to do—the problem is that they cannot perform or produce. They are *talkers* and not *doers*. An appropriate analogy is the "three o'clock wonder athlete" who talks a great "game" during the three o'clock, weekday practice sessions, but when it comes time to actually produce during the 8:00 P.M.. game on Friday night, the result is utter failure.

The "three o'clock booster wonder" frequently takes a significant toll in terms of motivation from others within the group, steals the time and drains the energy from those who are, or could be, the true producers. They end up taking far more—in terms of time, effort and resources—than they contribute toward the sports program. The best course of action in terms of handling these "three o'clock booster wonders" is to isolate them in such a fashion that they cannot do any real harm to the efforts of the organization, without (if possible) alienating them completely.

References

Briggs, J., Jr. & Duffy, J. (1987). *The official soccer fundraiser's guide.* North Palm Beach, Florida: Soccer Industry Council of America.

Bronzan, R. T. (1986). *Public relations, promotions, and fundraising for athletic and physical education programs.* Daphne, Alabama: United States Sports Academy Publishing House. Copyright 1977, by John Wiley & Sons, Inc., reprinted by permission of the author, 1986.

Kramer, W. D., et al. (1988). *Guide to Title IX & intercollegiate athletics.* Squire, Sanders & Dempsey and the National Collegiate Athletic Association. Mission, Kansas.

Lipsey, Richard A. (1992). *Sports market place.* New Jersey: Princeton.

Mauro, T. (1992, February 27). Sex bias law applied to schools. *USA Today,* p. 1-A.

May, Mike. (1990, April). A booster club can work miracles. *Athletic Director,* p. 24.

Official handbook, (1981). North Palm Beach, Florida: Booster Clubs of America, pp. 22–28.

Operating costs for athletics continue to climb. (1990, October). *Athletic Director.* 7(10), 10.

Oregon high school cancels athletics program. (1990, October). *Athletic Director.* 7(10), 15.

Stier, Jr., W. F. (1990, January 3). *Fundraising tactics and promotional practices for intercollegiate athletic programs.* Paper presented at the National Collegiate Athletic Association (NCAA)—Professional Development Seminar, Dallas, Texas.

Sunday Democrat and Chronicle, (1988, August 21). Rochester, New York, p. 3-C.

Yiannakis, A. & Braunstein, S. (1983). *The complete guide to successful fund-raising.* North Palm Beach: American Sport Education Institute.

Phon-a-thon in action. (Courtesy of Iowa State University/photo by Mike Despard, Iowa State Daily)

Staffing—Personnel and Working with Others

4

The Athletic Administrator

The athletic director is the keystone within the sports administrative picture—straddling the gulf existing between the school administration on the one hand and the various constituencies, including the booster club or athletic support group, on the other. The athletic director represents the interests of the athletes and the institution. The administrator also serves as a conduit for information and input between various constituencies and the sport entity. In terms of two-way communication, it is vital that the athletic director serve as *the* communication channel for all requests to the booster club from coaches and others who are seeking funds. It is the athletic director who serves as a leader by example, rather than edict, in terms of effort, enthusiasm, and optimism. Both enthusiasm and optimism are not only contagious but frequently a prerequisite for sustained, successful fund-raising.

Fund-Raisers Are Risk Takers

The sports administrators operating within the fund-raising and promotional umbrella are risk takers who understand the processes, theories, and principles, as well as the challenges, involved in generating support for the sports program. Fund-raisers, to be successful, must implement, adapt, and evaluate numerous tactics, techniques, and methods to fit specific situations in terms of available needs, resources, and circumstances in the pursuit of goals and objectives.

One must not be afraid to **dare.** One should not be fearful of failure. A popular poster is displayed behind the desk of a well-respected and known athletic director. The poster depicts a turtle walking down a path and has a most appropriate caption. Beneath the turtle are the words: *"You Can Only Get To Where You Are Going By Sticking Your Neck Out."* How true these words are in the world of sports fund-raising and promotion.

When Robert Hutchins assumed the post of President of the University of Chicago (at the time, the fourth richest university in the whole country), at the age of 30, in 1929, there was widespread criticism about this "boy wonder." On the day of his inauguration, his father was told by a friend: "I was shocked this morning to read

Principle 13
"No one ever kicks a dead dog."

49

that newspaper editorial denouncing your son.'' His dad replied, ''It was severe, but remember that no one ever kicks a dead dog'' (Carnegie, 1985, p. 54).

Those involved in athletics (at whatever level), and especially those involved in the promotional, public relations, and fund-raising aspects of athletics, must be like the turtle who only arrives at the appropriate destination by sticking its neck out. Such persons are risk takers, by the very nature of the activity in which they are involved. The successful fund-raiser makes things happen. The successful fund-raiser takes calculated risks and learns from mistakes, as well as from successes, of one's own and those of others.

Adequate, Skilled, and Viable Leadership

Identification of leaders as well as individuals with leadership qualities or leadership potential in the fund-raising arena is crucial. However, not everyone can be a ''chief.'' It is necessary to have followers as well. Obtaining and keeping the services and loyalty of an adequate number of skilled and motivated workers, both leaders and followers, is a major task for the sports fund-raising administrator. This remains true whether that person is the booster club president, the coach, the athletic administrator, or principal. What is sought are individuals who, as leaders and as followers, can work together and accomplish goals and perform tasks effectively in a timely fashion and at an acceptable level of competency.

Leadership is more effective if those individuals who are being led are able to feel confidence in the individual assuming the leadership role. Additionally, people are more receptive to having critical decisions made by a leader if they feel that they have some role to play in the decision-making process. Meaningful work toward goals and objectives is not possible without adequate leadership. Leadership is crucial and absolutely essential in the promotional and fund-raising arenas.

Contrary to popular belief, leaders are not necessarily born. Leaders in the fund-raising field can be taught and can be trained. One of the essential requirements of being a leader is that true leaders lead by example in terms of both quality and quantity of their efforts. This is a most important concept, especially when it comes to motivation of the staff.

One also leads by being loyal, supportive, overseeing actions of others in a fair and unbiased manner, reinforcing the efforts of others, motivating (through intrinsic and extrinsic means), evaluating, and giving credit to others. Just as the activities of sports revolve around a successful *team* concept, so too does the fund-raising effort of those involved in sports, whether they are coaches, booster clubs members, athletic administrators, or central administrators.

Responsibilities and Obligations of Others

Sports *administrators* have a job—that of administering and facilitating. *Coaches* have a job—that of teaching and coaching. *Boosters* have a job of supporting, in terms of spirit, services and finances. *Fans* have a job of providing moral and physical support as well as visible encouragement. *Parents* have a job of providing support, feedback, and reinforcement. *Everyone* within the athletic arena is part of the team effort. All of these individuals and constituencies should work in unison, guided and coordinated by the athletic administrator, toward a common goal. Each has a responsibility, an obligation to perform in a specific fashion, and to work toward objectives that, in turn, leads to the ultimate goal. The common goal remains the betterment of the sports program or activity.

The "Lone Ranger" Syndrome

The attitude, which sometimes is pervasive within athletic circles, that it is "far easier to get forgiveness than permission" *is not acceptable.* Such an attitude, and the resultant activities that such an attitude encourages, contributes to the negative image or reputation associated with some athletic fund-raising activities and plagues those involved in such activities. The "lone ranger" concept of doing it "my way and damn the consequences"—the concept that coaches or athletic boosters or others can do it "their way" and operate as independent entities—is long gone, if it ever existed at all. Today, more professionalism is expected of those involved in sport fundraising and promotions. Part of this professionalism is the *team approach* to promotions and fund-raising coupled with two essential components—sound planning and adequate assessment.

Dependency upon Others—The Team Concept

A critical resource of any sport program is the support organization and the individuals, both volunteers and paid staff, standing behind the athletic program. The effectiveness of the supporting booster organization has a great impact on the success of the fund-raising program for any sport team or program. Similarly, the quality, the skill of the people who make up the working staff of the booster club will determine, for the most part, whether or not the major fund-raising activity will be successful. Again, in the final analysis, it is the people involved who determine whether the fund-raising effort is a success or a failure. Usually, individuals do not work alone, especially in the area of generating monies for sport activities; rather, they rely on the team concept (fig. 4.1).

The building of a **team concept** in fund-raising will go a long way to serve as a strong foundation on which the fund-raising efforts can be built. This team concept of fund-raising is best illustrated by viewing the entire fund-raising and promotional arena as a row boat on a lake. *Everyone is in the same "boat," rowing different oars but all working together and heading in the same direction—with the leader(s) stationed at the rudder providing direction and shouting encouragement, keeping all informed of where they are, where they are going, and how well they are performing the appointed tasks.*

Another example used to illustrate the team concept is the attempt to break fifteen wooden match sticks, individually. Quite easy. However, when one attempts to break fifteen wooden match sticks collectively, it is virtually impossible due to the strength each individual match stick gains from the others. So, too, should there be tremendous strength with individuals and organizations working together for the common purpose of generating additional funds for the sports program.

One does not have to be an expert in all aspects of fund-raising and promotions. The key is not to have to know *everything.* Rather, the key is to know where to get the answers, or who to see about obtaining the answers. This means delegating tasks and responsibilities to others. It also means being able to work with and solicit assistance

Figure 4.1 Working together for a common cause.

from others, individuals and groups or organizations. It is important to be willing and able to obtain expert help (hired or volunteer status) to fill the gaps that may exist on the administrative or management *team.*

Delegation—The Key to Effective Administration and Management

In terms of delegation, there are two important rules to remember. *First,* one cannot ever truly delegate **total** responsibility. The athletic director or other appropriate person who has the primary responsibility for the athletic program is still held accountable. Specific tasks and responsibilities *can* and *should* be delegated to others. The person doing the delegating still retains ultimate responsibility for the tasks. One cannot give, as an excuse, that the job or task was delegated to a subordinate and therefore the delegator is not responsible. The buck does indeed stop at the desk of the person ultimately responsible for the sports program or the booster organization, etc. *Second,* when there is delegation, it is extremely important that the task that is delegated comes with appropriate authority to accomplish the task. Delegation without *appropriate authority* is worthless. In fact, it invites disaster.

The Use of "In-House" Staff versus Outside Personnel

One of the first questions to be answered when it comes time to attempt to raise monies revolves around **who** will actually be involved in the work. That is, will members of the athletic staff be involved in the day-to-day, hands-on activities associated with fund-raising? Will volunteer members of the booster organization be involved?

Or will so-called outside "experts," frequently referred to as professional "head-hunters," assume the role of the actual fund-raisers? Will there be a combination of all three?

Arguments can be made for a wide variety of organizational structures involving individuals, groups, and organizations when it comes time to determine who will be out there, on the "firing line," doing the actual work of raising money. The important point is that there is no one right answer for every situation. Much depends upon the specific circumstances that exist at the time for any sports program. That is why there is a need for skilled leadership capable of evaluating the situation and then, based upon facts, resources, and needs, making a decision as to how to structure the overall fund-raising efforts.

The Use of Athletic Staff. The case in favor of having members of an athletic staff actively involved in raising money rests on the fact that these coaches and administrators have a vested interest and are better able to recognize and represent the needs of the school organization, as well as articulate the objectives and goals of the athletic program or activities. There is also a viewpoint that holds that the coaches and/or the athletic director should devote the major portion of their time doing what they were hired to do, that is, to coach or to administer the athletic operation. In some athletic situations, there are athletic staff hired with the primary responsibility of helping to raise money.

On the college and university level today, usually only Division I institutions and a small number of NCAA Division II schools enjoy the luxury of having a full-time administrator responsible for the fund-raising activities of the total athletic department. Sabock and Bortner (1986) revealed that 88% of Division I schools had such a full-time staff member, and, of this number, 97% were male. In terms of background experience, 66% of these full-time fund-raising staff members at Division I institutions had backgrounds in either coaching or athletic administration. This leaves 34% who lacked background in sports, either as a coach or administrator, but yet held the post of full-time fund-raiser for the total athletic program.

In terms of the recency of full-time attention being devoted to athletic fund-raising at Division I schools, 41% of these full-time fund-raisers had been in their posts for three years or less (Sabock & Bortner, 1986). This may indicate that the position of full-time fund-raising staff member might be a transient one, that is, one that involves great mobility on behalf of such staff. It might also indicate that the positions of full-time fund-raisers are of recent origin. In fact, only 60% of all Division I institutions studied had had a formal athletic fund-raising program for more than 10 years. Even at Division I institutions (possessing the high visibility sports programs on the college and university level) the existence of a formal fund-raising program coupled with full-time fund-raising staff is a somewhat recent phenomenon in the United States.

Fund-raising on the NCAA Division II level is even more recent than among the Division I schools. Although today a majority of the Division II colleges and universities find themselves actively involved in external fund-raising, this has not always been the case. In fact, extensive fund-raising is rather recent. A national investigation by Marciani (1991) found 66% of Division II athletic programs had formal fund-raising programs in existence for less than ten years.

The Use of Volunteers or Boosters. Using the skills, time, and resources of volunteers, such as boosters, in lieu of or in conjunction with the efforts of the athletic staff, has the advantage of expanding the sphere of influence of the athletic program, thereby increasing the potential for securing more monies. The key to the successful utilization of genuine ''outside'' supporters or boosters rests in (1) making sure that they have an accurate and complete understanding of the athletic program they are assisting, and (2) insuring that these individuals follow established guidelines as to those activities and actions that are permissible and those that are not. A major benefit of using volunteers and boosters is that all of the monies generated through their efforts remain with the athletic entity for which they are raising the funds.

The Use of Professional Fund-Raisers—Headhunters. The use of professional **headhunters,** individuals, organizations, or companies whose business it is to raise funds on behalf of athletic organizations or schools, is more controversial. While professional fund-raising entities can be most successful, depending upon the situation, there are certain factors to be considered.

First, the headhunters are in the business of raising funds for a profit, their profit. While there is certainly nothing wrong with that concept, sufficient monies must be raised to pay the headhunters their fair profit while still generating sufficient monies to meet the needs of the athletic program.

Second, headhunters often do not have a long-term stake in the athletic program. Care must be exercised in the supervision of the actions (methods and style) of these headhunters lest their activities offend the various constituencies (individuals and organizations) who are being tapped for contributions. Sports constituencies often respond negatively to the ''hard sell'' approach. Here, too, as with formal booster organizations and friends of the sports program, there is a need to establish and to have followed specific guidelines and policies as to what type of fund-raising activities are permissible, when such activities may take place, and who may be solicited by the headhunters.

Third, headhunters usually possess extremely effective skills and have had successful experience in actually raising money. This fact, coupled with the high motivation usually possessed by these professionals, due to the fact that their compensation is dependent upon their actual successes in raising such funds, places the headhunters in an excellent posture to reap meaningful results for the sports program. The downside risk, in terms of expenses for the athletic entity, is almost nil, since no payment is due to the headhunters unless they are successful in generating monies for the sports program. Additionally, time and effort on behalf of the sport program's staff may be spent on other matters, thus reducing the risk of wasted effort on their behalf.

Advantages of Additional Assistance

The use of members of booster clubs, individual supporters, as well as the hiring of professional headhunters, enables the athletic department or program to significantly increase the fund-raising efforts and, hopefully, the amount of monies generated. The time and efforts of the athletic staff is freed up to attend to other essential tasks within the sports scene.

Figure 4.2
Confrontational relationships.

Soliciting the assistance of others—whether individuals, groups, or organizations—can often be a productive method of increasing the likelihood of successfully raising financial assistance for the athletic program. The athletic program is able, through the use of such outside assistance, to geometrically increase the number and type of tools, assets, and resources that can be called upon in the fund-raising process. The determining factors as to the advisability of utilizing outside personnel or organizations rests in the control exerted, the extent of the orientation or education provided, and the quality of monitoring of these outside individuals and groups by the sports administrator(s) in charge of the program.

Typically, outside experts are utilized to assist in such areas as (1) running the concessions' operations, (2) selling advertisements for publications, (3) producing various printed pieces, (4) conducting sports camps and clinics, as well as (5) providing various merchandise for resale.

The cooperative effort or **team concept** in promotions and fund-raising denotes the willingness to work together with a variety of constituencies for common goals and objectives. The atmosphere is one of a *help* mode—not an *interference* mode or a *hindrance* mode. Cooperation among all parties, the **team approach,** is the key. Toward this end, it is essential that all parties involved be willing to engage in a participatory type of working relationship with each other. Adversarial relationships, especially between those individuals who have to work together, not only create roadblocks in terms of current tasks and responsibilities, but stifle the potential creativity of those involved and drain energies needlessly (fig. 4.2).

Who are potential members of the team? The answer is simple—*everyone*—everyone and anyone who can assist in the fund-raising or promotion process. Too frequently, however, inexperienced sports fund-raisers assume an antagonistic posture with those who might not totally agree with them or those who do not completely support their cause. The results are hurt feelings and burnt bridges—both negative consequences for the sports fund-raiser.

Never take personally a disappointment, a rejection, or a setback. Nor should one ever be manipulated to act in a specific way by another person or another person's action(s). Being angry or harboring negative feelings about someone, an organization, or a program because of a personal feeling, resentment, or reaction is foolhardy and

▩ **Principle 14** ▩
Don't create an adversarial relationship with those with whom one works.

counterproductive. Leaving one's emotions out of one's decision making makes for a more effective and efficient sports fund-raising administrator. From a practical standpoint, one cannot continue to work effectively with others when one feels antagonistic toward them. It just doesn't work that way.

Centers of Influence

▒ Principle 15 ▒
Use centers of influence to help gain access to potential contributors.

Individuals who are in a position to influence the decision-making ability of others or who are able to gain access to other individuals or organizations are commonly referred to as **centers of influence.** These are individuals who are in a position to provide referrals or positive recommendations on behalf of the sports program and/or the fund-raising project. They provide introductions to others, thereby enabling the sports program to gain respectability via association, as well as entry to the inner sanctums of an even wider sphere of influence by "piggybacking" upon the reputation and status of the centers of influence. Most frequently, these centers of influence, who play and/or work within the same social or business circles with a wide range of influential individuals, are in a position to contact their peers, friends, close associates, and acquaintances in an effort to solicit assistance on behalf of the sports program.

In reality, the successful fund-raiser utilizes associates and friends to pave the way for requests for help from a third party through a prior call or meeting with the prospect. Even better, the center of influence accompanies the solicitor personally on the visit to the prospective donor.

Hints in the Utilization of Volunteers and Helpers

People are *the* essential ingredient in any fund-raising project—dedicated, interested, loyal, hardworking, sacrificing, cooperative, creative, talented people. The involvement of volunteers in the planning process is beneficial for two reasons. First, the added input and suggestions can be most helpful. Second, such involvement is a great motivating factor on behalf of the volunteers who correctly feel that they have a stake in the activities and the future of the program. When attempting to secure the services and skills of outside volunteers and helpers, it is necessary to realize that there are several general principles to be noted if full utilization and advantage of such individuals are to be realized.

▒ Principle 16 ▒
*25% Rule—
Involvement of others.*

A well-accepted fund-raising maxim that describes the willingness of potential volunteers to become involved in the fund-raising venture is expressed as the **25% Rule.** This rule states that 25% of volunteers will do nearly all that is asked of them. Thank goodness. The majority, the middle 50%, can respond to a cause with persuasive pressures and urging. They can have a significant and positive effect on the fund-raising program. There will, however, always be the remaining 25% who will rarely, if ever, contribute their time, skills, and effort. Recognizing who will and who will not be willing to be involved and capable of actually providing some real assistance is a meaningful skill (see fig. 4.3).

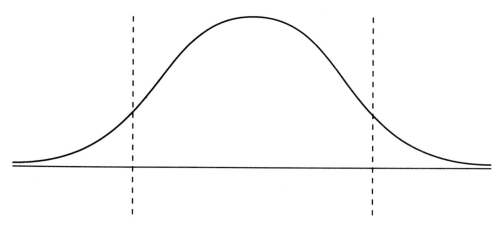

Figure 4.3 Willingness to become involved.

An interesting note regarding the segment of the population who are most immune to almost any plea or tactic regarding contributing as volunteers is that these same individuals are frequently most vocal in their criticism of the cause or of those who do volunteer. These same people seldom give of themselves to a campaign or project, and they frequently threaten to withdraw their supposed support unless events or courses of action are altered to suit their prejudices or desires. How ironic.

An example will suffice. Once upon a time there was a rather lengthy and heated debate among booster club members as they reviewed how a specific fund-raising project (raffle) should be organized, how the prizes were to be obtained, and in what manner the tickets were to be sold to the general public. One person at the meeting was very, very vocal—probably the most vocal person at the meeting. This individual was incessant in his repeated demands that the raffle be organized in a specific manner and that tickets be sold only in a special manner for a specific price.

When all was done and finished and the members in attendance were indicating how many tickets each thought *they themselves* could sell, this most vocal member simply said that he was not about to sell any tickets himself because he did not believe that he should be involved in such activity. Whereupon the other members present promptly threatened to "lynch" the individual on the spot. The point, however, is a poignant one. Sometimes the loudest complainer, the most boisterous loud mouth, is also the least productive and, too frequently, a real hindrance to progress. *Life as a sports fund-raiser is never easy.*

But then, who ever said that raising money for sports is an easy task? If it were, then every Tom, Dick, and Harry or Mary, Jane, and Sue could do the job. There would not be a need for a professional, highly qualified, and trained sports fund-raiser, such as yourself, to serve as the point person leading the charge for better financial footing for the athletic program or team.

Another truism in fund-raising is the **20% rule.** This deals with the area of productivity. Not all individuals are equally productive. The 20% Rule refers to those individuals who are truly effective, who are the real producers and "result-getters."

Principle 17
Beware of those volunteers who protest too loudly.

Principle 18
20% Rule—Productivity of staff.

Generally speaking, these are the individuals (comprising only 20% of the work force on a project) who will do 80% of the work while the remaining 80% of the people account for only 20% of the work. Sports administrators and fund-raising organizers who desire to have a more effective and efficient staff and organization must be able to recognize who are the producers and who are not, and plan accordingly. Much time and effort will be saved if the sports administrator is able to discern the "doers" from the "talkers."

One way to distinguish is to assign small tasks at first before giving individuals greater responsibilities. In that way, one is able to evaluate and discern how these individuals perform (under fire, if you will) in terms of specific tasks and responsibilities. When these individuals successfully carry out their tasks in an effective and efficient fashion, they may be given more difficult tasks that involve more and more responsibility. Conversely, those individuals who are unable to successfully perform simple tasks involving a minimum level of difficulty should not be expected to demonstrate proficiency in tasks that require more skills and competencies.

In effect, those who demonstrate an ability to perform tasks and to actually complete assignments effectively and efficiently are given additional tasks to perform and asked to assume more responsibility. Those who are not so highly skilled (and those who merely talk a great game) are relegated to spectator status. These individuals should not be counted on to actually do anything other than talk—based upon their past performance. The best judge of a person's future success in any task is that person's past record in similar situations.

▓ Principle 19 ▓

Sports administrators have an obligation to recruit, train, evaluate, and motivate volunteers.

A successful volunteer staff does not materialize overnight nor without effort. Quite the contrary. In order to have a consistently productive group of volunteers, it is necessary to make a conscious effort to recruit, train, evaluate, and continually motivate such individuals. Training includes all aspects of the fund-raising arena from dress, to salesmanship techniques, to time management, to motivational activities, to assessment, etc. Similarly, the recruitment of competent volunteers is an ongoing process and centers around the current volunteers and mutual acquaintances. Happy volunteers tend to attract like kind. Unhappy volunteers tend to quit and to bad-mouth the sports organization and/or support organization.

▓ Principle 20 ▓

Fund-raising and promotional activities should be satisfying.

Raising money for a charitable or worthwhile cause is an experience that should be satisfying for both the donors and the solicitors. People should feel good about contributing to a worthy cause. Similarly, people should feel good about soliciting for a meaningful, valuable, and worthwhile project. The activity of fund-raising itself should be exciting. The involvement should be enjoyable for all of the participants. Those who help, in whatever fashion, whether they be the solicitor or the person solicited, should receive positive vibes in exchange for their involvement.

In other words, some reward, some type of satisfaction, and some reinforcement, must be given to the workers who make it all worthwhile. It is wise to remember that administration of fund-raising and promotional activities is a *people business*. Successful internal and external personal relationships are crucial for the truly successful fund-raising or promotional effort. As a result, a sincere effort must be made to maintain high morale on behalf of all workers and to make their experience worthwhile in their own eyes. The result will be motivated workers (either paid or volunteer) willing and anxious to continue or expand their involvement in the future.

One should not be afraid or hesitant to give credit, privately and publicly, to others when due. Volunteers are a great source of untapped assistance, if properly utilized. Provide encouragement, treat them with due respect, thank them, interact with them, provide meaningful recognition, and make them honestly feel like valuable contributors to the *team* effort. Such actions can be a significant motivating factor, not to mention earning improved public relations and increased publicity. Remember, each volunteer has numerous friends and contacts with whom the experience with the sports fund-raising operation can be shared. Hopefully, the experience related to others by the volunteers will be a positive one, further helping the sports program in terms of public relations.

One sports program has a practice of awarding beautifully, expertly designed, three color certificates, suitable for framing, to those individuals who have played a meaningful, supportive role in that particular athletic program. The consequence is that many, many leaders within that community, as well as across the state proudly display the athletic department's framed ''Certificate of Appreciation'' on the walls of their offices or homes.

The end result is that the school and its sports program have profited two-fold. Not only is there a continual positive feeling on behalf of those who have received the framed certificates (at a formal ceremony with appropriate publicity), *but* the certificates themselves continue to create positive exposure, public relations, and publicity for the program. This is possible because the certificates are frequently displayed in a visible spot in the recipient's office or home for an extended period of time.

To keep the volunteers' energies charged up, their enthusiasm high, it is necessary to make them feel valuable and wanted. Motivated and loyal boosters and ''friends of the sports program'' have a high regard and respect for the sport program they are supporting. They have something at stake in the athletic program, *their* athletic program. The following are some key concepts to consider when working with volunteers within the fund-raising and promotional umbrella for sport (Heidrich, 1990; Tedrick, 1989).

■ **Principle 21** ■
Never hesitate to show that volunteers are wanted, needed, and appreciated —acknowledge those who have helped.

1. Volunteers have feelings; therefore, make them feel valuable and wanted, treat them with respect, and provide them with special privileges to reward them for their contributions and efforts.
2. Volunteers have needs; therefore, satisfy them.
3. Volunteers have suggestions; therefore, seek input from them.
4. Volunteers have specific interests; therefore, provide options and alternatives for them to do (there are a ''thousand ways to skin a cat'').
5. Volunteers have specific competencies; therefore, recognize these skills, and don't attempt to place square pegs in round holes.
6. Volunteers are individuals working with other individuals; therefore, encourage them to work as a team, not as competing individuals.
7. Volunteers are not (usually) sport professionals; therefore, treat them with special understanding and empathy.

8. Volunteers are not paid staff; therefore, don't involve them in staff politics.
9. Volunteers desire to be of assistance; therefore, let them know how they are doing (feedback), answer their questions, and provide good two-way communications.
10. Volunteers have the potential to be excellent recruiters, especially through networking, of other potentially helpful volunteers.
11. Volunteers can be trained to assume a variety of roles within the fund-raising process.
12. Volunteers are able to grow in professional competency with appropriate and timely training, guidance, motivation, and opportunity.

Communication
▒ Principle 22 ▒

Communication is an essential ingredient within the fund-raising process.

Techniques of Effective Communication

No normal man or woman can exist in today's society without being able to successfully communicate with others. Certainly the ability to communicate with one's co-workers, as well as with segments of the public through a wide variety of means, is crucial to the mission of the promoter and fund-raiser.

The objective of communication is simply to convey messages. The purpose of conveying messages may include attempting to inform and educate individuals, to create impressions, to change or reinforce opinions held by others, to affect behavior change in individuals or groups in some fashion, to reinforce habits, to develop allegiances, and to establish attitudes. Although the objective of communication may be simplistic, the process is far from simple. In fact, there are so many potential distractions and opportunities for interference between the sender of the message and the receiver that it is a wonder that any meaningful communication takes place in our society.

There are seven essential components for successful communication to exist (Jensen, 1988). These are:

1. Content (Is it accurate?)
2. Clarity (Is it clear?)
3. Credibility (Is it the truth?)
4. Context (Does it fit the situation or circumstances? Is it appropriate to the audience?)
5. Continuity (Do ideas flow from one to another?)
6. Consistency (Are thoughts and words consistent?)
7. Channels (Are adequate means established for the carrying of the message and the receipt of communication?)

▒ Principle 23 ▒

It takes two to communicate.

To be effective, communication must be a two-way process. That is, communication must flow two ways. Communication is impossible without at least two people—the sender and the intended recipient. There must also be a message that can take the form of either verbal or nonverbal communication. Communication can take place through a person's actions or inactions, as well as by one's speech and writings. Communication can be deliberate, incidental, or accidental; however, the fundamental concept of communication is clear. In order to have effective communication, both the sender and the recipient of the message(s) must interpret what is sent/received in

Sender of Message

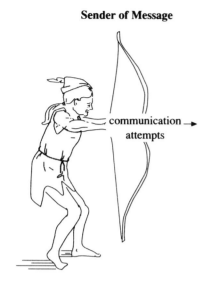

communication attempts →

Barriers to Communication

sexual differences
political differences
misinterpretations
age
religious belief
meanings of words
prejudices/biases
background
interference
words out of context
distractions
poor timing
distance
etc.

Potential Receiver

Figure 4.4 Components of communication.

an identical fashion. If not, the communication is flawed, and false messages and confusion can result. Additionally, listening skills are critical. The good Lord gave us two ears and one mouth—we should learn to utilize our ears twice as much as we do our mouths in communicating with others.

There are numerous barriers to good communication that lessen the effectiveness of the message(s) being sent (Horine, 1991). In fact, in some instances, the message may not even be received because of deficiencies in (1) the manner in which the message is communicated, (2) the message itself, (3) various obstructions, and (4) because of some defect with the intended recipient, (see fig. 4.4).

It is important for the sports administrator to recognize that there are numerous blockages or obstructions that may impede even the best attempts at communication. One has to really work efficiently and effectively at communicating one's ideas to others, whether in a one-on-one situation or in small or large groups (Zeigler & Bowie, 1983). Some of the factors that can affect the effectiveness of communication attempts are listed below.

1. Use of specific language (meaning of words).
2. Misinterpretations of words or terms
3. Political differences
4. Religious beliefs
5. Prejudices
6. Superstitions
7. Age
8. Social/economic background
9. Poor choice of communication medium
10. Interference
11. Lack of clarity
12. Words taken out of context

13. Use of words with more than one meaning
14. Timing of the communication
15. Circumstances surrounding the communication
16. Pride

In every language there are words and phrases that are overused or misused in everyday communication. As such, these words and phrases detract from the essence of the message. Effective administrators and people successful in raising monies and promoting sports must be good communicators and should refrain from repeatedly using such words. A partial list of these words or phrases are included below (Yiannakis & Braunstein, 1983). Essentially, any word or phrase repeated, incessantly, can also fall within this list of taboos.

Words to Avoid in Communication

1. "You know"
2. "As you know"
3. "For sure"
4. "Sure"
5. "You don't say"
6. "Not really"
7. "Don't you know"
8. "I'll tell you what"
9. "Old friend"
10. "Old pal"
11. "My friend"
12. "But honestly, now"
13. "How about that"
14. "How about it"
15. "Trust me"
16. "Believe you me"
17. "Yea"
18. "Uhn, uhn"
19. "You bet"
20. "Ahun"
21. "Yep"
22. "Well I'll be darned"
23. "I know, I know"
24. "Damn"—or any vulgarity

Communicating with Constituencies

Poor communication is deadly and a bane for the would-be fund-raiser or promoter of sports activities. In a sense, if one is not skilled in communicating with outside constituencies, it may be better to refrain from attempts that could be deemed by others as inappropriate, incompetent, or inadequate. This is especially true for the written or printed word.

Far too often the printed document, letter, or published piece coming from the athletic or booster offices lacks in professionalism, effectiveness, and style. This is unfortunate since the written or printed items, which are viewed by innumerable constituencies and segments of the public, can have such a significant and long lasting impression on others. Frequently, they can be the *only* link between the sports program and the recipient of the communication. Hence the advisability of doing everything within one's power to insure that all communication efforts, especially written or printed attempts, are perfect in every way. If it can't be done right (with the Ts all crossed and the Is all dotted), don't do it. Better yet, have someone who has the skills and competencies do it for you.

With whom does the fund-raiser communicate? Potentially, everyone. Communication is completed either through planned attempts via the printed and spoken word as well as by the time worn system of *word of mouth*. One of the oldest and still most effective methods of communicating is through word of mouth. Advertisers and merchandisers throughout human history have relied on word of mouth to communicate ideas and opinions.

In reality, a wide variety of constituencies and numerous segments of the general public are all potential recipients of the communication emanating from the sports administrator, sport booster, and fund-raiser. Some of these constituencies are:

1. Citizen's advisory groups
2. Students
3. Student-athletes
4. Parents
5. Teachers and other coaches
6. Employees
7. Booster club members
8. Business men and women
9. Service organizations
10. Fans
11. General public
12. Sport organizations, leagues, conferences, and associations

The use of any type of audiovisual aid, whether it be photos, graphs, displays, models, films, videotapes, slides, displays, demonstrations, graphics, records, or audiotapes is strongly encouraged in communicating information or attempting to convey an idea or create an image for another. Such efforts reinforce the impact of the actual message and increase the likelihood of the message being both understood and retained. This is true regardless of whether or not the communication is in a one-on-one setting or with large groups. Naturally, the larger the audience, the more essential role audiovisual aids play in the communicative process.

▒ Principle 24 ▒
Use audiovisual aids whenever possible to communicate and reinforce an image or concept.

The Telephone Chain

One of the challenges facing the sports administrator and booster leader is attempting to communicate with a number of individuals within a short period of time. One technique that has proven to be highly successful is the **telephone chain** (Briggs,

Figure 4.5 The telephone chain.

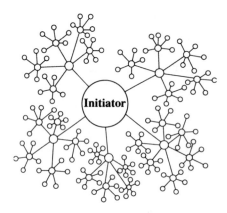

1984). This is a technique in which one individual is assigned to personally contact five others with a specific message (see fig. 4.5). Each of these five contacts in turn have the task for contacting five additional persons to whom the message is to be relayed. When each of these 25 individuals are in turn successful in contacting five additional people, the t tal number of individuals who would have been informed of the initial message numbers 156—quite a significant number in a minimum amount of time and, hopefully, a minimum amount of effort on behalf of any one individual.

Committees

The committee process is often confusing and frequently misunderstood. This holds true for school committees, college committees, and committees within booster groups. The committee process is not a cure-all. There are numerous pitfalls to the use of the committee process. Committees can easily be overused. Committees can consume much too much time on behalf of the members. The committee process is slow and often tedious and can be deliberately misused as a stumbling block or a delaying tactic by the unscrupulous. In short, the committee can become a burden to the sports administrator and to the booster organization.

If utilized in an appropriate manner, however, the committee process can become a great tool that, in turn, facilitates the work toward goals and positively enhances the group dynamics of any organization. The committee can facilitate communication to many constituencies. It is through the committee process that one can take advantage of the talents of others. There is, indeed, inherent strength in numbers. Seeking input from various individuals, through the committee process, enables the organization to tap the skills and energies of a wide range of diverse, highly trained, and skilled people.

The key to the committee process is two-fold: first, to select highly competent, motivated, and contributing individuals who are willing and able to really work in a productive fashion with the membership of the committee; and second, to have the inner workings of the committee structured so that the talents and attributes of the individual members will be facilitated, reinforced, and built upon by one another. The committee process is one example in which the principle of synergism can play a major role. That is, the sum total of the **collective** actions or talents of the members of the committee can have a greater total effect than their **individual** actions or skills.

Formation of a Committee

Whenever there is discussion regarding the need for a committee there are five questions to be initially considered. First, is there a provision for adequate representation from all important groups? Second, are the members of the committee well thought of by others in the community? Third, do the individuals possess the necessary skills and temperament to work together toward the objectives at hand? Fourth, is the committee of an appropriate size? Committees larger than 8 to 10 members tend to be unwieldy and unproductive. And last, are the potential members objective in their outlook and in their dealings with others in the committee process?

The composition of the committee will go a long way toward providing a sound foundation for future success. It is not that the makeup of the committee will insure the successful completion of the committee's tasks, but rather that an inappropriate makeup of any committee makes the tasks at hand just that much more difficult to do. Thus, in an effort to reduce the likelihood of difficulties and roadblocks, it is important to carefully consider potential members, and their strengths and weaknesses, prior to their appointment. After they are appointed, it is frequently too late.

Planning and Organizing an Effective Meeting

Since fund-raising is a people-oriented activity, and since booster clubs involve individuals, it therefore behooves any would-be successful fund-raiser to be competent in dealing with individuals and organizations *within a meeting-type setting*. It is imperative that meetings not consume too much time either in terms of the time spent by each of the individuals in attendance at the meeting and in terms of the actual length of the meeting itself (Byrne, 1987, July 13).

Generally speaking, meetings should have a definite time limit, such as an hour, in which to address the items on the agenda. Any meeting lasting more than 90 minutes should be suspect. It is important to be cognizant of the fact that three meetings, each lasting an hour and involving five people, in effect, consumes fifteen work-hours. Such meetings can be very expensive if they are not properly planned and orchestrated.

Exactly what are the requirements for a successful meeting that involves a number of diverse individuals? First, there is the matter of the purpose of the meeting. Meeting for the sake of meeting is not only unproductive but is a waste of time and effort. The purpose or need for the meeting should be such that the meeting is essential if the need is to be satisfied (Kiechel, 1986, May). An agenda must be established for the meeting. A suitable date, site, and time for the meeting are as essential as is setting a cap on the length of the meeting. Of course, all members receive an advance copy of the agenda items for the meeting. Then, the actual meeting should take place in an efficient and effective fashion in light of the factors cited below.

▒ Principle 25 ▒
The mind will absorb only what the seat will endure.

Working with Committees in Meetings

Once committees have been formed, there are some guidelines that, if followed, will facilitate the total committee process. These following guidelines will enable the committee to effectively and efficiently work toward the stated goals and objectives at hand (Tropman & Morningstar, 1989; Nisbet, 1989).

In order to have well-run and productive meetings:

1. Schedule meetings on a regular basis.
2. Start meetings on time.
3. Take roll call to determine whether or not there is a quorum.
4. Recognize and introduce all guests.
5. Solicit additions to the agenda and approval of the final agenda items.
6. Prepare an agenda well in advance.
7. Stick to the agenda.
8. Be sure that the goals of the committee are clearly understood by the members.
9. Keep accurate minutes of the meeting.
10. Distribute minutes of the meeting as soon as possible after the meeting.
11. Keep discussions open, brief, and germane to the topic(s).
12. Establish a warm and friendly (help mode) atmosphere conducive to decision making and answering and exploring questions.
13. Encourage frankness among committee members (telling it like it is).
14. Keep all reports and open discussion brief and pertinent to the subject(s) at hand.
15. Make the members aware of the subject of the meeting.
16. Encourage members to become knowledgeable and to do their homework (reading) *before* the meeting.
17. Require those individuals desiring to comment to seek recognition from the floor.
18. Discourage aimless discussions.
19. Stipulate that a group or subcommittee be appointed to study the subject and report back to the full committee when situations warrant it.
20. Keep all responses short and to the point.
21. Remind members to speak in a clear and audible voice, so others can hear clearly.
22. Insist that members talk to the entire group and not segments of the committee or to individual members.
23. Influential people (those who speak "softly but carry a big stick") often save their comments until they really have something to say and are able to back up their statements with facts.
24. Sum up salient points of the discussion at the end of the presentation or discussion.
25. Ask dissenters to summarize their convictions in a direct statement, thus permitting a thorough examination of the idea(s) that could be highly constructive when understood.
26. Decide which generally accepted parliamentary procedures are to be used at the meeting, such as Roberts Rules of Order Newly Revised.
27. Assign as tasks the gathering of needed information. Decisions depend on advice given that, in turn, should be based on data and information.
28. Delegate tasks to appropriate committee members.
29. Be sure that committee assignments are clearly stated and understood, including priorities.

30. Hold members accountable for specific tasks and responsibilities.
31. Follow the advice and recommendations of the committee unless there are specific circumstances or justification that warrants other courses of action.
32. Be sure to adjourn at a reasonable hour.
33. Express thanks and appreciation to all the committee members at an appropriate time and place (preferably publically).

Taking Advantage of Advisory Groups (Committees)

Advisory groups are a special form of committees. Examples of advisory groups might be "Athletic Advisory Committees," "Parents Advisory Committees," "Community Advisory Committees," "Facility Advisory Committees," and "Financial Advisory Committees." Such groups or committees are usually formed to take advantage of the expertise of the membership and to seek input from the members in any number of areas.

There are two cautions to be aware of when dealing with such advisory groups comprised of "heavy hitters." First, the members of such advisory groups, being "heavy hitters" and respected individuals in the community, should never be assigned menial tasks to perform. Nothing discourages these highly skilled and respected individuals from continuing their association with the advisory group than to be asked to become involved in Mickey Mouse activities.

The second caution centers around accepting the input or recommendations of such a powerful committee. Generally speaking, the recommendation(s) of the advisory group should be accepted and acted upon unless there is a very strong reason not to do so. And in this case, it is absolutely essential to adequately and clearly communicate the reasons for not following the advisory group's recommendations and suggestions.

Scheduling Meetings for a Specific Fund-Raising Campaign or Project

When organizing a specific fund-raising campaign, it is necessary to establish meetings at strategic times during the campaign so as to properly organize the overall activities. Another reason is that this keeps the personnel who are involved with the project both informed and motivated. Usually, four general meetings will suffice (Briggs & Duffy, 1987). Specifically,

1. The *kick-off meeting* should be an exceptional gathering. Window dressing and excitement are essential. Use of a key motivator to kick off activities is frequently helpful.
2. The *second meeting* might take the form of a luncheon or dinner. It is at this time that progress reports are made and evaluated. Hopefully, by this time up to 75% of the stated goal would have been achieved.
3. A *third meeting* is a near final review of the status of the effort. If necessary, final changes can be made at this gathering for the extra effort that might be needed the remaining week or two of the campaign.

4. The *final gathering* is the wrap-up meeting and might center around either a luncheon or dinner. This is the time for the fund-raising teams and individual producers to be thanked, to be recognized, and given awards, if any. Outstanding achievers are noted, and selected notables receive special momentos (wall plaques or certificates suitable for hanging on their office or den walls).

Results Orientation

Deciding on a specific campaign strategy or fund-raising tactic is often easier said than done. As anyone who has ever been involved in athletics knows all too well, "talk is cheap." What counts are results. Nowhere is this more true than in the area of fund-raising. Although there are over a thousand and one different promotional tactics and fund-raising activities that could be attempted, not every school or sports organization can utilize such projects in an identical fashion without some customizing and adapting of the activities to fit the specific circumstances, resources, and parameters that exist with one's school or sports program.

Going through all of the motions of attempting to raise monies, doing all sorts of work, and spending inordinate amounts of time attempting to raise funds are meaningless unless the results, the actual resources sought, are realized.

▒ Principle 26 ▒

*Mere practice and effort do not produce results—*quality *practice and* quality *effort produce results.*

It is not how hard one works or how long one works. Rather, it is how effective one is in doing those things that end in desired *results.* We are living in an age of accountability. We work in a results-oriented society. Rightly or wrongly, we are judged by results, not how long or hard one works at the job. This is especially true in terms of the sports fund-raising and promotional arena.

Individuals involved in the area of sports promotions and fund-raising must be **goal oriented** and **success driven.** While effort expended and good intentions are important, it is far more important to have concrete results. Of course, that is easier to say than to accomplish. Many would-be fund-raisers and/or promoters exist. The number of successful, effective, and efficient fund-raisers and promoters are fewer in number.

How does one measure success? What criteria are used? Are anecdotal stories sufficient? Are mere feelings adequate? Or is there a real need for hard, concrete data that stands up to the scrutiny of close examination? Although everyone believes that results are important, it is obvious that it is easier to measure results in some areas than in others. All too frequently, and sometimes most unfortunately, especially in the world of amateur sports, anecdotal information and gut feelings form the foundation for many decisions.

It is, therefore, of the utmost importance to attempt to obtain objective, measurable data and figures, whenever possible. Doing so prevents projecting an image of a "hit-or-miss operation." Doing one's homework by planning, conducting *feasibility research,* and assessing prior activities is indicative of a professional approach. Such action helps to establish confidence and provides much needed experience to those involved in the work of fund-raising and promotions.

Collecting Data for Decision Making

Hard Data Collection. Some examples of measured results and data that can easily be collected include such information as the amount of money raised, the number of tickets sold, the number of people within a community, the number of specific organizations in the community, the number and type of other sports organizations within a geographical area, the demographic snapshot of the community, the number of prospective contributors within a specific area, the number of prospects contacted, the number of phone calls made, the number of individuals attending an event, the number of people contributing specific sums of money, and the number of programs printed and sold. This may be referred to as **hard data** collection. A variety of decisions can be made on the basis of such information, and it is possible to compare the information with other data in a comparative analysis so that appropriate decisions can be made.

The local chamber of commerce, local newspapers, area libraries, schools, and even the community city hall are key sources of hard data about the community in which the sports program finds itself. Also, one's own records and files may well contain valuable information that can aid in future fund-raising efforts. This is why record keeping is so vital. The ultimate objective is to be able to find, collect, and present, in a meaningful and understandable format, information that will prove to be helpful in making sound and defensible decisions relative to one's own fund-raising and promotional efforts.

Soft Data Collection. There is another type of data collection and assessment that is often helpful when dealing with sports promotions and fund-raising called **soft data.** An example of soft data is commonly referred to as opinion research. Although more difficult and challenging to obtain, the data and results dealing with the opinions of individuals, the acceptance of ideas by others, the perceptions held by others, and reasons people act as they do, can be of great help in the decision-making process. This type of data can be obtained through the use of surveys, as well as informal input gathered via conversations with others.

It is important to note that individuals' opinions are generally determined more by actual deeds and events than by words. Also, opinions are essentially determined and shaped by self-interests and tend to diminish without acute reinforcement by words or actual happenings. Individuals tend to form more opinions, more easily, regarding specific goals and objectives than about the means and methods to reach these same goals and objectives.

Conducting opinion research involves three distinct but related activities. First is to assess the current situation. That is, what do people currently think about the sports program and why? Second, determine how public opinion operates in the community in which one operates by attempting to identify the various forces that help shape public opinion. Every community has a different power structure that helps to formulate public opinion. Third, utilize testing before and after a specific period of time during which one's promotional and/or fund-raising efforts will take place. For example, test a certain segment of the population for opinions and attitudes before and after a season of the specific sport or before and after a specific promotional project or change in personnel.

Those involved in sports fund-raising need to build upon a *data base* of knowledge, information, and facts so that *accurate* and *timely decisions* can be made. A partial list of such information includes: (1) names of donors (past, current, potential); (2) past ticket sales (regular, special event, seasonal); (3) mailing list of representatives of news media (print, television, radio); (4) identification of current and potential centers of influence; (5) summaries of past fund-raising and promotional activities (successes and failures); (6) updated list of various publics and constituencies; (7) needs assessments of various constituencies; (8) membership list of the booster organization; (9) mailing addresses of parents; (10) mailing addresses of businesses and corporations; (11) activities of other sports related organizations; (12) listing of dates on which other sports activities are being held; (13) amounts of money previously raised, etc.

▨ Principle 27 ▨

Sports fund-raisers and promoters are in the business of determining the publics' needs and then meeting these same needs.

There is a real advantage to ascertaining what people think about specific topics. With this knowledge, sports promoters can plan an appropriate course of action to meet the needs of the public(s) and to take advantage of people's perceptions. There is even an urgency to keep up-to-date as to what regard (whether positive, neutral, or negative) various constituencies and segments of the general public hold one's sports program. It becomes profitable to know the actual, as well as the perceived, needs of individuals and groups within the community.

Fund-raising is really a matter of determining needs on behalf of the consumers, constituencies, or publics (or even creating the needs themselves, in some instances). Then it behooves the fund-raiser to do whatever it takes to satisfy these same needs. Unless the sports fund-raiser is cognizant of the feelings and opinions of the potential donors, contributors, supporters, and consumers, and unless the sport promoter recognizes the so-called needs of these same individuals and groups, how can the sports program(s) be marketed and promoted in an effective and efficient fashion?

Simply stated, there should be a match between the real and perceived needs of the various constituencies or segments of the public and the offerings of the sports program so that these programs can meet these needs.

Criteria for a Successful Sports Fund-Raiser

In the evaluation of fund-raising efforts, a key determinant is how cost effective the project or activity becomes in terms of *time spent, effort expended,* and *resources utilized.* Additionally, there are three factors exhibited by most successful sports promoters and fund-raisers at every level. These attributes or characteristics, in terms of a person's actions, are (1) quality of work, (2) consistency in performance and (3) systematic continuity of effort (fig. 4.6).

There is a need for **quality** in everything one does: quality in terms of time spent, quality in terms of one's efforts, and in terms of one's accomplishments. It is the quality of what an individual accomplishes rather than the **quantity** of one's work that garners respect for one's efforts and places value upon one's contributions.

In addition to quality, there is a need for **consistency** in one's actions. Anyone can be successful once, a flash in the pan, so to speak. A mark of a truly competent

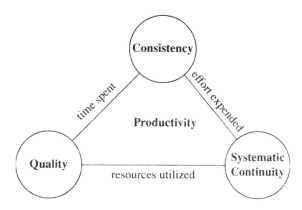

Figure 4.6 Productivity of fund-raising efforts.

fund-raiser is one who can consistently, over a period of time, produce positive, quality results (measurable) that can be directly attributed to the planned, systematic, and well-coordinated activities.

Finally, there is a need for systematic **continuity** in one's efforts. That which is accomplished should have some long-term, positive, residual effects so that further efforts will be able to be built on what has been previously achieved.

Hindsight is indeed a wonderful teacher. Too often, however, we fail to learn from the past, ours as well as others. One does not have to reinvent the wheel in terms of what has been tried before. This is an important concept to follow throughout one's involvement in sports fund-raising and promotion.

A helpful tactic in assessing the effectiveness and efficiency of a fund-raising activity is to take the time to periodically review what has already taken place. This is especially useful once the task has been completed. It is then that the staff can sit down, with the added value of hindsight in a calm, cool, and collected atmosphere, and review what could or might have been done differently, as well as what should be repeated to improve the project and enhance the likelihood of greater success, should the task be attempted in the future. Learning from one's successes and failures, as well as those of others, only enhances the likelihood of success in the future.

Globally speaking, continually appraising one's efforts by conducting a periodic public relations, promotional, and fund-raising **audit** is beneficial. An ongoing process of error detection and correction is mandatory (Hardekopf, 1989). The highest priority should periodically be given to assessing the public relations effectiveness and efficiency. Far too often, however, public relations is wrongly equated with publicity. As stated earlier, publicity is only one of the many tools used in a comprehensive public relations program. A desire to maintain a high level of quality in all that is done within the promotional, public relations, and fund-raising arena is essential. Similarly, one must be willing to ask oneself searching, pertinent questions and be able to provide honest responses. Discovering what various constituencies feel about the sports program, what they know about its accomplishments, goals, and objectives and its needs, will help direct future promotional and fund-raising activities. In short,

Principle 28

Use hindsight as a tool to assess one's work.

Principle 29

Conduct a periodic "audit" of one's fund-raising and promoting efforts.

there needs to be an honest, continuous, comprehensive effort to assess the effectiveness and efficiency of the public relations, promotional, and fund-raising efforts. Without knowing where one is, it is awfully difficult to plot, with any accuracy, what one needs to do or what path to choose to follow to reach the ultimate goal.

Steps in Assessing Fund-Raising Activities

Once the campaign or project is over, there is still much work to be done. One of the first things that should be done is to adequately thank all those who played a role in the success of the campaign or activity. *This is an absolute must.* The more professional and visible this expression of appreciation can be made, the better.

Additionally, there is a need to review the activities and the accomplishments during and immediately after the conclusion of the campaign, while things are still fresh in one's mind. This is the time to review the written reactions and suggestions that had been made throughout the campaign. In this way, it is possible to have ready reference to ideas and suggestions that, if implemented, would improve and enhance the operation in the future. Thus, maintaining detailed records of what takes place in any fund-raising activity is an important requirement. Such record keeping is the first step in establishing a meaningful and complete evaluation of the activities.

There should also be a checklist of things that had to be accomplished and an indication whether they were accomplished in a timely and acceptable manner. There will need to be a recommendation sought as to whether or not the project should be repeated in the future, and if so, what changes should be implemented to improve the campaign. This is where the value of hindsight comes into play. However, one must work at using hindsight by keeping explicit records and seeking input and recommendations immediately after such a project has been completed. Waiting several months will dilute the ability of those who worked with the project to remember details.

Why Fund-Raising Efforts Fail

There are numerous reasons why fund-raising tactics fail. There are almost as many reasons for failure as there are different projects. However, a few of the reasons stand out above the rest and deserve mention here. One reason efforts at raising money for sport programs meet with less than success is that individuals try to copy *exactly* another program *without* taking into consideration the different circumstances, limitations, and resources that exist in their particular athletic situation.

A second reason is the expectation of immediate gratification. There is an expectation that the so-called successful fund-raising project will take place almost immediately, without adequate, advanced planning. Finally, there is the attempt to substitute quantity for quality in terms of both individual and group activity. It is still better to do a few things correctly than attempting to spread oneself so thin that the result is less than a quality effort.

Naturally, a lack of any of the essential ingredients necessary for a successful fund-raising effort will significantly hinder the attempt to generate funds. The absence of proper leadership, as well as "followship," the absence of periodic assessment of efforts, the lack of necessary resources, inadequate allocation of resources, lack of priorities, poor timing, outside competition, misunderstanding of the needs of the publics, absence of a marketable product, absence of a good cause, poor or adverse publicity and/or public relations, failure to emphasize the urgency of the fund-raising opportunity, tasks that are too complicated, campaigns or activities that last too long, a lack of motivation to act (lack of urgency), and poor implementation tactics can hinder or even doom the fund-raising project.

References

Briggs, J. Jr. (1984). *The official football fund-raiser's guide.* North Palm Beach, Florida: Boosters Clubs of America.

Briggs, J. Jr. & Duffy, J. (1987). *The official soccer fund-raiser's guide.* North Palm Beach, Florida: Soccer Industry Council of America.

Byrne, J. A. (1987, July 13). Making the most out of meetings. *Business Week,* p. 120.

Carnegie, D. (1985). *How to enjoy your life and your job.* New York: Pocket Books, a division of Simon & Schuster, Inc.

Hardekopf, B. (1989). Developing the campaign. *College Athletic Management (CAM),* p. 36.

Heidrich, K. W. (1990). *Working with volunteers in employee services and recreation programs.* Champaign, Illinois: Sagamore Pub., Inc.

Horine, L. (1991). *Administration of physical education and sport programs* (2nd ed.). Dubuque, Iowa: Wm. C. Brown Publishing.

Jensen, C. R. (1988) *Administrative management of physical education and athletic programs.* (2nd ed.) Philadelphia: Lea & Febiger.

Kiechel, W. III. (1986, May). How to take part in a meeting, *Fortune.* pp. 177–180.

Marciani. L. (1991, May). Mining for Division II gold. *Athletic Business,* pp. 49–52.

Nisbet, M. A. (1989). Meetings-Keeping minutes losing hours. *Canadians Banker,* pp. 48–51.

Sabock, R. & Bortner, J. (1986, September). Fund-raising: High priority in Division I-A. *Athletic Business,* pp. 80–83.

Tedrick, T. (1989). *Volunteers in leisure*: A management approach. Reston, Virginia: American Alliance for Health, Physical Education, Recreation and Dance.

Tropman, J. E. & Morningstar, G. C. (1989, Fall). *Dividend.* Ann Arbor, Michigan: University of Michigan, School of Social Work and School of Business Administration, pp. 28–33.

Yiannakis, A. & Braunstein, S. (1983). *The complete guide to successful fundraising.* North Palm Beach: American Sports Education Institute.

Zeigler, E. F. & Bowie, W. (1983). *Management competency development in sport and physical education.* Philadelphia: Lea & Febiger.

Bernie and the Bandit. Burt Reynolds, star of the "Bandit" movies visits with Florida State University President, Bernard "Bernie" Sliger, who dressed up like the sheriff in the "Bandit" movies for the dedication of the Burt Reynolds Hall on the Seminole campus. (Courtesy of Florida State University)

Publicity and Public Relations— Working with the Media

5

One of the best advantages a sports practitioner can enjoy is a professional relationship with members of the news media. Anything that facilitates this relationship is to be encouraged. Conversely, anything that hinders such a relationship is inherently dangerous, if not disastrous, for the sports program. It takes work, true effort, to develop and nurture this professional relationship.

Fund-raisers being involved as they are in the very visible task of generating monies for their sports programs must develop and cultivate positive and productive relationships with all members of the media, print, television, and radio. Those involved in the fund-raising and promoting processes must possess knowledge and develop competencies that will facilitate their working with the news media. All too frequently the promoter and/or the fund-raiser will need to exercise skill in dealing with the various representatives of the media in the process of implementing the fund-raising plan or a specific promotional effort.

Frequently, athletic personnel, booster club members, and general fans become irritated with what they view as failure of the news media to provide what the sport fans and boosters view as supportive news, positive exposure, and favorable publicity, either for their sports program or for a specific promotional or fund-raising project. *However, that is not the goal of the news media.* Nor should it be. The media has two major responsibilities to the public. The *first* responsibility revolves around the reporting of the news, the facts, in an unbiased fashion, period. The *second* responsibility is to report news that the general public is interested in and finds informative and satisfying.

There can never be any guarantees that the media, whether it be the print or electronic media, will provide the type or extent of sports coverage those involved in athletics desire. This is especially true for those who are involved in fund-raising and those who desire extensive media coverage to help reinforce or facilitate the fund-raising process itself. One of the difficulties is that the news media (radio, television, or print) cannot assume the role of providing free advertising for the fund-raising effort or promotional project. Those involved in sports fund-raising must recognize that the duty of the representatives of the various news media is to report the news. The media has an obligation, a role to play, and that is to meet the needs of the public by providing supposedly unbiased news and information. Editorial comments

Developing Professional Relationships with the Media
▬ Principle 30 ▬

Establish consistent and positive working relationships with the media.

are also appropriate provided they are identified as such. The ultimate determination of what is news and what is not news is made by the news media.

Determination of What Is News

What exactly is considered news? When people do something of significance or accomplish something of value, it is news. The significance of what is accomplished or achieved depends on what is being done, who is doing it, and the difficulty or uniqueness involved. Announcements of a specific fund-raising project might be news in one community or in one situation and not be worthy of even a mention in other circumstances. Periodic reports on progress toward a goal might be newsworthy.

Similarly, a report on a significant achievement, such as the completion of a fund drive with the goal being reached or surpassed, is certainly a candidate for mention in some media vehicles. Perhaps an announcement of the election of officers for the booster group (including photos) might be of sincere interest within some communities. The more visible the individuals serving as officers, the greater likelihood of their being mentioned by the media. Of course, any unusual special event is a possibility for inclusion within a newspaper or on a broadcast. Again, it varies from community to community.

The size of the community has a significant effect on the extent of news coverage for any sports program. News coverage of a high school team in Chicago and coverage of a school within a small community in the deep south can significantly differ. That is just reality. In large metropolitan areas, the secondary and small college sports programs always have to compete for available space, in both the print and electronic media, with the national news, the major university athletic programs, and professional teams. The result is that the major sports programs and professional teams always seem to garner greater exposure. Such is life.

Negative News versus Positive News

Although sports people hate to admit it, negative or controversial news does deem to "sell" better than positive news. Negative news may be considered to be more newsworthy in the eyes of many reporters and editors as well as members of the public. Sometimes this can have unfortunate consequences. For example, during the same season a college had a number-one ranked wrestling team within the NCAA, Division III (per the NCAA poll), and also had an ice hockey team that had over 15 players threatening to quit unless the head coach was fired. The resultant publicity from the two events was totally lopsided in favor of the hockey situation and the complaining athletes. The athletic director investigated the circumstances surrounding the ice hockey situation and found that there was absolutely no substance in the players' charges and the dissident players were subsequently dropped from the squad. In terms of column-inch coverage within the area paper, the ice hockey controversy received 40 times the amount of space (plus a 5" x 7" photo on the front of the sport's page) that the wrestling team received during the same regular season. The wrestling team *finally got a total of one column inch on the fifth page of the sports section.*

One of the area sports writers was asked by the athletic director why so much attention and space were being devoted to the negative ice hockey controversy and hardly a mention was made of the school's number-one national ranking of the wrestling team. The reply was, "Every year someone in this country is ranked number one in wrestling." Additionally, the sports writer pointed out that it was a rarity that a majority of team members at a college threaten to quit unless the coach is fired. Besides, the writer pointed out that people really want to read about negative and controversial happenings; that is what sells papers, that is what keeps editors happy, and that is what enables writers to keep their jobs.

Principle 31
It may not be fair, it may not be just, it may not be "right"— but it does happen. It is reality.

Although this may seem like small consolation, there is something to be said about receiving any kind of publicity, even so-called negative publicity. Public exposure is still exposure. Sometimes it is possible to turn around what had initially been perceived as negative publicity to something more positive.

Principle 32
There is almost no such thing as completely negative publicity.

Witness the above example of negative publicity with the ice hockey team and the dissenting and disgruntled athletes. Certainly, the college initially received bad press. However, the athletic department, through an open communicative posture on behalf of the athletic director and the coach with the media, parents, fans, and the general public, was able to appraise and educate these constituencies as to the proper role of athletics within an educational setting. The end result was a better understanding by numerous segments of the public (both internal and external to the institution) of the ice hockey program, the athletic department, and even the institution itself. In fact, in the second season after the dissident athletes had been removed, this same team under the auspices of the same talented head coach finished with the sport's best win/loss record in the history of the college.

The job of the fund-raiser is to facilitate the job of the news media staff. Don't make it hard for representatives of the media to help you. Provide them with exactly what they need, when they need it, and in the style and format that they can use, with as little inconvenience or need for change as possible.

Principle 33
Make it as easy as possible for the representatives of the media to utilize the news items you send to them.

Dos and Don'ts of Working with News Media

Things to Do. Be cooperative at all times, and be accessible by phone. News is a highly perishable commodity. It should be remembered that the newspapers and the electronic media want *news* and not *publicity,* and they need it while it is still news and not history (Frost, Lockhart & Marshall, 1988). In an attempt to facilitate relationships with news media, the fund-raiser should:

1. Become personally acquainted with the news people. The personal touch goes a long way in developing a positive professional relationship.
2. Call and visit the media representatives to find out what they want, what they need, and when they need it.
3. Send the news releases to the correct department and person. Be aware of personnel changes within the news media (such changes are indeed frequent and often without notice).

4. Treat media representatives appropriately, honestly, and fairly. Develop a reputation for honesty through one's actions.
5. Give timely, accurate, and updated materials; meet all deadlines consistently.
6. When news occurs, get the story out as fast as feasible—**hot** news is needed.
7. Give as much service as needed to the media. Go the extra mile in terms of effort.
8. Be ready to supply the print media appropriate pictures and correct statistics in addition to stories—on time.
9. When talking with the media, keep responses brief and to the point so there is less chance of being misquoted.
10. When dealing with student representatives of the media, tape interviews openly to encourage accuracy in reporting.
11. Be candid—answer questions as best you can.
12. Nip a rumor as soon as it becomes known.
13. Provide news, not publicity.
14. Provide media with good feature material.
15. Make time for the press on a reasonable basis.
16. Respect media problems.
17. Always call in scores of wins and losses; only calling in wins and good news is a major professional gaffe.
18. In providing information, use proper grammar and spelling and appropriate semantics. Be precise, concise, accurate, polite—*do it right*.
19. Be familiar with the deadline of every radio station and newspaper on your list of media when calling with final scores.
20. Be sure to have all the material you need when you call in your scores—final statistics, score books, quotes, key plays of the game, top performers, correct final score, team records, and upcoming games.
21. Know your mail distribution time systems and the deadlines of the media. Specifically, know times and dates when news media go to press or on the air, and send materials accordingly—know when to mail any releases.
22. Determine the light days of the media, and plan to distribute releases for these days.
23. Check with the public affairs director or program director of the station in terms of getting on the air with a public affairs type program.
24. Say "thank you" for a good story on a team, etc.
25. Arrange to involve, recognize, and/or honor media personnel at public functions, such as dedication ceremonies and special events.
26. Have an "open door" policy in terms of sharing information.
27. Provide free tickets and appropriate notices of all events to media representatives.

Things Not to Do. There are some things that fund-raisers and promoters should avoid in their relationships with representatives of the news media (Yiannakis & Braunstein, 1983). Specifically:

1. Don't make careless and indiscreet statements to news personnel.
2. Don't attempt to bribe or buy favors with gifts and promises beyond the usual and accepted practices—no exclusive stories, etc.

3. Don't take it personally when the media fail to include stories about one's program and/or when negative news is included.
4. Don't become angry or confrontational with members of the media.
5. Don't seek trouble or controversy.
6. Don't stress or depend on off-the-record accounts.
7. Don't pad a weak story.
8. Don't beg or demand to have a story used.
9. Don't threaten to withdraw advertising or to seek support of advertisers (this is coercion).
10. Don't ask media to kill or suppress a story except under the most dire circumstances.
11. Do not employ publicity stunts that border on press-agentry.
12. Never ask for a retraction—if necessary ask for a "correction."
13. Do not "double plant," that is, give the same story to two different departments of the same media outlet.
14. Don't be an obvious promoter of unimportant items.
15. Don't try to block news by evasion, censorship, pressure, or trickery.
16. Don't give "scoops," and don't play favorites.

The ability to recognize when one makes an error coupled with the ability and willingness to admit one's mistakes and then go on with the tasks at hand are valuable traits for any individual, especially for the person involved in the action-packed and hectic world of sports promotion and fund-raising. The time spent in attempting to cover up errors or in denying one's involvement or responsibility for errors or misjudgments is not only wasteful in terms of time and effort but can actually be detrimental in terms of one's image in the eyes of others. No one appreciates an "excuse maker." One should be willing to recognize and admit errors in judgment and to learn from one's mistakes. One should not allow such mistakes to serve as hindrances to further efforts on the tasks at hand, that is, attempting to raise resources for the athletic programs.

▒ Principle 34 ▒
Admit mistakes— never try to cover up errors.

A helpful hint when attempting to address controversial issues and the news media is to always deal with the written or printed word rather than the spoken word when one provides information or data to the news media. It is just too easy to be misinterpreted and misquoted when speaking over the phone or in a personal interview situation. Besides, taking time to create a written news release in response to a controversial topic provides the sports information director and the fund-raiser with the opportunity to check all of the facts and to have appropriate athletic staff double check the release for accuracy and appropriateness, prior to its being distributed to the media.

▒ Principle 35 ▒
When dealing with controversial issues, provide written releases to news media.

Never overstate the facts. Never fluff things beyond proportion. Sport people must retain respect and integrity in terms of public relations, promotions and fund-raising. If these are lost through unprofessional conduct, exaggerations, half-truths, or outright lies, they become most difficult to regain. The old adage of "Fool me once, shame on you, but fool me twice, shame on me" is applicable here.

▒ Principle 36 ▒
Tell the truth, the whole truth, nothing but the truth—If one is to have credibility.

▓ **Principle 37** ▓

*Keep the public and
the news media
abreast of
developments at every
step or stage of the
fund-raising project.*

Keep media representatives cultivated or properly informed at each step of the campaign or at strategic times of the year. The more the general public and various constituencies know about one's program, its goals, its efforts, its needs, and the organization's purposes, the better. This can be facilitated by keeping the media (television, radio, newspapers) up-to-date on all activities. Additionally, since public relations is an ongoing activity, one should attempt to keep the public aware of what the sports program is all about by taking advantage of opportunities to spread the "good news" to various publics, via speaking engagements, involvement in charity activities, etc.

Involvement of Media (Radio, Television, Print)

There are several ways to become involved with representatives of the media in terms of one's own sports program. First, there is the communication process by which the coach or sport official communicates pertinent information to the media representatives to insure effective coverage by the media. Second, there is the business relationship in which agreements are consummated for trade-outs and/or payment for various services, advertisements, etc. Third, there is the reciprocal type of involvement in which a media representative is asked to become professionally associated with the sport or sports program. An example of this reciprocal type of involvement is when reporters, announcers, or editors are requested to throw out the first ball at the baseball game, to serve as a master of ceremonies at a banquet, or to serve as a member of an evaluation team assessing the total program's effectiveness in reaching the public. Media representatives might serve on the selection committee for a Hall of Fame or an All-Tournament athletic event. The objective is to become involved with the media in a professional manner.

Essentials of Publicity

Publicity is the process of planned sharing of specific information in an attempt to inform or influence others. Publicity has a specific and limited "life" in that its usefulness diminishes rapidly if not utilized and shared within a reasonable period of time after its occurrence. Thus, it is imperative to disseminate news items as soon as possible. In terms of media, the objective is to be mentioned frequently for positive reasons in a variety of media so that members of the public will remember the sport or program and its achievements and will hold the program and its personnel in a positive light.

Generally speaking, publicity can play a role in winning friends and supporters, influencing individuals and groups, promoting events and programs, sharing new ideas or reinforcing previously held concepts, and promoting the organization and the individuals associated with the program. On the other hand, publicity is a poor substitute for the truth, and it certainly cannot be a lasting substitute for good works. To paraphrase Abe Lincoln, one can fool some of the people all of the time, all of the people some of the time, but it is impossible to fool all of the people all of the time.

Publicity works best when it is supported by truth and a sound program. Attempting to publicize untruths is like attempting to build a house on quicksand. Neither will stand for any length of time.

The vehicles through which publicity can be disseminated may take many forms (Bronzan, 1986). Some of these vehicles or mediums are listed below. A well thought-out publicity and promotional program may involve many different vehicles. The key is to utilize these tools in a professional manner so that the communication process will be effective with the appropriate audiences.

Tools and Mediums of Publicity (Print and Electronic)

1. Daily newspapers
2. Weekly newspapers
3. Magazines
4. Professional journals
5. Trade and business magazines
6. School, club, and organizational publications
7. Newsletters
8. Radio Stations
9. Wire Services
10. Cable Television
11. Regular Television stations
12. Syndicated columnists, feature writers
13. Films and filmstrips
14. Videotapes
15. Slides and photos
16. Direct mail
17. Organized word-of-mouth campaigns
18. Displays
19. Posters
20. Fliers
21. Public address or special announcements at local events and activities, such as sports events
22. Bumper stickers
23. Feature stories in magazines
24. Free and paid classified ads
25. Graphic and pictorial materials
26. Radio and television ads
27. Bulletin boards
28. Annual reports
29. Speakers bureaus

Radio and Television

Radio and television, although electronic media, have different needs. Slides and film clips are appropriate for television but would not be for radio. Television needs brief (literally seconds), dramatic, visually or acoustically appealing stories. A local television station might control a limited amount of air time (often less than two hours) each day. Usually, the total sports segment of the televised news show is around 4 to 6 minutes. Thus an individual story on the evening newscast might be measured in seconds in contrast to column inches in a newspaper. The impact of TV on sports is tremendous. This is especially true with the advent of cable television. Never under-estimate the importance of the media in influencing others.

Radio and local cable television stations have a looser format and can usually devote more time to shows of local origin. This has significant implications for sports programs. Of course, different radio stations have different themes and formats, and this factor will affect what each station will be willing to air. However, even local radio stations have only minutes, if not seconds, to devote to sports stories in their customary sports report segments of the regular news block.

Daily and Weekly Newspapers

There are different needs for the newspapers published daily and those papers published on a weekly or biweekly basis. The weekly or biweekly publications are commonly referred to as the neighborhood papers. These smaller "hometown" newspapers primarily concentrate on a smaller geographical area as their primarily coverage responsibility. These weekly and biweekly publications (sometimes called "suburbans") are often able to provide much more extensive *local* sports coverage than the major dailies.

The "hometown" or suburban weekly papers frequently have a more narrow interpretation of what qualifies as news worthy, and therefore suitable for inclusion within their papers, in terms of sports. Sometimes these papers will only provide coverage for specific levels of sports activities while completely ignoring others. Some weekly or suburban papers have the philosophy that they will carry sports news only for the noncollegiate sports programs and nonprofessional teams. They leave the dailies with the responsibility of providing coverage for the college and university programs as well as for the professional teams. This is beneficial for the junior high and high school athletic programs as well as for youth sports because it means more column inches available for coverage of their sports activities. However, such a situation can play havoc with the suburban college sports program.

The colleges or universities located in smaller suburban communities that have weekly neighborhood newspapers might not enjoy the sports exposure provided for high school and youth sports by these suburban or weekly news publications. There is never a guarantee that coverage will take place in such papers.

Some suburban or weekly papers, as part of their editorial policy, will not provide any coverage for the suburban college sports programs. This is because of the assumption (sometimes an erroneous assumption) that the larger, daily newspapers in the nearby major metropolitan city will be able to provide these colleges with adequate sports coverage. Of course, if the major, metropolitan daily papers have an editorial policy against providing sports coverage for nearby suburban colleges because it is expected that the weekly, neighborhood papers will be providing this type of coverage, there really are problems for these colleges' sports information and athletic administration staff.

Wire Services

The two major wire services within the United States distribute news stories, features, film, tape, and photographs to over 6000 newspapers, radio, and television stations throughout the United States. These two wire services are the Associated Press

(AP) and the United Press International (UPI). Both have local bureaus in most sections of the country and are excellent sources for dissemination of news items about sports teams. Promoters should take advantage of these news services in an effort to obtain a wide dissemination of information about their programs and projects.

Criteria for Production of Publications—Programs, Brochures, and Other Printed Pieces

Printed Materials—Guidelines. Printed sports programs and brochures are frequently used to help promote and publicize athletic teams, individuals, and organizations at all levels. It is advisable for those involved in the promotion of sport and in athletic fund-raising to be knowledgeable in some of the basics of the print world. With all of the rapid scientific advances made within the past few decades in the area of graphic arts and printing, this is not always an easy task. However, it is important for the sport promoter and fund-raiser to be familiar with the basic areas essential to the planning, creation, and evaluation of any type of publication, brochure, or printed piece. For example, it is important to be able to be apprised of some of the very basic, fundamental questions that must be addressed in the decision-making process regarding the creation, design, and printing of a brochure or other printed piece. Some of these questions deal with the following areas:

1. Size and quality of the piece (8" × 11" or 8" × 14"; folded to fit into #10 envelope or larger; self-mailer; etc.)
2. Set-up and printing costs (total costs and cost per piece)
3. Structure of the piece (use of a "common" cover but changing inside pages with rosters, etc., or creation of entirely new content for subsequent printings)
4. Advertising rates (price of front and back covers; inside covers; plus price of special inside insert section and features)
5. Use of front and back covers and the inside of each for advertisements; general advertising rates and percentages
6. Advertising and printing schedules (deadlines for copy)
7. Advertising sales force (who is to sell; use of headhunters or local sales force to sell advertisements)
8. Advertising sales strategies and techniques (phone, door-to-door, person-to-person, business contacts, etc.)
9. Graphics, layout, and design (content and who is to create it)
10. Involvement of modern computer desktop publishing capabilities
11. Layout standards—the percentage of ads in comparison to printed copy
12. Quality of paper (glossy or flat)
13. Use of photos (black and white or color)
14. Use of color (1, 2, 3 or 4 colors; using 1 color ink on a different color paper to create a two color image)
15. Typesetting versus typing for copy (computer enhancing capabilities)
16. Creating a proper image with the program (first class, professional image)
17. General cost estimates (financial, time, resources, effort, etc.)
18. Size of press run (the more copies the cheaper per item cost)
19. Special inside inserts

20. Special game promotions to increase program sales
21. Pricing of the printed product (how to market, sell, or give-away)
22. Determination of program sales force
23. Determination of extra benefits, if any, to go to advertisers (tickets, souvenirs, etc.)

The use of color within printed pieces is strongly encouraged. The use of multi-colored brochures, if the budget will permit, is the most effective, especially if glossy paper is used. If multicolor inks are not feasible, the alternative might be the use of one or two ink colors (other than black) on a different color paper, thereby creating the impression or image of multiple colors. In today's highly sophisticated world of printing, the black on white printed piece is rather dull and drab in comparison with what other sports programs are currently producing.

When planning the creation and printing of any piece, it is essential that one examine the cost per printed piece. In so doing, it is important to remember that the biggest expense in the printing of items is associated with the initial design and the initial press run. What this means is that the cost difference between the printing of 100 and 1000 programs is frequently negligible, running between 3% to 10%.

In visualizing the brochure's role in a direct-mail campaign, the outer envelope can be considered to replace the sign in a store window while the letter itself replaces the salesperson. Additionally, "the order card becomes the cashier while the brochure itself becomes the product which is being marketed or sold" (Grazian, 1988, p. 7).

Grazian (1988) also reported that the majority of readers of brochures usually do not read the piece word for word. Rather, they skim through the publication. Thus, it is important to highlight the information that you want to stand out on each page of the brochure. The brochure should be conceptualized as a magazine in that the information in the brochure should be broken down into articles, editorial panels, news updates, and feature paragraphs.

▓ Principle 38 ▓

Utilize photos to convey feelings and attract attention in publications and printed pieces.

Photos enhance the visibility and impact of any brochure or printed piece. In fact, if one had the choice in terms of space shortage and faced the dilemma of choosing between narrative and photos to fill the space, always lean toward the photos. Photos catch the eye of the reader, draw attention to the printed piece, and effectively communicate an image or concept in an efficient manner. Hence, the use of photos in brochures is very important in any sports program.

Newsletters

Preparing the Newsletter. A typewriter and a piece of paper was all that was needed in the past for someone to be able to create and distribute a sports program newsletter. Today, however, with the advent of sophisticated computers, accompanying hardware, and desktop publishing software, a highly sophisticated and impressive newsletter is only as near as one's fingertips. With the accessibility to computers and accompanying desktop publishing software comes a greater responsibility to produce a quality newsletter if one is to be produced at all. This is true, if for no other reason, because of the fact that the capability for producing *quality* newsletters does exist.

An ever increasing segment of the public has a greater and greater expectation of sophistication and quality in terms of a wide variety of printed publications, including newsletters.

If one has to compete with the beautiful and artistically attractive printed publications emanating from all of the businesses and advertising agencies, and one must, it is necessary to produce competitive, beautiful, and artistically attractive pieces. The time of the two-bit, poorly-written newsletter is a thing of the past if a positive impression is to be created and a message is to be successfully conveyed to the readers.

Before the newsletter can become reality, there are some decisions that must be made. Some of these decisions revolve around:

1. The publication schedule of the periodic newsletter
2. Who will serve as the editor
3. The purpose of the newsletter
4. The recipients of the publications
5. How the newsletter will be printed (computer, typeset, typewritten)
6. Size of the printed piece (number of pages; size of pages)
7. Quality of paper, selection of colors, and any special requirements relating to the style of the piece
8. Quality control (neatness, accuracy) for the newsletter

The newsletter can be very helpful in disseminating a wide variety of information about the sports program including, but not limited to, the following:

1. The purposes of the program
2. Upcoming season projects
3. Publicity for fund-raisers, trips, special projects
4. Membership drives
5. Solicitation of contributions
6. Athletic accomplishments of teams—summary of past and current accomplishments and achievements
7. Synopsis of a sport season
8. Announcements concerning staff (coaches, specialists such as physicians and trainers, retirements, departures, honors, distinctions)
9. News of players, player profiles, awards, news of graduates
10. Alumni news—successes of former players, alumni organizations and activities in the field and nation, comments by famous alumni
11. Comments by school or legislative officials

News Releases

Preparing the News Release. In preparing the typical news release, the following questions are answered. *Who? What? Where? Why? When? How?* All press releases should be written in the **inverted pyramid style.** That is, the first paragraph should say it all and could stand alone, if need be. The least important information should appear at the end of the news release. This is done to facilitate the adapting of the news release to the space or time available. If the space or time requirements are such that not all of the release can be used, it is easier to cut from the bottom up to make the piece the appropriate length. All news releases need to be free from bias, yet appealing and interesting. When sending releases to athletes' hometown papers, the inclusion of black and white photos are frequently helpful to the editor and, when utilized, greatly enhance the impact of the story, as well as the resulting exposure of the athletic program.

There are three types of news releases: the advance story, the follow-up story, and the feature article. When writing for the news media, the copy should be written with clarity involving short, sequential sentences. There should not be a headline for the story, as the headline is written by the newspaper staff (Bronzan, 1986).

Minimum Standards for a News Story (Yiannakis & Braunstein, 1983).

1. Essential facts of major importance contained within the first paragraph
2. Paragraphs arranged in descending order of importance (inverted pyramid)
3. Short sentences and short paragraphs—appropriate content (usually about people or one individual rather than conditions, situations, or dilemmas)
4. Accuracy in facts, correct spelling, correct grammar, and good sentence structure are minimal
5. Typed double or triple space
6. Normal type and normal capitalization
7. Suitable photos (information on back or attached to photo—identify all individuals)
8. Inclusion of the name, address, and phone number of the organization submitting the release, release date, on the top left of the first page
9. Inclusion of release dates on top left of first page (*immediate* or *specific date/time* or *preferred date/time*)
10. Avoidance of:
    a. Cliches
    b. Humor (unless one is very good at it)
    c. Emotional statements
    d. Biased statements about opponents and officials
    e. Profanity
    f. Highly technical language
    g. Excuses
    h. Distortions and inaccuracies
    i. Information about disciplinary action, if athletes (that is between the athlete and the coach)

Reasons for Rejection of Releases. Being aware of the reasons for the rejection of news releases by the news media is half the battle. By knowing why the news media does not use releases, those involved in sport will have a better understanding of the requirements for acceptable news releases and can work to improve future releases. Some of the reasons why a news release is not used by the media are (Bronzan, 1986):

1. The information has limited appeal to potential readers.
2. The story is dated, that is, stale news.
3. The story is not well written.

4. Other stories have higher priority or are of more interest.
5. The information is exaggerated.
6. There are apparent inaccuracies or omissions in the story.
7. The information is a duplication of previous stories.
8. The information is stretched too thin.
9. The story is an attempt to receive free advertising.
10. There is insufficient space available.
11. The story is in conflict with a newspaper policy.

It is not enough to merely write news releases and distribute them to all of the appropriate news media. *Do more than that.* It is important to make others aware of the work and effort that has been completed. For example, one college has a practice of sending a duplicate of all news releases concerning athletes to the individual athlete, to the athlete's coach, and to the parents of the athletes, when appropriate. This is done in an effort to gain additional positive public relations on behalf of the athlete, the coach, and parents. Since the sports information director writes the news release, anyway, it was decided to send a copy to these individuals in an effort to make them aware of the athletic department's effort to gain publicity via the news release. Again, the concept is to take full advantage of what an athletic program accomplishes by making others aware of these achievements and efforts.

For this same reason, another college displays copies, on a biweekly basis, of all news releases within a special, highly visible, display board within the athletic complex. Additionally, a copy of all news releases are kept in a special 3–ring binder displayed in the reception area in the athletic office. Thus, the concept of a simple news release can be parlayed into multiple opportunities for increased exposure with a number of individuals—the athlete, the parents, the coaching staff, individuals visiting the athletic office, and members of the public viewing the display board.

Of course, if the news release is actually published or carried by the news media to which it was mailed by the school, so much the better. If it is not, at least the effort to write the news release is not for nought as the news release is utilized in other ways, as cited above, to create positive publicity and public relations.

▒ Principle 39 ▒
Make known efforts and successes involving publicity and promotion— Make others aware of one's activities.

Press Conferences

Press conferences can prove to be utter disasters or can be highly successful. The determining factors that distinguish the two results rests on many variables, not the least of which is the purpose for the press conference. Unless there is a real drawing card to motivate the media representatives to take time to leave their offices to attend, there is always the danger that the worse possible scenario will take place, that is, no one will show up. What an embarrassing catastrophe that can be for all concerned. In an effort to lessen this eventuality, the following list has some hints in terms of what to do and what not to do in scheduling press conferences. The basic premise holds true; that is, hold a press conference only when there is no other way to adequately disseminate the information coupled with a dynamite news breaking story.

What to Do When Holding a News Conference.

1. Use only for a special, newsworthy situation.
2. Schedule the event at an appropriate date and time convenient to the members of the news media.
3. Provide sufficient advance notice.
4. Secure a proper facility (access to phones, electrical outlets, lighting).
5. Provide a fact sheet plus photos to the media.
6. Make personal phone calls prior to the date to confirm if media will be present.
7. Schedule the meeting at a site convenient to media.
8. Start on time.
9. Provide opportunity *and* time for questions and answers.
10. Introduce the spokesperson for the conference.

What Not to Do When Scheduling a News Conference.

1. Don't schedule press (news) conferences unless there is no other way to successfully disseminate information.
2. Don't schedule press conferences (time/date) in conflict with any other significant news announcement.

Public Service Announcements (PSA)— Obtaining Free Time for Your Messages

Federal law requires electronic media to contribute free time in the course of their daily broadcasting for the purpose of providing general information of interest to the general public. Since it is good public relations for the media to support the efforts of nonprofit organizations whose activities and causes affect many members of the public, the needs of both the media and the charitable organizations can be met through carrying these public service messages. It is only up to the energetic sport promoter to take advantage of these opportunities. In planning for such public service opportunities on radio and television, being aware of the following guidelines can be helpful.

Forms of Public Service Opportunities:

1. Editorials, prepared *by station personnel* and delivered over the air by the station's professional staff
2. Editorials, prepared *by a member of the public* and delivered either by a station's announcer or delivered over the air in person by the writer of the editorial
3. Personality **spots** (announcements by on-the-air personalities such as disk jockeys, hosts of panels and games, and other staff)
    a. The most popular spots for radio are 10, 20, and 30 seconds in duration. The 10-second spot usually takes 20 words of text, while the 30-second spot consumes 60 words of text, and the 60-second spot consumes approximately 125 spoken words.

      b. Television also uses spots in varying duration, usually from 30 seconds through 60 seconds. Since television is a sight as well as an audio medium, however, it is necessary for the station to utilize a visual image, such as a slide, film, live television shot, etc. Slides of sport logos or of staff members are frequently utilized within the various spots.

4. Special programs, a one shot deal or a series of programs, interviews or discussions on shows that are relevant to the work of one's organization
5. Segments of programs that are similar to "specials" but are generally briefer presentations that are included as a "piggyback" type of feature in existing shows or programs

Examples of the Use of Tangible Tools for Publicity, Public Relations, and Fund-Raising Purposes

There are numerous physical *objects* that may be utilized in the overall scheme of publicity, promotion, and fund-raising. These tangible, visible tools are most helpful in creating and reinforcing an image of the sports program and those involved with it. These tangible assets may be used in activities designed to (1) generate publicity, (2) promote the program, and (3) to generate fiscal resources.

While the representatives of the news media are the sole determinants as to what is actually carried through the print and electronic media, not so with other means of communication (print and other) available to various sports programs at all levels. These "controlled tools" or "managed assets" help to establish a communication link (to carry messages) with various constituencies. The quality of these tangible tools or assets is solely determined (within the bounds of good taste) with the initiator of the message, the sport personnel. Too often these tools of communication are overlooked or not utilized to their full potential when it comes to the areas of public relations, promotions, and fund-raising. Alert sport administrators and coaches will take advantage of these tools that can frequently be put into play with a minimum of effort and expense (Bronzan, 1986). These same devices can be very effective in carrying a message to various constituencies. In short, each of the following can be thought of as tools or resources that can be used to *facilitate* the promotional and public relations process. These tools include:

1. Official school or organizational publications
2. Handbooks and manuals
3. Letters and printed bulletins
4. Bulletin boards
5. Posters
6. Outdoor billboards
7. Information and magazine racks
8. Institutional advertising
9. Public meetings (open forums)
10. Speeches by staff members
11. Public address system
12. The grapevine
13. Motion pictures, filmstrips, slide films, videotapes

14. Television clips
15. Displays, exhibits, and trophy cases
16. Campus tours and visits
17. Staged events, homecoming weekend, old timer's day, reunions, senior citizen's guest day, dedications, pioneer's day, festivals, etc.
18. Inserts within publications and printed pieces
19. Photographer's day
20. Open houses
21. Banquets and other food gatherings
22. Faculty-student sports contests
23. Tributes to support staff
24. Letters to parents
25. Invitation to parents
26. Participation in faculty affairs
27. Club awards
28. Letter writing
29. Monthly tabloid
30. Newsletters
31. Periodic reports (report cards) to publics
32. Annual reports
33. Photo albums and scrapbooks
34. Team calendars—photos of team, individuals, logo along with schedule of the upcoming sport, with advertisements of the sponsors of the calendars
35. Team/game programs
36. Schedule cards—piggyback on company's products (grocery bags, shopping bags, milk cartons, napkins, etc.)
37. Posters
38. Special "congrats" cards (including newspaper article/photo, etc.)
39. Creation of logos (quality control)
40. Stationery (letterhead and envelopes) and business cards, etc.
41. Christmas cards
42. Awards for letter winners—certificates and cloth "letters"
43. Thank-you notes
44. Mascots
45. Window displays in local or community outlets
46. Passes—for game and field (complimentary and sale)
47. Welcome signs
48. Tickets
49. Scoreboard advertising
50. Highlight films or videotapes of contests—Sell and/or allow local video stores to rent out.
51. Display of photos of staff, graduates, alumni, students-athletes, facilities, historical perspective, photos in hallway, photos in businesses
52. Pamphlet or handbook explaining the objectives of programs and facilities for students and visitors
53. Bumper stickers

54. Signs—Use outdoor signs and bulletin boards and billboards to announce upcoming attractions and achievements of your program.
55. Advertisement on buses (donated ad space) to highlight your program, etc.
56. Stickers on windows
57. Fliers
58. Door-to-door drop-offs
59. Souvenir programs for sale on day of contests and at school
60. Graphic and pictorial materials

Selective Binding Capability in Advertising Efforts

A relatively new technology that has been available on a limited basis only since 1977 is called selective binding. This technique enables advertisers to utilize specific inserts in magazines to reach specific, targeted subscribers. These subscribers would be targeted on the basis of specific demographics that the advertisers have identified as being desirable recipients of a specific advertising piece designed to have the greatest effect on the reader (Guy, 1992).

In the future this technology holds significant promise and potential for fund-raisers who desire to reach a specific population of subscribers in their advertising and solicitation efforts. Selective binding could be used to even target individual homes where different or slanted advertising in magazines would be directed and reach single readers or readers with young children or women or individuals of a certain age level or occupation.

Creation of Stationery—Letterheads and Envelopes

Coaches and athletic administrators wishing to communicate with others in writing naturally find themselves using stationery and envelopes. Such communication attempts can be much more effective if artistic stationery with matching envelopes is used to convey messages. The careful design of appropriate, distinctive, and attractive stationery is an essential element in the written communication process. Part of the challenge in creating stationery and envelopes is designing and using an appropriate sport logo. The sport logo is that identifying trademark automatically associated with the athletic program. If the logo helps in the positive identification of the athletic program, then it has done its job. The logo can be a variation of the athletic team's mascot, some graphic design, or a combination of the two.

A wide variety of variables can be taken into consideration in the creation and design of stationery and envelopes. The paper stock can vary from expensive high rag content paper to the less expensive plain paper. Color paper can be utilized to provide a distinctive look. Similarly, different ink colors can be added to increase the visual impact of the stationery itself.

One coach has expressed the concept that she wanted the stationery for her athletic sport to be viewed by the recipient as something very special and distinctive, so distinctive that the recipient of the letter would be able to identify it at once and would want to open it immediately. Distinctive stationery that is pleasing to the reader and that conveys a degree of professionalism is often prima facie evidence of a sound sports program. That is the image sports administrators and coaches want to project to the various constituencies.

References

Bronzan, R. T. (1986). *Public relations, promotions, and fund-raising for athletic and physical education programs.* Daphne, Alabama: United States Sports Academy Publishing House. Copyright 1977, by John Wiley & Sons, Inc., reprinted by permission of the author, 1986.

Frost, R. B., Lockhart, B. D. & Marshall, S. J. (1988). *Administration of physical education and athletics—Concepts and practices* (3d ed.) Dubuque, Iowa: Wm. C. Brown Publishers, pp. 294–295.

Grazian, F. (Editor) (1988). Creating a successful brochure. *Communication Briefings, 8*(2), 7.

Guy, P. (1992, Thursday, April 23). Newsweek folds in something extra for readers. *USA Today,* p. 7–B.

Yiannakis, A. & Braunstein, S. (1983). *The complete guide to successful fundraising.* North Palm Beach: American Sports Education Institute.

"Mascot Mania"—half-time entertainment. (Courtesy of University of Tennessee at Chattanooga, Department of Intercollegiate Athletics)

Public Relations and Promotional Activities — Working with Various Constituencies

Essentials of Public Relations

Public Relations is a broad, all encompassing concept that involves *everything that influences the image of the program in the mind of the various constituencies and publics.* With that definition it is imperative that those individuals who are involved in the fund-raising process be constantly aware that everything they do (or don't do) associated with the fund-raising project can have a direct impact on the public relations of the entire sports program as well as the fund-raising effort. Thus, it behooves the fund-raiser to remain cognizant of and alert for opportunities that will enhance the public relations image and reputation as well as the successful completion of the fund-raising project.

Those attempting to promote the value of sport need to sponsor an excellent program in itself and must effectively and efficiently communicate that fact to others (Lewis & Appenzeller, 1985). Those attempting to generate additional monies via a fund-raising activity must successfully communicate in a positive manner, through an effective and efficient public relations effort, with one or more publics.

Bucher (1971) indicated that public relations involves the process of disseminating information and accurate data to appropriate individuals and groups, in a timely fashion and in an acceptable way. Chapter one introduced the concept that public relations involves everything associated with the sports program as well as with the fund-raising effort. In essence, public relations is the process of getting the right facts to the right people at the right time in the right way (Mason & Paul, 1988).

A public relations (PR) plan must be flexible, adaptable, and adjustable. **PR** is both an *attitude* and a *process*. As an attitude, it involves realistic optimism and positive thinking. As a process, it involves open and effective communication, with emphasis on the good and the positive. Sound public relations seeks to bring about a harmony of understanding between the sport program and the various publics and constituencies the sport program serves and on whose good will it depends.

Good PR can affect individual and group perceptions, attitudes, and public opinion, and, consequently, can significantly influence human behavior. This is accomplished by reinforcing the truth, eradicating negative attitudes and feelings, as well as correcting erroneous perceptions. The end result is a better *positive image*, which in turn can create true, long-lasting, and meaningful support from segments of the community.

There are five ways to effect a good public relations program. First is through the actual athletic program itself; second, through personal contact between those involved in the sport program and members of the general public; third, through professional working relationships with representatives of the news media; fourth, through formal public speaking efforts on behalf of those who are part of the sport program; and last, through actual demonstrations, exhibits, and tangible objects or tools that are seen by the publics.

Objectives and Goals of Promotional Activities

One of the objectives of a sport program's public relations effort is to create confidence within appropriate constituencies in terms of the value(s) of the total program as well as the specific athletic activities. Toward this end, public relations can prevent misunderstandings and can create positive morale as well as tangible support for the sport arena. This is accomplished by stimulating an awareness of how the sport offerings and sport involvement can contribute to a healthy life-style and meet the psychological, social, mental, physiological, and recreational needs of members of the society. Finally, a sound perspective of the value and role of athletic competition can likewise be enhanced by an appropriate public relations program.

If public relations can play a part in the above scenario becoming reality (and it can), there is a great opportunity, through appropriate sport promotional activities, for the sport program to receive increased revenue through donations, as well as via increased attendance at sporting events. This is possible due to the increase in the interest, exposure, and positive acceptance of the sport program by those who might not have otherwise been associated with the sport program to any great extent. Promotional and public relations activities should also provide a means for recognizing the contributions and achievements made by team members, coaches, boosters, and sponsors. This in turn aids in greater recognition and acceptance of the value or worth of the program and the prestige of those associated with the athletic program.

The Foundation of Public Relations

The foundation of good public relations is *communication*. This communication with various publics and constituencies can be facilitated by the use of both electronic and print media. The objective is to keep the publics sufficiently informed in order to make appropriate and wise decisions concerning the athletic program. This communication process is a function of what is called public relations. It must be emphasized, however, that what is communicated *must* be based on truth. This communication of accurate information is continuous and involves the total effort of everyone (especially the athletes and athletic staff) involved with the sport program. How these individuals within the inner sanctum of the sport organization act and behave and represent the athletic program is very influential in terms of how the total athletic program is viewed by the publics. A key component to any public relations effort is its flexibility and adaptability in light of changing circumstances.

The best public relations proponents for any sports program are the student-athletes themselves, those youngsters who are current or past participants in the program.

This is simply because these athletes have direct contact with many other individuals, including their parents, and are able to spread the word about the positive sports experience they are experiencing and have experienced in the past. They have first-hand knowledge of the sports experience. Thus, the ideal public relations program starts with the athletes themselves.

The athletic staff, both paid and volunteer, form the next important category of individuals who have a major role to play in the promotion and public relations arena of sports. These individuals, like the athletes themselves, have such a major role in communicating on a personal and professional level with a whole range of individuals and groups. These individuals are able to significantly promote and establish positive public relations on behalf of the athletic program with many so-called "outsiders."

Conversely, nothing hurts an athletic program like dissatisfied athletes and/or staff members who criticize the sports program. If sufficient numbers of athletes (past or present) or staff (paid or volunteer) fall into this category, the sports administrators have a real challenge facing them. If the athletic organization cannot convince those actively involved, the athletes themselves and those having some responsibility for or associated with the program, of the value and benefits resulting from the athletic experience, how can others who are not so intimately connected with the program be convinced?

Use of Facilities and Equipment for Promotional Purposes

The presence and proper use of facilities and equipment can greatly facilitate the creation of a positive image of the sport program in the eyes of the general public. Similarly, the proper upkeep of such equipment and facilities is absolutely essential.

In terms of facilities, the first mark of vandalism is somewhat reluctantly committed when the facility is kept spotlessly clean. However, when the facility has been marked by vandalism, subsequent marks by the same or another vandal are made with less trepidation. And, the third act of vandalism (unless the facility is repaired and again kept in tip top shape) often follows in quick succession to the second act of vandalism.

Facilities must be reviewed constantly in an effort to detect any damage or act of vandalism. If such damage has occurred, it is essential that the repairs be effected *immediately* lest additional subsequent damage is done to the same facility. In short, it is easier to commit acts of vandalism against marred or damaged facilities. Clean facilities seem, to some extent, to deter many would-be graffiti artists.

The reason that it is so important for sports organizations to attempt to keep facilities in excellent shape is because, for many members of the general public, the only glimpse of the sport program may be the periodic visitation to a contest or a tour of the facility. The image created by this exposure can be significant and long lasting. The existence and care of scoreboards and trophy cases; the availability of sufficient and suitable lighting; the condition of the hallways, bleachers, and playing surfaces (paint, etc.); the availability of picnic pavilions, as well as grills and picnic tables, jogging trails, professionally created signs, clean restrooms and locker rooms; and attractive, well-fitting uniforms, all help create lasting and positive impressions in the eyes of the public(s) that can transfer to the actual athletic program and staff. In short, the general upkeep of all facilities and equipment should be maintained as another means of influencing the opinions and attitudes of others.

Use of Specific Image-Enhancing Tactics for Promotional Purposes

Other image-enhancing tactics and activities that can play a significant role in the promotion of the sport program are associations or liaisons with various national organizations such as local charities, Special Olympics, service clubs, and professional sport and nonsport organizations. It is through such close association with other visible and highly regarded entities and individuals that the sports program is capable of gaining added esteem and respectability within the community by piggybacking onto the reputation and image of other organizations and activities.

For example:

1. Involve special populations by inviting individuals to attend athletic contests as guests. These special populations might include handicapped persons, disadvantaged youths, scouts, senior citizens, residents of retirement homes, family nights, fraternity or sorority organizations, as well as service groups (Masonic Temples, Elks, Lions, Moose, Order of the Eastern Star, Knights of Columbus, B'nai Brith, Shriners, JCs).

2. Develop community programs that allow school facilities to be utilized by various local, state, or national organizations, thus creating an awareness and appreciation of the sport program, the facilities, and the organizational skills of the athletic personnel behind the scenes. A college encouraging the use of the athletic facilities by area elementary and secondary schools, as well as other nonprofit organizations (Special Olympics, Big Brothers, Big Sisters, various state games, etc.), can pay big dividends in terms of immediate and long-term public relations, promotional, and publicity consequences.

A small college and its athletic department that have been very successful in becoming associated with, as well as significantly helping, a well-known and respected local charity in western New York is St. John Fisher College in Rochester, New York. On February 28–29, 1992, $75,000 in pledges were generated via a 24–hour dance marathon for the Teddi Project of Camp Good Days & Special Times, a camp for sick and handicapped children in the Rochester area. This was an increase of some $8,000 from their 1991 marathon. Earlier that month, the football coach at the college organized another dance marathon at a local public school, and those students were able to raise an additional $10,050 for the same project.

Use of Operational and Home Event Activities for Promotional Purposes

■ **Principle 40** ■

Everything associated with the sports program promotes the image of that program.

Every action your program takes sends a message to someone (Hartman and Browkaw, 1988, p. 90). The conduct of the sport program and the conduct of the fund-raising and/or promotional activities themselves promote the image of your sport program. The professionalism with which the fund-raising efforts are conducted have an effect not only on the success of the *actual fund-raising effort* but also upon the *image of the sport program itself.* Similarly, the operation of the sport program can either facilitate or hinder the efforts to raise money. Thus, it is important that the management of all aspects of the athletic operation, as well as the conduct of the sport participants themselves, be exemplary.

How athletic events are conducted (home management), how the participants and spectators act at these events, and how the participants and the actual athletic events are perceived by others affect the image of the total sport program. This includes the conduct of athletes, coaches, and administrators as well as parents and boosters. It even includes such areas as the public address operation, half-time programs, adequacy of seating, ushering, cheerleading, etc. *Everything and anything associated with the sport program can and does contribute to the creation of an image and a reputation and is part of the public relations effort.*

A well-balanced public relations effort should include a variety of approaches. There is no simple solution. There is no one way or approach. The total public relations effort extends beyond just specific, deliberate public relations tactics and involves every source of information and type of impression given to the public by the school personnel, facilities, and programs—whether intentional or unintentional.

Daily Operational Aspects of the Athletic Program

How the sport program is conducted, on a day-to-day basis, helps establish its reputation and its image with others. Thus, it pays big dividends to see that the operational facets of the sport activities are conducted in an exemplary fashion. The home event activities, dictated by the organization's procedures and policies are the visible components of any sport picture and are easily seen and evaluated by others. Some suggested tactics, in the day-to-day conduct of sport activities, that can help promote the athletic program as well as individual team sports include:

1. Securing the labor for the preparation of site contests and home event management.

    a. If manual labor is needed, attempt to have the labor donated.
    b. If manual labor is needed and cannot be donated, hire one's own athletes or teams or those otherwise associated with the sports program to do it—keep it in the "family."

2. Provide adequate sports offerings, including an adequate number of contests to insure a competitive schedule.
3. Provide a suitable medical support program (trainers, physicians, medical coverage, etc.).
4. Provide adequate sports information, that is, publicity for the various athletic activities.
5. Establish an *athletic hall of fame.*
6. Establish an *academic hall of fame.*
7. Establish an *academic honor roll* (emphasize the positive).
8. Establish *codes of conduct* for spectators, participants, and coaches, and publicize these codes.

9. Publicize accomplishments of athletes (grade-point averages, graduation rates, honor societies, etc.).
10. Publicize achievements of staff and alumni (honors, distinctions, job promotions, etc.).

Handbooks—Policies, Procedures, Practices, and Priorities (4 Ps)

The existence of a departmental or athletic handbook can prove to be valuable not only in assisting in the operation of the sport organization but also in terms of public relations and fund-raising. Having a document that specifies the policies, priorities, procedures, and practices of the sport organization enables those involved with the program to become aware of the organization and familiar with its operation (Stier, 1988). The existence of such a document also can make a positive impression with others—higher administrators as well as individuals who are outside the sport entity—by making them aware of the organizational and administrative professionalism that exists in order to develop and refine such an important document.

The presence of a handbook containing information regarding promotions, publicity, fund-raising, as well as many other facets of administration and organization, can be used as (1) an actual tool in the operation of the sport program *and* (2) a public relations device to make others aware of the sophistication that exists within the administrative structure of the overall athletic program.

Maintaining Quality and Professionalism

■ **Principle 41** ■

It is the little things that count.

One must pay attention to the details—the dotting of the Is and the crossing of the Ts—of any fund-raising activity. Details form the foundation of the entire promotional, publicity, and fund-raising effort. Without a firm foundation, the walls of any promotional, publicity, and fund-raising plan come tumbling around one's head.

In *everything* the fund-raiser does, there should be a significant degree of professionalism, a high level of competency. This is no idle generalization. It is a fact. Paying attention to small details is a crucial element in the overall strategy of successful individuals engaged in promotions and fund-raising. This includes written and verbal communications, handling of phone calls, conducting meetings, professional dress, use of time, etc. There is indeed a need to demonstrate competency in *all that one does*. The following are some examples that illustrate the importance of paying attention to the seemingly simple task of utilizing the written word.

1. All professional communication should be *personally* typed, rather than sent as a form letter or printed via mimeograph.
2. Letters should be signed with blue ink rather than black to emphasize that the letter was actually individually signed. Signatures with black ink can be misinterpreted as having been duplicated via a mass production process.
3. Written communication should be free of grammatical as well as typing errors, both of which are sources of embarrassment for any organization.

The desire for so-called perfection should not be taken to the extreme. To feed the bureaucracy or encourage procrastination, and thus destroy the timeliness, in the search for perfection in any project, is counterproductive. For example, in one school, the chief administrator insisted upon *personally* reading, proofing, and approving most news releases that left the campus, as well as all articles to appear in the publications of the alumni office. One such article slated for the quarterly alumni publication was to describe the school's oldest (100-plus years old) living alumna. The final draft was given to this administrator for his usual review in early fall. The release of this article was held up while being read and reread numerous times over the next three or four months by the chief executive. The approval of the article was postponed over and over.

In fact, the article was never approved for printing and distribution because of the administrator's failure to act in a timely fashion. The result was that the oldest living alumna of that school died four months later with the article still sitting on the desk of the administrator. *This moral is simple. Timing is everything and its mortal enemy is procrastination—for whatever reason.*

Principle 42

Don't become obsessed with details and the search for perfection to such an extent that you lose sight of the ultimate objective—the generation of support.

This principle is not expressed as a tongue-in-cheek joke but is made quite seriously. Much of the effort spent in promotional and fund-raising projects is actually not truly productive. For example, in attempting to obtain 10 contributions, it may be necessary to make 100 initial phone calls and/or personal contacts. If we knew, in advance, which of the 100 initial contacts would end up actually making a contribution, a lot of effort and time could be saved by just concentrating on these 10 individuals. Of course, in most instances, one doesn't know who will actually become donors, and the effort has to be made to convert as many of the initial 100 candidates in the prospect pool as possible. Effort can be made, however, to critically assess the prospect pool so that some of the potential prospects might be culled from the pool, leaving room for the addition of more likely prospects.

Additionally, this same principle points out the necessity of evaluating exactly how to spend one's time and in what direction effort is expended. With experience and increased skill, the fund-raiser and promoter will be able to discard those activities and tactics that have proven not to be highly productive in the past. This reinforces the importance of learning from previous experience (one's own and the experience of others) and in critically assessing possible consequences and results of one's efforts. That is why experience *can be* so important. People learn and make better, wiser decisions when they have meaningful prior experience to draw upon.

Principle 43

Sixty percent of the effort expended in promotional activities is wasted—but one doesn't know which sixty percent.

There is always the danger that the promotion activity itself will receive more attention than what is to be promoted. When this happens one loses sight of the ultimate objective being sought and falls in love with the process itself, which can be both addicting and self-destructive. Promotional activities must be viewed as being simply means to an end and nothing more.

Principle 44

Promotional activities are a means to an end—not an end in themselves.

Concepts for Promotional Activities

A good promotion, per se, is **attention getting, legitimate,** and **appropriate for the situation.** It should have the power to inform, remind, and persuade (Successful Promotion, 1985). It should also be **capable of being adapted or changed to meet specific needs,** needs that can and do change as time passes. Further, promotional activities must be appropriately planned, frequently around themes and slogans. Finally, such activities must be adequately implemented and periodically evaluated if they are to be successful in reaching stated objectives and goals.

▨ **Principle 45** ▨

Promote the promotable—that which is successful.

Promote what is successful. If the team's win/loss record is significant, promote that. If the team has a very competitive and attractive schedule, promote that aspect, that is, the competitiveness of the sport. If the sport has excitement, promote the exciting experience. If the team has an outstanding academic record and scholarly achievements, then highlight the academic standards of the athletes and their achievements in the classroom. Successful promotional activities emanate from successes, achievements, and accomplishments.

An underlying premise in the world of fund-raising, promotion, and marketing is that there be a real or perceived need to possess a product or service or to accept an idea. Schneider (1992) suggests four basic rules for marketing and selling. These are:

1. Must have a good product, service or concept
2. Must have a good product, service or concept
3. Must have a good product, service or concept
4. Must be sure and let people know about the product, service or concept

When examining whether or not it is appropriate to promote a specific sport or activity, the following questions should be reviewed:

1. What is the quality, the competitiveness of the program—the squad's win/loss record?
2. What is the public relations ability and enthusiasm of the coach—is the individual a natural salesperson or public relations person, that is, is the coach marketable?
3. Is there public interest in the sport as a spectator event?
4. Is there interest in the sport by individuals or businesses with money to donate (potential major donors)?
5. Are there adequate facilities for spectator and/or support groups?
6. Is there available VIP seating and hospitality areas?
7. Is there available VIP parking?
8. What achievements or accomplishments have been made or earned by the sport program itself, the athletes, and the staff?

▨ **Principle 46** ▨

Sport promotors and fund-raisers are only limited by their imagination and the imagination of others.

This key concept must be kept in the forefront of the minds of all successful sports promoters and those involved in athletic fund-raising. Being aware of the general guidelines and principles supporting sound promotional and productive fund-raising efforts is only half of the battle. The other half involves the presence of creative, imaginative, and innovative coaches, administrators, and supporters who are able to plan, evaluate, adapt, and implement possible strategies and tactics suitable for their own particular schools and programs.

Just as there are numerous tactics and techniques that can be used to *publicize* a sport program, there are many strategies and tactics that can be utilized to *promote* the sport program and its participants. Some of these are:

1. Establishing *natural rivalries*—the use of the natural rivalry that can exist between teams or schools or organizations provides the basis of numerous promotional activities. For example, the establishment of a "Little Brown Jug," "Bell," or trophy to travel with the victorious team.

2. Instituting a *speakers bureau*—in which the athletic staff and boosters become roving ambassadors on behalf of the sport program to segments of the general public. Having staff members and supporters willing to spend time speaking before numerous groups and organizations on behalf of the sport program is an excellent promotional strategy.

   It is helpful for each speaker to be given written background information on topics that they might be asked about during their speaking engagements. In addition, speakers should periodically be given updates on new promotional events, upcoming games, and achievements of both teams and athletes as well as other newsworthy facts dealing with the total sport program (Sutton, 1990).

   The use of speakers out in the community is a method of spreading the gospel according to "St. Coach." These opportunities to provide 10–12 minute speeches or presentations at schools, service clubs, youth groups, and church organizations are often numerous. Of course, those who go on the lecture and banquet circuit must be attractive, articulate speakers, who are excellent ambassadors of the sport program. In many instances, the only firsthand, face-to-face contact many members of the general public will have with the sport program will be the representative of the athletic organization speaking before their group. Thus it is essential that the speakers serve as effective ambassadors of the sport program.

3. Erecting *suggestion boxes*—provide excellent opportunities to receive feedback and suggestions from various constituencies. The practice of placing suggestion boxes throughout the athletic facilities is nothing new. However, the proper use of the suggestion box can go a long way to make this traditional tool into an excellent promotional and communication experience in more ways than one. This can be done by actually doing something—in a visible manner—with the suggestions that are made.

   One technique to accomplish this is to have a professionally created glass display case next to each suggestion box. Inside each display case are typed lists of previous suggestions (cumulative over a 2–3 month period) *and* a typed list of administrative steps, with specific dates, taken in response to these suggestions. In this way individuals can see that their suggestions are

▩ Principle 47 ▩

Use a variety of promotional tactics to expose the sport program to the general public.

taken seriously and are appropriately acted upon. If the suggestions placed within the suggestion boxes cannot be actually put into practice, reasons are given and placed within the display case adjacent to the suggestion box.

The practice of honoring and rewarding those individuals who contribute the better suggestions at a year-end banquet or luncheon goes a long way to (1) motivate future contributors of suggestions and ideas and (2) to convince others of how seriously the suggestion process is taken by the sports administrators.

4. Involving *"outside" notables*—to take some part in the athletic program or activity. For example, inviting the mayor of the community or some other notable to throw out the proverbial first ball, to cut a ribbon dedicating a new trophy case or a new facility, or to assume some other visible role in the sport program.

5. Inviting *fans, special "friends," members of booster organizations, faculty, administrators to be special guest "coaches"* for a specific period of time, for example, a week or a day.

6. Involving *special organizations*—by inviting their members to be guests of the athletic program at contests. For example, inviting individuals from senior citizen's clubs, boy and girl scouts, etc., to watch games and matches can pay big dividends in terms of promotional and public relations benefits for the athletic organization.

7. Extending *thanks to people*—by publicly expressing appreciation for their support and work. Taking time to provide certificates, congratulatory notes, Christmas cards, and/or letters of thanks to individuals and organizations and seizing opportunities at banquets and social occasions to publicly thank others, helps to insure the promotion of the athletic program.

8. Holding *open houses*—provide excellent opportunities to show off the positive aspects of the athletic program, both programmatic aspects and facilities. This is especially effective when the open house is coupled with some type of demonstration or exhibition conducted by the staff and involving the athletes themselves.

9. Providing *annual* (seasonal) *dinners or luncheons* to honor specific individuals and/or groups.

10. Erecting *special display* cases to exhibit newsworthy items (academic honor rolls, list of staff accomplishments, news releases and/or news clippings, photos of athletes and/or staff, etc.).

11. Displaying *banners and signs* inside and outside the sport facility highlighting achievements of athletes and teams.

12. Showing *exhibits of photos of athletic teams* (including athletes' names, team achievements and records, and scores of contests against opponents).

13. Constructing *trophy cases* for championship awards for teams.

14. Establishing *a "Hall of Fame" exhibit* within the sport facility.

15. Establishing an *"All-American Wall of Fame"*—containing photos of All-American athletes along with the All-American certificates.

Merchandising Novelty and Premiums Items

When the subject of premiums comes up, there are four questions to be answered by the sport promoter. The first question hinges upon whether or not so-called premiums should even be used as part of one's arsenal in promoting (and fund-raising) for the sport program and, if so, what type of premiums should be used. The second question to be answered is for what purpose shall the premiums be used? In other words, what are the actual benefits to be derived from the use of premiums on behalf of the activity or program? The third question revolves around whether or not the premiums will be used as a giveaway type of promotion or will be sold, that is, merchandised for cash? And, the last question hinges on whether or not the premiums should have advertisements printed on them.

It is absolutely essential that all premiums be of high quality and that they have some value to the potential recipients. Offering numerous "cheap" and/or inappropriate trinkets or premiums such as decals, key chains, visors, pins, and thinking that this equates with a quality promotional activity is foolish. It is important to remember that offering premiums is only a small facet of a promotional effort.

Premiums sometimes have negative connotations with some sport promoters. For example, the practice of giving premiums (hats, shirts, etc.) to the first 500 in attendance might be frowned upon by some athletic administrators and coaches. These people feel that the attempt to distribute such premiums is often wasted since some research indicates that most of the people who receive such premiums in this type of giveaway would have come anyway.

On the other hand, there are those promoters who feel that there is nothing wrong with loyal fans receiving such premiums. They point out that if the premiums are given to someone, why shouldn't the loyal fans receive some gimmick? The giveaway of premiums might well be worth the effort as long as the fans and the actual recipients find it acceptable and enjoyable. Besides, what is wrong with rewarding those loyal fans who come to the contest? What does it cost the sport program? If the "word" gets out in the community regarding the fun promotional giveaway, and if people react positively, and if the 500 fans are satisfied with the promotional tactic, is this not a positive consequence?

A study conducted by the Arizona State University for the Specialty Advertising Association International (SAAI) revealed that business gifts accounted for 38 percent of the $4.16 billion spent nationally on *all* advertising specialties in 1988. Sixty-one percent of another national survey by SAAI revealed that general businesses use premiums and inexpensive gifts to thank consumers while 54 percent utilize gifts or premiums to build goodwill and cultivate further business with the recipients (*Entrepreneur*, September 1990).

Premiums or trinkets distributed, sold, given away, or exchanged may be almost anything. The objective is to help *promote* and *publicize* the sport and the athletic program while generating interest in the premiums or trinkets. It is essential that such items have at least some intrinsic value to the potential recipient lest the premium generate more negative reaction than positive. Of course, tying the theme of the gift or premium to your event or program can enhance the likelihood of the recipient remembering your event or program over a longer period of time.

▓ Principle 48 ▓

First-class premiums can promote the sport program as well as generate revenue.

A Hampton Falls, New Hampshire, consultant, Delahaye Group, claims that coffee mugs that have logos and advertising on them catch people's eyes as many as ten times a day. If such a coffee mug costs the promoter or fund-raiser $5.00 each that amounts to less than six-tenths of a cent per view over a one-to-two year life of the mug (Wall Street Journal, Thursday, June 20, 1991). A few examples of the more common types of inexpensive premiums or gifts utilized in the world of sports promotion are:

1. Car decals
2. Buttons
3. Ties
4. Special pins
5. Cloth patches
6. Shirts
7. Scarfs
8. Shorts
9. Visors
10. Baseball type hats
11. Painter hats
12. Miniature balls
13. Towels
14. Golf towels
15. Miniature megaphones
16. Bumper stickers
17. Balloons
18. Bookmarks
19. Cups
20. Coffee mugs
21. Glasses
22. Key chains
23. Ribbons
24. Stick-on pins

To insure that the premiums are identified with the sports program, promoters frequently have the program's logo or mascot printed or otherwise placed on the premium that is distributed. If the premium is paid for by an outside company or organization, the question of whether or not the name of the outside organization or group should appear on the premium must be addressed by the athletic administration. There are arguments for and against allowing companies to place their advertisements on the premiums distributed through the athletic program. The answer to this dilemma depends on the philosophy of the athletic program and the circumstances that exist in any particular situation. It is not possible to make a definitive statement that would be applicable and appropriate for all situations.

Another question to be addressed regarding the use of premiums is whether or not the premiums should be distributed free or whether they should be sold. If they are to be given away free, exactly how should the distribution be completed? For example, are premiums going to be given away at contests? If so, to whom? Everyone who comes to a specific contest? To youngsters accompanied by parents? Will the premiums be literally thrown into the stands at a certain time (miniature footballs thrown by cheerleaders during the halftime ceremonies)? Again, there is no single, simple answer. That is why there is a need for qualified, trained, and experienced sports administrators to make such determinations.

Of course, in utilizing premiums for game promotion giveaways or awards it is important to have people at the game or the contest and to publicize the fact that the premiums will be distributed. Toward this end, it is helpful to widely communicate, in advance, *how* the premiums are to be distributed; that is, given to the first 500 people at the game, to be thrown into the stands at halftime, to be given to spectators who have specially marked programs, etc. This sometimes helps to create an interest in the contest and can increase attendance if the premiums are of worth, if the premiums are of value, and if there is an interest in the athletic contest.

References

Bucher, C. A. (1971). *Administration of health and physical education programs including athletics* (5th ed.). St. Louis: C. V. Mosby, p. 585.

Give and you shall receive. (1990, September). *Entrepreneur,* pp. 42, 44–45.

Hartman, C. & Brokaw, L. (1988, October). Everything you always wanted to know about PR . . . but were afraid you'd have to pay for. *INC.* , pp. 32–35.

Lewis, G. & Appenzeller, H. (1985). *Successful sport management.* Charlottesville, Virginia: The Michie Company.

Mason, J. G. & Paul, J. (1988). *Modern sports administration.* Englewood Cliffs, New Jersey: Prentice Hall.

Not a penny for your thoughts. (1991, Thursday, June 20). *The Wall Street Journal,* p. 1-A.

Schneider, R. E. (1992). Don't just promote your profession—Market it. *Journal of Physical Education, Recreation and Dance. 63* (5), 70–73.

Stier, Jr., W. F. (1988). Policies, procedures, and practices for intercollegiate athletics. (2nd ed.). Brockport, New York: State University of New York, Brockport. (ERIC Document Reproduction Service No. ED301558).

Successful promotion: Identify the problem before trying to solve it. (1985, March). *Athletic Business,* p. 22.

Sutton, B. (1990). Off-the field coaching. *College Athletic Management (CAM),* pp. 27–29.

Southwest Missouri State University All-Sports Auction. One thousand supporters in attendance generated net proceeds of $84,000 in 1991. (Courtesy of Southwest Missouri State University Photo Services/photo by Kevin White)

Promotional Activities and Fund-Raising Techniques—The Art and Science of Raising Money

7

The success of fund-raising strategies and promotional activities revolve around seven essential components, shown in figure 7.1.

Historical Perspectives

Without the establishment of agreed upon or recognized objectives and goals, there is little possibility of meaningful or purposeful activity in the future. Planning is an essential ingredient in the establishment of objectives or goals of any fund-raising or promotional effort. In the planning process, however, it is imperative that one does not lose sight of what has been attempted—successfully as well as unsuccessfully— in the past.

We learn from prior successes, as well as prior failures, our own and those of others. The important thing is to *learn*—period. Taking stock of what has been successful previously, in similar and dissimilar situations, is important. It enables us to assess, evaluate, and eliminate errors and time wasters. It enables us to replace such ineffective, inefficient efforts with tactics which are effective, efficient, and successful in reaching objectives and goals. This is because recognizing the critical factors that determine success and/or failure enables us to identify those principles that might be applicable in circumstances that currently exists. Thus, we learn from the mistakes as well as the correct decisions of others. We don't have to reinvent the wheel when planning and implementing fund-raising programs. Don't be too proud to borrow, beg, and adopt ideas and successful techniques, tactics, and activities relating to promotional activities and fund-raising efforts.

The concept, *be willing to learn from others,* is clear, in terms of (1) the setting of reasonable objectives and goals, (2) the selection of appropriate tactics and strategies, (3) the actual implementation process of those programs, activities, and projects designed to meet the then established objectives and goals, and (4) the assessment of one's activities insofar as their effectiveness and efficiency in getting the task successfully completed.

▬ Principle 49 ▬

Learn from others—build upon prior experiences, one's own and those of others.

Figure 7.1 Components
of fund-raising.

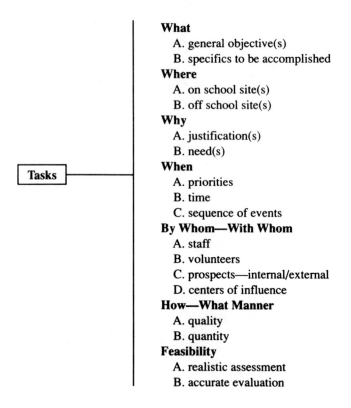

```
                    What
                        A. general objective(s)
                        B. specifics to be accomplished
                    Where
                        A. on school site(s)
                        B. off school site(s)
                    Why
                        A. justification(s)
                        B. need(s)
                    When
                        A. priorities
                        B. time
          Tasks          C. sequence of events
                    By Whom—With Whom
                        A. staff
                        B. volunteers
                        C. prospects—internal/external
                        D. centers of influence
                    How—What Manner
                        A. quality
                        B. quantity
                    Feasibility
                        A. realistic assessment
                        B. accurate evaluation
```

Determination of Needs

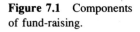

Principle 50

Develop a strong case for your needs (justification for support and assistance).

There must be a good reason to be involved in fund-raising. Don't become involved merely because others do it or because fund-raising is perceived as glamorous or "big time." The best position for an athletic administrator or coach to be in is to have the school or organization take the posture that there will be adequate funds available for the sport program via the regular budget process of the school, etc.

This means that there might not be a need to raise funds. While this is undoubtedly true in some situations, in the vast majority of sport organizations and schools this is far from the case. In the majority of schools, colleges, and other sport programs there is a real need to raise supplemental funds for the enrichment (if not for the bare essentials) of the sport experience for the participants.

Of course, even in those rare situations in which outside funding is not required there will still be a need to promote the athletic program, and there still exists a need to implement a positive public relations program.

Principle 51

Tap a variety of fund-raising sources.

When one hears the phrase "fund-raising," one immediately thinks of attempts to raise money by going to outside individuals and organizations with a request for contributions or, perhaps, attempts to sell merchandise to members of the general public.

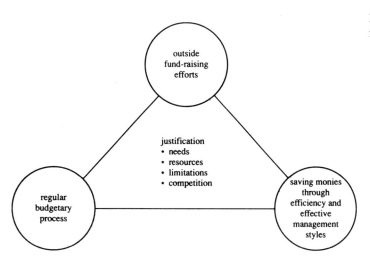

Figure 7.2 Sources of financial support.

One should not neglect two other avenues where much-needed support may be generated. Specifically, the coach and athletic administrator should be aware that there are actually three sources or ways of gaining much-needed support—three sources of monies, for the sports program, shown in figure 7.2.

The *first* source of money lies in the general athletic operation itself. For every dollar that is saved through wise and efficient fiscal management within the sports organization, there is a corresponding reduction in the need to go "outside" to raise that dollar. In other words, one can raise money by saving money.

The *second* source of money is through the sponsoring organization itself. Whether it is a high school, a college or a youth sport organization, the organization should be targeted for additional financial request(s) prior to attempting to go "outside" for funding. Being able to justify to the sponsoring organization the need for a greater share of the financial pie and to actually receive such monies reduces the amount of outside fund-raising needed.

The *third* source of obtaining funding involves fund-raising "outside" of the school or athletic program itself. The objective, of course, is to raise sufficient funds and/or support that will enable the sport program to meet the specific needs of the athletes and the various constituencies. Tapping a combination of sources as outlined above enables the sports administrators to take full advantage of every means possible to generate sufficient funds to support the various segments of their program.

Regardless of how the financial resources are obtained, the money must be put to productive use by purchasing such items as uniforms, new lights for the field, team trophies, upgrade in terms of facilities, additional staff, etc., for the greater good of the athletic program. The important point to remember is that these specific objectives (trophies, facilities, lights, vehicles, uniforms) are merely means to an end, merely tools to enable the sport program to achieve a higher, more important, and essential goal, that of meeting the needs of the participants, the athletes themselves, so that the athletic experience is indeed a wholesome, safe, and significant learning experience.

Figure 7.3 Realization
of objectives and goals.

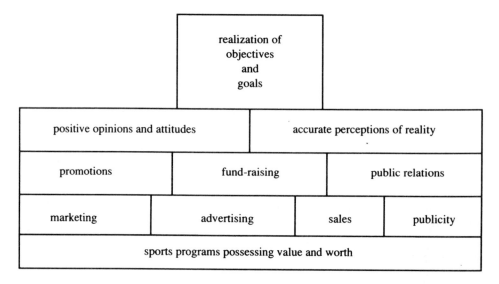

Realization of Goals and Objectives

The realization of goals and objectives is a multifaceted challenge for those involved in promotional and fund-raising efforts. The tasks involved in reaching any specific goal, whether that goal is an increase in generated revenue, additional spectators at a contest, increased public exposure or an improved positive image of the program or specific event, are frequently affected by a wide variety of activities (fig. 7.3). These activities can be carried out under the auspices of (1) marketing, (2) advertising, (3) sales, (4) publicity, (5) promotions, (6) fund-raising and (7) public relations.

Philanthropic Activities

Fund-raising is big business in the United States today for charitable, philanthropic, and nonprofit programs. Philanthropic contributions have continued to increase within the United States in recent years. Contributions to charitable causes come from individuals, from foundations, and from the business world.

By the year 2000, according to Bill Olcott, editor of *Fund Raising Magazine,* total contributions will reach $230 billion (Fund-a-thon, May 3, 1991). Total gifts from individuals, corporations, foundations, and other sources rose some 5.1% per year during the decade of the 1980s. During the previous 25 years, donations from all sources rose only 3.3% per year, according to the Center for the Study of American Business.

Corporate Giving. From 1975 to 1985, corporate annual giving increased from around $700 million to approximately $4.3 billion. In 1990 corporate America gave a record $5.9 billion to charity and other nonprofit organizations. Estimates for 1991 ranged in the neighborhood of $6.2 billion. Corporate contributions are seen as being good for business. Such contributions help the community while permitting the company to take tax deductions as well as to attract new customers. In reality, contributing is a good marketing tool for businesses in this country (Corporations find, August 1991).

Although on the surface it might seem that the majority of contributions would be forthcoming from the world of big business (corporations, industries, etc.) or from foundations, in reality, this is not the case. In this country, it has been individuals who have contributed the greatest amount in terms of actual dollars to charitable causes than either foundations or the business sector.

Sources of Charitable Contributions. In 1986, $93.7 billion were donated by philanthropic organizations to all types of charities, nonprofit organizations, and programs in the United States. During both 1988 and 1989, contributions *from all sources* exceeded the $100 billion mark for the first time. Gifts from individuals alone in 1989 totaled some $96.43 billion, an increase of 11.7 percent. This was approximately two-and-a-half times the rate of inflation that year. In that same year, some $114.7 billion were donated to all nonprofit causes from individuals, foundations, bequests, and estates. This was an increase of $10.83 billion (10.4%) over the $103.87 billion given the previous year in 1988 (McMillen, 1990).

In examining all charitable contributions made in 1989, categorized according to the source of donations, the vast majority ($96.4 billion, 84%) of philanthropic contributions were from living individuals in contrast to individual donations made via wills ($6.6 billion, 5.75%), foundations (6.7 billion, 5.85%) and corporations (5.0 billion, 4.40%). In fact, more money has traditionally been contributed by individuals than from all other sources combined (McMillen, 1990).

Charitable contributions made in this country during 1990 continued the trend in which individual contributions represented the vast majority (83%) of all contributions to nonprofit causes. In 1990 all such contributions totalled $122.57 billion, an increase of 5.75% (Charitable Contributions, June 12, 1991). A breakdown of the sources of contributions in 1990 is provided here.

Contributions to Educational Institutions. In terms of contributions to educational institutions, some $2.35 billion was donated in 1989 by United States corpora-

Sources of Charitable Contributions in 1990	$ Amount (in billions)	1-year Growth	Percent of Total
Individuals (both current and deferred contributions)	101.80	5.19	83.05
Foundations	7.08	8.09	5.78
Bequests (wills)	7.79	11.76	6.36
Corporations, businesses, and industries	5.90	5.36	4.81
TOTALS	$122.57	5.75	100.00%

Check for $500,000 donated to Dee Rowe Scholarship Fund at Dee Rowe retirement dinner at the University of Connecticut. (Courtesy of University of Connecticut/photo by Bob Stowell)

tions alone. This significant amount was a 3.7% increase over 1988 and marked the thirteenth straight year in which corporations have increased their contributions to nonprofit educational institutions (Grassmuck, 1990).

Today, there are 26,000 foundations headquartered in the United States. Of these, there are nearly 400 large general purpose foundations that control about two thirds of the total foundation assets in this country. These 400 super large foundations also distribute approximately two thirds of the grants in terms of dollar amounts. While one might think that grants from foundations and other sources involve so-called "big dollars," 50% of all grants are under $1000 and 80% of grants awarded for charitable purposes are under $5000.

Types of Donations

What exactly can be donated? What should one seek as contributions? The answer is simple: **everything and anything of value**—*money, products, services,* as well as *ideas.* For example, there are (1) cash or negotiable instruments, (2) real and personal property, (3) equipment and supplies, (4) stocks, (5) bonds, (6) life insurance policies (proceeds to beneficiaries), (7) time (donated), (8) expertise (donated), (9) advice, and (10) donated services.

Timing of Fund-Raising Efforts

Generally speaking, fund-raising activities can be thought of in three ways in terms of the time or frequency in which such efforts take place. The three classifications are: (1) one-shot or one-time events or activities, (2) events or efforts that can be repeated a second time at some point in the future, and (3) those events that are annual or continual in nature.

One-Time Events. Some fund-raising and promotional activities by their very nature are best thought of as **one-time events.** An example of such a one-time activity might be a wine & cheese reception for initial (charter) memberships within the new booster club organization. Once this event takes place, it is over and will not be repeated since there can only be one "initial charter membership kick-off drive."

Repeatable Activities. A **repeatable fund-raising and promotional activity** is one that can be utilized more than once but is not of a nature that lends itself to being an annual event or a continuous activity. An example is a typical car wash as a fund-raiser. Although this event can be repeated, and often is, this event does not lend itself in terms of importance or significance to become a real tradition or an annual event within a sports program. Perhaps the car wash might be repeated but, it nevertheless lacks that certain something that would be necessary to become a tradition, an annual promotional and fund-raising activity.

The Annual Event. The **annual or continual promotional and fund-raising event** is such that, by its very nature, the activity lends itself to being repeated year after year, on an annual basis. For example, the typical Annual Hall of Fame Induction Ceremony for a school, held each fall during homecoming weekend, is an ideal annual promotional and fund-raising activity. Such an event will be conducted each and every year and is expected to be held by specific internal and external publics. Such an event becomes, after a number of years, part of the sports tradition of the organization. In fact, if such an event would not take place one year, it would be sorely missed.

Categories or Vehicles of Giving

In the world of fund-raising today, donors are frequently asked to contribute or make commitments for future contributions in response to a variety of different programs or vehicles designed to generate monies for the sport program. Eleven of these vehicles are:

1. Major donors programs—solicitation of large contributions from individuals and/or organizations.
2. Capital campaigns—providing for capital funding, new construction, renovation of existing structures, purchase and/or gifts of land, buildings, and equipment.
3. Annual scholarship appeals—providing money for student scholarships (in the form of room, board, tuition, etc.).
4. Annual giving campaigns for a total program—providing for ongoing needs of the sport program supplementing the regular sources of income. Between major fund drives, the annual giving programs receive a high priority.
5. Annual special event or projects—contributions generated from such activities as dance productions, sport medicine seminars, hall of fame ceremonies, social functions, etc.
6. Annual giving campaigns *for specific purpose*—designated giving to support a specific sport or cause.

7. Annual giving campaigns *on an unrestricted basis*—donations that are not specifically designated for a special purpose. This permits significant flexibility in the support of programs.
8. Deferred/planned giving programs—take place over an extended time period and involve estate planning, assignment of life insurance annuities, securities, as well as real and personal property.
9. Memorial giving programs—gifts made in memory of deceased individuals.
10. Gifts in kind for the total sport program or specific teams—contributions in other forms than money, such as, products, advertising, services, expertise, etc.
11. General endowment programs (scholarship, coaching stipend, facility upkeep, etc.)—establishing athletic or coaching "chairs," research programs, and student scholarships. Such programs can provide operating funds from the interest generated from the endowment monies.

Endowments Provide for Long-Term Support. The purpose of endowment programs is to provide for long-term support over a number of years. Endowments are created when the original gifts, money, and/or stock, etc., accrue interest indefinitely. The annual proceeds (profits) from the endowment provide available monies throughout time to provide support for the program, while leaving the original money intact. Thus, there is the potential for continued benefits accruing to the sport program generating from the interest earned, as well as from profits from wise investments made with the original gift(s). These benefits may be enjoyed in perpetuity as long as interest and/or profit is generated from the use of the original money contributed.

It would be a mistake to assume that endowments are the exclusive property of large colleges and universities. Not so. The concept of establishing endowments for the benefit of a wide range of worthy causes can include all levels of athletic programs including youth sports and secondary schools. All that is needed is the concept of a plan and the successful solicitation of potential donors.

There are numerous types of endowments. One type is the scholarship endowment trust. In this instance there is a permanent scholarship fund established by the contributor who may be allowed to name a scholarship as well as to designate the sport for which the scholarship may be used. As in any endowment, the interest generated each year on the principle money donated is used toward tuition, etc. A second type of endowment might provide for payment of a coaching stipend or salary. On the college level, this might be termed an Endowed Chair for Coaching, similar to the Endowed Chair for Physics—paying for the salary of a specific coach rather than the physics professor. A similar situation could exist on the high school level where the salary of the coach would be paid with the interest generated from the monies placed in an interest-bearing bank account. A third variation of the endowment concept calls for the interest (profit or proceeds) earned from the principle (contributions) to be paid for the maintenance on the facilities. Since there will always be costs associated with maintaining sport facilities, it is wise to plan for a steady source of income to help offset this perpetual expense.

Deferred/Planned Giving Programs—Proceeds from Life Insurance. A growing emphasis is being placed on what is called the **Living Life Insurance Trust,** which is a type of a deferred, planned giving program. In this instance, the premium is paid by the contributor as a donation to the sport program. The sport organization in turn makes the premium payment on a life insurance policy that provides coverage for the contributor. The beneficiary of the policy is the sport organization. When the policy reaches maturity, its value will be placed in the Endowment Trust (for whatever purpose the endowment has been established) in honor of the designated donor. Upon the death of the donor (the insured) the proceeds of the life insurance flow to the endowment of the sport organization.

Attempting to Influence Opinions of Others—Use of Centers of Influence. Those who are associated in fund-raising and promotional activities are, for the most part, involved in changing or reinforcing opinions of others and getting people to act in a specific fashion—that is, to contribute money or some other commodity of value. In attempting to approach potential donors, it is often wise to obtain the assistance of an intermediary (*center of influence*) to introduce you.

A center of influence is an individual who has influence with the prospect. This is especially important if the potential donor is a stranger and/or someone who travels in a different social or business circle. Obtaining a mutual friend to serve as that all important "bridge" via an introduction can be a significant boost in building one's credibility. In addition to the use of centers of influence in an attempt to influence opinions of others, there are six other tactics commonly utilized in attempting to exert an influence on the decision-making ability of others.

These include the (1) use of authority figures, (2) use of respected individuals, (3) use of popular idols, (4) use of persuasive arguments, (5) use of emotional statements, and the (6) use of needs satisfaction. Naturally, use of any of the above tactics depends upon the circumstances one finds oneself in, as well as the status of the prospective donor.

Who Contributes

Earlier it was pointed out that individuals, businesses, corporations, and foundations are potential donors to charitable causes, such as educational and sport organizations. Since we have already seen that the vast majority of charitable dollars come from individuals and from businesses, it is only natural to concentrate on these sources of monies. Identifying and cultivating potential donors for one's own program is very, very important. The **donor** is the key element to a successful development program. Naturally, the more sources (individual donors and organizations) of revenue you have, the more stable your fund-raising program will be and the greater the likelihood for substantial and continual success.

Facts to be Considered in Soliciting Support. When considering the potential for receiving assistance (money, time, goods, services, volunteering, etc.) from individuals and organizations, it is useful to note the following information regarding people who tend to contribute to sports programs (Yiannakis and Braunstein, 1983).

1. Contributors tend to follow certain patterns. Approximately one-half tend to match their previous donations; about 20% will give less, while 20% tend to make a larger contribution. New or reactivated donors will be the remaining 10%.

2. The *more individuals have given in the past,* the more likely they will increase subsequent donations.

3. Those who *have or have had a family member* associated with the program are more likely to contribute, help, or volunteer.

4. Those who *attend the sport activities* or *related activities* tend to be more receptive to assisting and contributing.

5. Those who *have an interest in sport activities* or *related activities* (fans) are more prone to give of themselves.

6. Those with an *interest in the goals and objectives* of the organization and its activities are potential supporters.

7. Others who are prime candidates to become contributors include:
   a. Those who are *members and employees* of the sport organization.
   b. Representatives of *other sport businesses.*
   c. *Vendors* associated with one's sport organization.
   d. *Area business owners and managers.*
   e. *Alumni* (athletes, coaches, administrators) of athletic organizations and programs.

8. People *tend to contribute in round numbers;* therefore provide such opportunities in the areas of donations, as well as in the pricing of items for sale.

9. Individuals and organizations *favorably disposed* (for whatever reasons) to such worthy sport causes will contribute.

Known Characteristics of Givers (Briggs, 1984).

1. *Age:* Historically those 30 and over tend to be more responsive to appeals for funds because of their financial situation and experience.

2. *Sex:* Males still tend to be more responsive to contributing to sport causes than females. However, this may be changing with the emerging women who are involved in sports and who are financially independent.

3. *Social Class:* Middle and working class people are excellent sources for fund-raising for sports and sports related programs. Those in the lower social/economic class, due to their economically deprived position, are often incapable of sizeable donations. However, there continues to be a growth potential of middle class contributors. At the other end of the spectrum, those who might be considered to be the so-called higher social class are often difficult to reach for the typical sport fund-raiser. The one exception might be if these potential donors are approached by centers of influence who are of equal or higher social/economic standing.

4. *Income:* When sizing up potential donors it is important to look at total family income rather than focusing only on the primary income earner. From experience, it is safe to assume that the probability of contributing decreases as the amount of discretionary income decreases. Extremely wealthy people give the most. An experienced fund-raiser once revealed that contributions of $5000 and above account for almost 70% of total gifts nationally to education.

5. *Proximity to the cause or program:* It seems logical that the closer the prospect is to the cause (such as an alumnus or alumna), the more likely the

person is to contribute. Also, those closer to the cause or sports program are more susceptible to emotional appeals. Thus, those individuals who are farther removed from the cause of the campaign should be approached for contributions through more of an intellectual rationale.

6. *Residential proximity to school:* In a school setting those who live close to the facility are prime candidates to become donors.
7. *Property owners:* Individuals owning property in the general geographical area are more likely to contribute than renters.
8. *Area of residence:* Solicitation seems to be more productive in rural areas than suburban.
9. *Marital Status:* Married persons with children are more likely to contribute to sport causes than those without children.
10. *Economy:* Individuals tend to contribute more in sound economic times. Corporations give most when profits are up, and they also tend to give more to sports organizations within close geographical proximity.

In summary, contributors to sport-related entities tend to be older, middle, or working class members of society, with a combined family income of more than $30,000. They tend to be male rather than female, married rather than single, and are likely to have children residing in close proximity to the school. Further, those who contribute have a tendency to have given previously, are graduates of colleges and universities, are often teachers or former teachers, have or had children in the same or similar school or organization, and/or are close to someone who participates in the program. Further, contributors to school athletic programs tend to be alumni, students, general activity consumers, owners of related businesses, owners of community dependent businesses, and community property owners (Yiannakis & Braunstein, 1983, p. 23–25).

When examining the question of **who** contributes to worthy causes, be aware of a general rule of thumb that commonly is referred to as the **90–10 rule.** This implies that, generally speaking, 90% of the monies generated in any given fund-raising effort comes from only 10% of the donors. Conversely, 10% of the money comes from contributions comprising the remaining 90% of the donors.

▬ Principle 52 ▬
The 90–10 rule.

Another axiom in fund-raising, in terms of *direct contributions* made to charitable causes, is the **one-third rule.** This states that one-third of the monies raised usually come from the top ten contributors, the second one-third of contributions (in terms of money raised) are generally derived from the next 100 contributors, and the final one-third of contributions are attributable to all other contributors and donors combined (however many that happens to be).

▬ Principle 53 ▬
The one-third rule—in terms of direct contributions.

In light of the above two rules or principles, the initial step in planning for direct contributions is to accurately identify the top ten probable contributors and then pinpointing the next 100 or so likeliest prospects. Fund-raisers need to identify and prioritize those who could very well be actual contributors and those who will probably not be contributors or significant contributors, and then concentrate on the prime prospects.

Potential contributors, once they are identified, become the prime targets of solicitors as they have the potential for producing the most on behalf of the fund-raising effort.

Why People Contribute

Advantages to Advertisers, Contributors, Supporters, and Sponsors. When attempting to plan and organize a fund-raising effort, there are two basic questions to ask. These are:

■ **Principle 54** ■

People support deserving causes, successful individuals, and meaningful programs.

1. Why would or should someone contribute to the effort?
2. What are the real appeal factors of the fund-raising activity to potential donors?

The answers to these two questions may very well reveal whether or not the proposed fund-raising activity meets with success or failure. There is another factor, however, that the fund-raiser needs to be cognizant of in the attempt to garner support—namely, that there is a need to show that the sports program or activity is of value and that the present management is currently doing a good job with what resources are currently available. People do indeed support what they perceive to be deserving causes, successful people, and significant programs.

In real life, individuals contribute for all sorts of reasons. Some reasons are logical. Others are emotional, and still others defy reason. In real life there are almost as many reasons for contributing as there are benefactors. It is important to remember that there are indeed real benefits that can accrue to individuals, as well as businesses, contributing to worthy sports causes. It is up to the promoter, the fund-raiser to match would-be contributors with benefits that they desire or need.

In addition to the satisfaction gained from knowing that a meaningful contribution had been made for a good cause, there are other intangible *and* tangible consequences of such generosity. Some give because of a genuine and generous desire to assist or contribute to worthy and/or charitable causes. Others contribute their money, goods, time, and skills because there are tangible and intangible benefits which may accrue to the giver. A partial list of the reasons why benefactors contribute to sports programs is provided below (Lopiano, 1983; Yiannakis & Braunstein, 1983; Briggs, 1984; McDermott-Griggs & Card, 1992).

1. Need to belong
2. Loyalty
3. Pride (personal, community, and school)
4. Desire for some benefit—season tickets, name in publications, gifts, premiums
5. Tax advantages
6. Membership benefits
7. Guilt elimination
8. Personal satisfaction (feeling good)
9. Opportunities for input and influence
10. Religious beliefs
11. Need to achieve
12. Indebtedness (gratitude) and obligation

13. Ego satisfaction
14. Permanent remembrance—facility named after oneself
15. Identification through children or youth
16. Desire to help others
17. Publicity and public relations
18. Group pressure (internal and external)
19. Personal recognition
20. Elimination of fear
21. Desire for association with an organization (achievement or respectability by association)
22. Vote casting privileges and opportunities
23. Identification with an image or a cause
24. Self perpetuation (to be remembered in some fashion in the future)

Lopiano (1983) cites the ''guilt and glitter'' syndrome as being a significant motivating factor in people's tendency to contribute to sports programs. In this respect, people tend to contribute because of the desire to be associated with the so-called ''glitter'' of the sport world. There is something exciting about sports teams regardless of the level at which they compete. Whether one is talking about youth teams, high school sports or collegiate athletic programs, there is an excitement, a thrill, a unique ''experience'' that attracts people and motivates them to become involved. That they become associated with the sports program through their contributions speaks towards the ''glitter'' aspects of motivation.

The second part of the syndrome as expressed by Lopiano refers to the concept of ''guilt.'' That is, individuals are sometimes motivated to contribute because of the guilt or uneasiness they tend to feel in having more resources and advantages than the average person in society. Being able to share with the less fortunate is a worthy motivational concept that has resulted in numerous contributions to worthy causes, including those within the sport umbrella. Acting upon these twin motivating factors, ''guilt and glitter,'' as well as any of the others listed above, can significantly increase the fund-raising efficiency and effectiveness of any sport organization.

Appropriate Strategic Planning

Fund-raisers, as strategists or tacticians, must be able to decide on a specific master plan of attack. They must agree upon a strategy involving tactics, resources, and timing designed to raise money within the confines or limitations of available resources, established priorities, and within a specific timetable. The use of a *strategy* enables knowledgeable decisions to be made. Planning also involves the setting of priorities coupled with realistic timetables, the elimination of conflicts, the securing of sufficient lead time to allow for proper preparation, and the involvement of adequate staff in the project.

Initial Steps

In the initial stages of fund-raising, there are really three very important steps that must be completed. The first is the determination of the need to raise money. That is, can the fund-raising efforts be justified? The second is the decision-making process

**Strategic
Planning for
the Generation
of Monies for
Sport Causes**

itself—deciding what exactly will be done and how; that is, deciding upon tactics or strategies. The third is the approval process, the gaining of approval, of permission for the actual implementation of the plan from all appropriate parties, prior to the initiation of the activities.

Before One Starts—Important Early Decisions to Make

There are several key decisions that must be made prior to the actual initiation of any specific attempt to raise funds. These decisions will help forge the direction in which the fund-raising activity will take in the future and will define the parameters of the fund-raising efforts. These decisions will also help gain the approval of the appropriate higher administrators by revealing that a sound examination has been made of all aspects of the proposed project(s). These decisions revolve around the following:

1. Realization that promotion and fund-raising starts at home. Just as the ripples expand outward when a pebble is thrown into a pond, so, too, should efforts to promote and raise funds start at the very center of the sport program—with the participants, the staff, and members of the athletic entity. If those close to the sport program will not participate and significantly contribute, how can outside constituencies be expected to do so?

2. Determination of whether the fund-raising activity is to be considered a *one-shot effort* or as a *repeat* activity. Could or should the activity become an annual event? This reaches to the basic philosophy of the organization itself and the purpose for which the fund-raising activity is being established. If the activity is an annual event, during the second year the homework time is reduced by 80%–90%, the planning or meeting time could be reduced by 50%–60%, while the project development time may be reduced by as much as 40%–50%.

3. Determination of the *number* of fund-raising activities that will be undertaken within a specified period of time. In terms of major fund-raising efforts, it is generally conceded that the mastery of a single successful fund-raising project, in a professional fashion, should be achieved before a second or a new fund-raising activity is undertaken. Spreading oneself or an organization too thin to be able to do justice to any one single activity is a common fault and should be guarded against. When a major fund-raising activity has proven to be successful and when the multitude of tasks involved with the project have been mastered, then it might be appropriate to think about planning for another major project.

4. Determination of whether the **shotgun** or the **rifle** approach should be used in dealing with prospective contributors. The shotgun approach involves attempting to blanket a wide range of potential prospects. For example, sending out a mailing containing a request for contributions to everyone in the community. Contrast this approach with the rifle technique, which involves zooming in on a select but smaller target population, for example, mailing the same request as cited above, but only to parents who have had children who were involved in sports at the school.

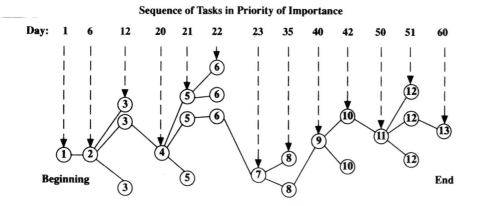

Figure 7.4 Modified PERT Network.

5. Determination of the worst-case scenario in an effort to determine what could possibly go wrong at the worse possible time and then planning for that eventuality. Be aware of Murphy's Law, which states, *"Anything that can go wrong will go wrong at the worse possible point in time."*

6. Determination of the *criteria* by which the fund-raising activity will either continue or be terminated. At some point in time during every fund-raising effort, there comes a time when a decision has to be made whether or not to continue the effort or activities to their ultimate conclusion. However, the criteria underlying this decision must be made prior to the actual start of the fund-raising efforts.

The Program Evaluation Review Technique (PERT) is a system or method of planning and controlling any project. The PERT system assists with identifying and prioritizing all key components, steps, or activities that must be completed in order to accomplish a given project or to successfully reach a specific goal. The PERT concept can be used to greatly facilitate the successful planning and implementation of any sophisticated fund-raising or promotional project.

A simplified version of the PERT system involves the identification of all individual activities or steps that must ultimately be completed in order for the fund-raising project to be successful. This listing of each and every major task or step is paramount for the successful utilization of the PERT concept. Essentially, once a complete and detailed list of such tasks and steps involved with the project is completed, the fund-raiser then constructs a flow chart involving a *time line* or *critical path,* shown in figure 7.4. On this flow chart the fund-raiser can then categorize the major tasks according to priorities and places each task, step, or component along the time line or critical path.

This flow chart can also include the (1) amount of time, (2) the kinds of resources needed, and (3) specific performance that will be required to accomplish each task. When viewing the PERT flowchart the fund-raiser should be able to easily determine which task or job must be completed at any given point in time as well as which components or resources must be in place prior to tackling a specific activity or task.

▨ Principle 55 ▨

Use a variation of the Program Evaluation Review Technique (PERT) to plan the timing of appropriate steps in the fund-raising and promotional process.

Kraus and Curtis (1977) suggest utilizing a "network" of essential activities established and plotted on a chart in a logical time sequence. Starting as well as completion times for each component or activity should be shown to create a pictorial description of the time relationships of all of the steps, the activities, or the components involved in the complete project.

The major advantage for the PERT-type analysis is to keep the planners and administrators abreast of the progress of the ultimate task or project at hand. The identification of each component or activity necessary to be completed prior to the realization of the ultimate goal is essential. So too, is the allocation of the amount of time necessary for the completion of each component or activity. Thus, the planners are able to better understand not only what must be accomplished prior to reaching the ultimate objective but are able to monitor the progress of the attempt to do so throughout the time spent on task(s).

Team Concept for Direct Contributions—One Plan of Attack

Use the team concept of fund-raising. Employ the spirit of competition among individuals involved. Each team has its owner, coaches, and players. Prizes and awards are given to owners, coaches, and individuals. Have a kickoff dinner or luncheon, a midway progress lunch, and a final victory banquet meeting.

One of the more successful organizational techniques for soliciting donations is the **squad concept** (Briggs, 1984). This concept calls for the formation of squads structured within a league in an effort to generate motivation and to stimulate production. Each squad has an elected captain chosen on the basis of proven leadership. Using names from one of the national sports leagues, the squads or teams compete for group and personal prizes on the basis of sales production.

After 100 to 200 top donor prospects are identified, they are allocated among the various squads. There is a 24-hour trading period during which target donors are traded. Upon receiving the final prospect list, a squad may assign one of the members to contact each potential donor without fear of competition from another squad or member until, after a specific predetermined amount of time passes, the so-called commissioner declares that particular prospect as a free agent.

Free agency may occur during the last week of the campaign when it is apparent that a prospect had not been approached or not been effectively approached or had resisted all appeal attempts. In this event, the individual deserves to be considered fair game for any solicitor with the ability to persuade the prospect to action.

This technique can also be used in other activities, such as ticket and product sales and using geographic zones instead of prospect lists. The concept itself, however, is sound.

▬ Principle 56 ▬

Prior to the start of the fund-raising effort, establish the exact point of no return or determine—in advance—when to "cut your losses".

The essential factor in any major fund-raising project is simply this. Before ever beginning a fund-raising activity, a decision should be reached as to whether or not there are criteria that must be met or satisfied in order for the fund-raising activity to continue. Knowing when to call it quits and to cut one's losses is as important in fund-raising as it is in gambling.

Far too often sport organizers become enthralled with the "hunt" and with their own efforts and time expenditures in working toward a goal. The end result is a poor decision made in the heat of battle, based upon one's emotions, rather than with cool logic. One should never change the "rules of the game," that is, the guidelines as to whether or not to continue the fund-raising activity, merely because one is emotionally involved and excited about the project and/or with one's efforts expended up to that date. Throwing "bad" money after "good" is foolish. Throwing good effort after unproductive effort is foolish. Knowing when to stop the downside risk and to call a halt to the activity takes great courage. But, it must be done.

For example, let's examine the scenario in which a booster organization decides (on December 1) to kick off the sale of 400 tickets ($50.00 each for $20,000.00 in gross sales) for a brand new automobile on March 15. The scheduled date for the actual raffle is set for May 1. The car will cost the club $12,000.00 with the anticipated maximum net proceeds of some $8,000.00 remaining with the booster organization. The final commitment to the dealer must be made by the club no later than April 15.

When April 14 rolls around, only 150 of the 400 tickets have been sold (generating only $7,500.00 of the $12,000.00 needed *to even pay for the cost of the car,* much less make any profit). The officers of the club need to decide whether to call off the raffle or to continue and hope that the remaining number of tickets can be sold so that there would be at least sufficient money to pay for the cost of the car being raffled.

This decision should have been made back on December 1, when the officers of the booster organization were in a *calm, cool, and collected frame of mind.* The thinking and the decision-making process should be unaffected by the emotions attending the fund-raising activities and excitement on April 14. Far too often, decisions are made in the heat of the movement and are made with emotions rather than logic, much to the detriment of the image of the organization and the fund-raising activity.

Of course, if new information becomes available prior to April 14 that would shed a different light on the prospect of successfully meeting the ultimate goal, then by all means, a re-examination of the earlier decision (to cancel the activity if less than 350 tickets were sold) might certainly be warranted.

Many promotional and fund-raising projects involve the use of student-athletes in a variety of different roles. While there is nothing inherently troublesome in involving student-athletes, it is important to remain up-to-date in terms of the various eligibility rules and regulations promulgated by various conferences as well as state and national governing bodies.

The NCAA has placed certain restrictions in regard to the use of student-athletes for promotional activities. Several years ago Steve Alford, a basketball star on the Indiana University men's team, took part in a promotional effort that involved pictures being taken of the athlete and used as part of a fund-raising calendar. The athlete received no direct or indirect benefit by posing for the photographer. In fact, the calendar was sponsored by one of the University's sororities, and the proceeds from the sale of the calendar were earmarked for a nonprofit, worthy organization. Nevertheless, when the NCAA found out, the basketball player was punished by being declared ineligible for one basketball game. Since that time the NCAA has instituted a

▩ **Principle 57** ▩

Be cognizant of and adhere to all conference, state, and national rules and regulations pertaining to student-athletes' involvement in fund-raising.

less stringent policy regarding such involvement. However, there are still several sections within the current *1992–1993 NCAA Manual* (1992) applicable in this type of situation, specifically, sections 12.5.1.A-F.

High school athletic associations or conferences may also have eligibility rules restricting the role athletes may play in terms of promotions and fund-raising. Competent sport administrators and promoters should anticipate potential problems. Thus, before embarking on any scheme involving the direct participation by athletes in promotional or fund-raising activities, double check with the appropriate governing organization.

▧ Principle 58 ▧

Be cognizant of and adhere to all state and federal laws, as well as insurance requirements.

Another general topic that must be addressed when dealing with promotion and fund-raising activities is that of the legal ramifications. Under this category are four general areas that deserve the close attention of competent fund-raisers or promoters and will be discussed in the following pages. These areas are (1) legal liability, (2) insurance considerations, (3) applicable federal and state laws, and (4) licenses and permits.

Liability Considerations—Fund-Raising and Promotional Activities

Promoters and sports fund-raisers must be constantly aware of the potential for litigation as a result of the activities they sponsor, and litigation is increasing each year. In fact, we have almost become a society of litigants.

▧ Principle 59 ▧

In terms of legal liability one is judged by what a similarly educated, trained, experienced professional would have done in similar circumstances.

Negligence is the failure to act as a *reasonable* and *prudent* professional would have acted in a similar situation, assuming the person possessed similar educational credentials, practical experiences, training, and expertise. In short, we are judged by the standards set by our peers in similar circumstances when it comes to legal liability. The determination of what is reasonable care is directly affected by the age, sex, health, skill, maturity, and reputation of the individuals involved in the activity or program. Naturally, greater care and closer supervision must be shown when dealing with youngsters in grade school than with 21-year-old college students or other adults.

Generally speaking, there are *five factors* that must be present to be guilty of negligence. First, there must be a duty or obligation that an individual has for the person who becomes injured. That is, a person must have responsibility for another person. One must have an obligation for caring or protecting another individual. Second, was that duty breached? Did the person fail to perform the assigned duty, either by an act of omission or through commission of an unsafe act? Third, was the act of omission (*not doing what one should do*) or commission (*doing something one should not have done*) the result, the proximate cause of the injury? Fourth, was the injury avoidable or unavoidable? Or, was the injured person partly at fault or was there a third party/person who shares the blame for the injury? Fifth, did the plaintiff actually receive an injury, physical, emotional, or psychological?

In defending against the charge of negligence, one attempts to prove that one of the five factors listed above are not applicable. Other possible defenses against being found negligent are:

1. Assumption of risk—the person involved in the activity recognizes and assumes that there are specific risks associated in the activity.
2. Contributory negligence—the injured person was at fault (more difficult to prove when the person is a youngster).
3. Comparative negligence—the person who is injured is only partially deemed negligent. There is an apportionment of guilt or fault between the plaintiff and the defendant. As a result, there is a weighing or sharing of responsibility of negligence.
4. Act of God—an unforeseen and unpreventable act or event took place resulting in injury.

Administrators and coaches need to be reminded that the majority of litigation areas in sports revolve around seven specific areas. Hence, it is advisable for the fund-raiser, in the planning of the sponsored activities, to take into consideration the need to insure that proper safety procedures are followed in terms of:

1. Supervision of the specific event by qualified and trained adult supervisors.
2. Use of safe equipment and supplies.
3. Use of appropriate and safe facilities, inspected prior to use.
4. Proper instruction of those being asked to perform specific tasks.
5. Use of appropriate vehicles driven by qualified adults.
6. Warning of the dangers and perils that might be inherent in the activity.
7. Provision of first aid and emergency care in the event of an injury.

Principle 60

Practice foresight ("ounce of prevention") when it comes to preventing accidents—prevent, don't merely react.

Risk Management for Preventing Exposure to Negligence Charges

Risk management are popular "buzz words" in legal circles today (Maloy & Vivian, 1992). Risk management implies evaluating the risk(s) involved in any activity and planning for the worst-case scenario. It is a matter of asking "what if" and then planning to prevent accidents from taking place. Essentially, risk management involves three major factors (Figone, 1989): First, the study of the hazards that might or do exist; second, the planning as to how to eliminate such hazards or potential for injuries; and, third, planning the course of action to take in case of accidents that might occur in spite of one's best efforts.

Factors taken into consideration in determining whether or not one is negligent in the conduct of a fund-raising activity include (Nygaard & Boone, 1985):

1. Who sponsored the activity (school or booster club).
2. Age of the individual injured in fund-raising.
3. The type and extent of training provided.
4. Whether or not directions were obeyed.
5. Whether or not adequate supervision and warning were provided by appropriate persons.

6. Any hazardous conditions and specific dangers inherent in the activity or product.
7. Extent of product liability for those products sold by the athletic program (Dennison, 1985).
8. Where the injury occurred and if there were witnesses.
9. Whether the accident/injury was foreseeable or preventable.
10. The approximate cause of the accident/injury.
11. Who was responsible for the accident/injury?
12. If a standard liability release was obtained from the participants if the event or activity could be considered inherently risky, such as a 10–K race, a marathon, etc.

Insurance Considerations—Fund-Raising and Promotional Activities

Check with the school attorney and with the school insurance company to determine liability insurance coverage for activities in which the booster club is engaged, both on the school grounds and away from the school. Similarly, booster clubs need to be concerned about securing adequate insurance in their own right if they cannot be covered under the school's umbrella policy.

Naturally, all activities and all actions by individuals associated with the booster club and the athletic fund-raising activities should be beyond reproach. Everyone associated with the fund-raising effort must exercise extreme caution in their daily actions in order to reduce the likelihood of improper action (negligence through omission or commission) that could result in the legal wrong to another person or person's property. The goal is to adhere to the necessary standards of performance, supervision, and safe and prudent conduct by *all* personnel—paid and volunteer—associated with the sport fund-raising efforts.

Applicable Federal and State Tax Laws—Fund-Raising and Promotional Activities

The process of incorporation in most states is not a complicated one. The laws governing businesses and the creation of corporations vary from state to state. In some states it is not mandated by law that an attorney file the necessary incorporation papers. However, it is wise to consult with a lawyer conversant with corporation law prior to making a final decision whether or not to incorporate.

To obtain definitive information regarding the laws in one's own state, one has only to contact the Secretary of State in the state in which the organization exists to obtain up-to-date facts relative to incorporating the fund-raising entity as a not-for-profit organization.

The Internal Revenue Service (IRS) has specific tax laws governing organizations formed for profit, as well as for those organized (and meeting the requirements of the laws) for charitable, education, and religious purposes. There are three categories recognized by the IRS under which organizations might be categorized as not-for-profit. These include (1) charitable, education, and religious agencies, (2) social welfare organization and civic leagues, and (3) social recreational clubs.

In this respect, it is highly advisable to contact the Internal Revenue Service and/or a knowledgeable accountant or attorney to examine the benefits, limitations, and requirements applicable for the so-called profit and not-for-profit businesses and corporations.

Licenses and Permits—Fund-Raising and Promotional Activities

In some communities it may be necessary to obtain licenses to peddle merchandise or to distribute leaflets. Some municipalities require a special permit and insurance for sky divers to jump into a football stadium. It is also frequently necessary to obtain city, township, county, or state permission (via permits) to conduct gambling-type activities or games of chance. In short, it is always best to check with local, county, and state authorities to insure that the proposed promotional and fund-raising activity meets all legal requirements.

It is indeed embarrassing and counterproductive to find out after the fact that a law or regulation was violated out of either ignorance or negligence, or that a required permit or license was not obtained, or a mandated report not appropriately filed in a timely fashion. When these mistakes and oversights take place, it reveals that the fund-raising organizers and managers were not operating at an acceptable level of competency. The result is a potentially embarrassing and damaging situation in terms of public relations and publicity—a fact that can quickly erode confidence in the competency levels of those involved in the fiasco when viewed by others.

References

Briggs, J., Jr. (1984). *The official football fund-raiser's guide.* North Palm Beach, Florida: Boosters Clubs of America.

Charitable contributions. (1991, June 12). *USA Today.* p. A-1.

Corporations find giving pays in hard times. (1991, August 29). *USA Today,* p. 1-B.

Dennison, M. (1985). Product liability: A legal dilemma. In H. Appenzeller. (ed.). *Sports and law, contemporary issues.* Charlottesville, VA: The Michie Co.

Figone, A. (1989). Seven major legal duties of a coach. *Journal of Physical Education, Recreation and Dance, 60* (7), 71–75.

Fund-a-thon season hits full stride. (1991, May 3). *USA Today,* p. 1-D.

Grassmuck. (1990, September 5). *The Chronicle of Higher Education, XXXVII* (1), 31-A.

Kraus, R. & Curtis, J. (1977). *Creative administration in recreation and parks* (2nd ed.). St. Louis: The C. V. Mosby Company.

Lopiano, D. A. (1983, November). More on developing a successful fund-raising program for non-revenue sports. *Athletic Purchasing & Facilities,* pp. 32–37.

Maloy, B. P. & Vivian, J. (1992, May). Risky business. *Athletic Business,* pp. 43–46.

McDermott-Griggs, S. & Card, J. (1992). Creating a successful fund-raising letter. *Journal of Physical Education, Recreation and Dance, 63* (1), 57–58.

McMillen, Liz. (1990, June 13). Philanthropic contributions. *The Chronicle of Higher Education, XXXVI* (39), A-1, A-23.

1992–1993 NCAA manual. (1992). Overland Park, Kansas: The National Collegiate Athletic Association, p. 74.

Nygaard, G. & Boone, T. (1985). *Coach's guide to sports law.* Champaign, Il: Human Kinetics.

Yiannakis, A. & Braunstein, S. (1983). *The complete guide to successful fund-raising.* North Palm Beach, Florida: American Sports Education Institute.

Money scramble—promotional activity at a baseball game at Florida Southern College. (Courtesy of Florida Southern College, Office of Sports Information.)

Pragmatic Approaches to the Raising of Resources

Two Approaches to the Raising of Monies

The raising of money (resources) can be accomplished through two approaches. First, is the so-called **supermarket** or **merchandising model.** The second method is through the formal **solicitation model.**

In the *supermarket* or *merchandising model* there is an actual sale of items or services directly related to the organization to the various publics. Items such as pennants, ashtrays, t-shirts, publications, car washes, or coupon redemption plans with various kinds of retail establishments can all be sold. Additionally, other things that can be marketed include drawings of one kind or another (with prizes going to the winners) and various gambling activities.

This model has also been called by others the **business revenue approach,** highlighting the value of the product or service to the customer/donor. The buyer purchases and/or donates monies, products, or services in exchange for an expectation of something of value (a benefit). In this situation, the motivating factor underlying the purchase of the benefit is *the benefit itself,* while the worthiness of the sport program frequently plays a secondary role in the motivation scheme (Bronzan, 1984).

The *solicitation* or *appeal model* involves the solicitation or asking of money, services and/or products from prospective contributors. The motivational force behind the donation, on behalf of the donor, lies in the charitable, intangible, or worthy cause aspect or facet. That is, the donor gives primarily because of the worthiness of the cause and only secondarily (if at all) because of any real or tangible benefit reverting to the donor.

There should be a full understanding on behalf of the prospective donor of the *urgency to act* as well as the *worth, value,* and *importance* of the sports program. Finally, there must be an appreciation of how the actual contribution will lead to the realization of specific needs of the program, which are of value and worth supporting.

It is the responsibility of the sports fund-raiser to insure that the potential donor is made aware of these facts. Donors must be motivated to act. These factors can serve as motivators. Unless there is a real urgency, in reality, why should the prospective donor make the contribution *now* rather than at some time in the future? It becomes too easy to procrastinate and to put off the act of actually making the donation until

■ Principle 61 ■
Develop a sense of urgency to act when discussing or presenting needs to prospects.

a future time unless there is a real need (an urgency) for the act to be consummated at the present time. This urgency or need to act can be further facilitated by the presence of excitement and enthusiasm (which is contagious) derived from the association with the sports program and the fund-raising activities.

■ **Principle 62** ■
Don't cry wolf.

To successfully raise funds, it is not necessary for the athletic staff or booster club to always cite an emergency situation with potentially dire consequences if monies are not forthcoming. Sometimes additional resources are needed to provide for enhancements of an athletic program. Without these additional resources, however, the athletic program will not wither, die, and blow away in the sunset. There are other justifications for soliciting support than citing potential catastrophes. In fact, if one always solicits contributions on the basis of averting some calamity (the "Chicken Little syndrome") it does not take too long for the prospective donors to grow tired and wary of such thinly veiled attempts. No one wants to repeatedly give to a perpetually sinking sports program.

The Feasibility of Raising Funds

The answers to the following questions will go a long way to determine whether or not a specific proposed activity is worthwhile in terms of expenditure of money, time, effort, etc.

1. Does the fund-raising activity meet the needs of the sport program? Is there really a need?
2. Is this the only way, or the best way, of meeting this need?
3. Is the program itself worthy of support?
4. Is there adequate and competent leadership available?
5. Is the necessary "followship" available? Are there sufficient volunteers?
6. Is there an athletic support infrastructure capable of achieving the successful conclusion of the fund-raising effort?
7. Is there is a support organization or booster club in existence? Is this organization recognized as the official representative of the athletic program in terms of fund-raising?
8. Is there a positive image of the support organization in the eyes of the various constituencies?
9. How much will it "cost" to raise the desired amount?
10. What are the downside risks? Is the effort cost effective in terms of money, time and effort, personnel, and other resources?
11. Are the necessary resources available (budgeting, publicity, office management, etc.)?
12. What are the requirements in terms of time to reach the objective(s)? Can the objectives be reached in that time?
13. Are legal matters taken care of (incorporation, taxes, special permits, etc.)?
14. Is the image of the total sport program a positive one as viewed by various constituencies?
15. Can the end results stand up to close scrutiny of various constituencies?
16. Is the financial and political climate conducive to success?

When soliciting contributions, one should be willing and able to fully discuss with potential donors the needs and strengths of the organization, the institution, the program, as well as how the money will benefit the program and the participants with the prospect(s). Donors like to know how their contributions will be used to facilitate the program. People like to see tangible results of their efforts.

Although this seems like an overly obvious statement, this principle is violated repeatedly. Citing a problem or deficiency with the support received from the central administration as the reason that additional funds are needed creates as many problems as may be solved. An athletic program may be in need of additional monies or services without having to place *blame* on any one individual, group, or organization. It isn't necessary or appropriate to criticize or to cast a negative light on others to raise money for athletic programs. An upbeat, positive approach is far more productive, both in terms of internal and external public relations and in terms of actual dollars raised. No one likes to hear individuals speak ill of others, and that is just what fund-raisers do if they cite the lack of support by the central organization or by athletic administrators as the justification for why they "have" to raise *outside* funds for the sports program.

Principle 63
Don't bad mouth the school or athletic program when attempting to raise money.

Too frequently fund-raisers attempt to garner funds by stating—either outright or through implication—that the school or the athletic program is unwilling or unable to adequately support the athletic or sport program in the manner in which it should be supported. As a result, the present fund-raising effort has to be implemented. Naturally, the impression left is one of negativism toward the school and/or the athletic program, not to mention the staff and administrators within the school and athletic program. Such an approach is needless and counterproductive. The end result will often be ill will and the creation of an adversarial relationship.

It is all in the way the fund-raising activity is approached. If approached in a positive vein, from a perspective that the sport program will be *enhanced* with additional financial resources, etc., the end result will more likely be positive both financial contributions and positive public relations. It is important to remember that athletic fund-raising efforts will have an important impact on the public image and on the public relations perception of the total sport program, as well as on the total school or organization. If approached from the positive aspect, everyone can win.

If approached from the negative aspect, and the justification for the fund-raising causes the overall organization or school or athletic program to look like it is not fulfilling its responsibilities to the sports and the athletes, the fund-raising effort will have certainly failed in terms of creating a positive public relations image. In fact, just the opposite would have taken place, that is, the creation of a negative image.

Principle 64
Never pay for anything you can get for free or for a reduced cost.

A key concept is to never pay for anything—whether a product or a service—that can be obtained for free via a contribution. Spending money for tangible resources or services that can be obtained for free or on a reduced-cost basis is an important goal of any sport program. Doing so is the same as generating real cash, for it allows the sport organization to free up the hard cash that would have had to be spent for the acquiring of these resources for other purposes.

If resources cannot be obtained via actual cash donations, attempts should be made to barter or trade for needed resources. Exchanges or trade-outs of *athletic resources* such as tickets, appearances by members of coaching staff, provision of advertising space, and so on, can be effected for such *needed assets* as cash, advertising space, services, supplies, equipment, etc. The object is clear. The sport program is in need of resources. These resources can be obtained either via contributions or via an exchange of assets (which may or may not be discounted) with individuals or organizations. The possibilities and opportunities are endless, and yet the concept is simple.

Another wrinkle in this whole area of utilization of resources obtained through charitable contributions or through exchanges of assets revolves around what is actually done with the resources or assets once they are on hand. For example, merchandise, services, or products, once obtained can be utilized in the *general operation of the sport program* or can be used as a *resource that can generate additional resources*. For example, a side of prime beef donated or exchanged for something of value can become (1) steaks for the athletes at their training table or (2) can be used to generate actual cash via an auction held in conjunction with a formal fund-raising event.

▨ Principle 65 ▨
It is easier to raise money when one can show sound fiscal management in the current operation of the sports program.

Sports people interested in increasing the financial base for an athletic program should make known to potential contributors that the internal fiscal management of the athletic program is conducted on sound principles. This includes the assurances that the day-to-day management operation is sound and that the fiscal or accounting procedures meet all generally accepted criteria. It is vital that the current fiscal management of the athletic operation be viewed as being responsibly managed. That is, that the dollars available to the sports program within the budget are well spent. It becomes increasingly difficult, if not almost impossible, to generate additional funding from outside sources when the fiscal management of the resources that are available leaves much to be desired.

Another area that is a concern to donors is the amount of money being raised that will be allocated to overhead expenses. A recent study of 51 colleges revealed that it costs the institutions' development offices an average of only 16 cents to raise each dollar in their general fund-raising effort. This 525% return on investment included all directly related fund-raising expenses (McMillen, 1990).

No one likes to contribute money and see a high percentage of the contribution go to pay for the actual cost of raising the money. People contribute to see their money go for worthy causes—to help the sports program, to meet the needs of the athletes, etc. One tactic that has been used to counteract this potential problem is to have two separate income accounts. One of the accounts is structured in such a fashion that 100% of all donations placed in that account are actually used for the benefits of the sports program. All overhead expenses are to be taken from the second account.

In this situation, the prospective donor who expresses concern about what percentage of the contribution will actually go to the sports program can be assured that 100% of the funds contributed to the first account will be funnelled to meet the actual needs of the program, with none of those funds being diverted for overhead costs. Money for the second account can be solicited from those contributors who either do not express a concern about exactly where their money goes or from those

John Mahlstede, co-chair of the implementation committee, Iowa State University President Martin Jischke, and athletic director Max Urich help plant the first tree east of Cyclone Stadium as part of the All-American Grove Committee project. One tree will be planted (sponsored by a $300 donation) for each Iowa State athlete named All-American in the past 100 years. (Courtesy of Iowa State University Intercollegiate Athletic Department)

contributors who understand that in almost any fund-raising effort, there are necessary and ordinary expenses that must be taken care of and are customarily covered from the gross proceeds of the contributions collected.

A generally accepted assumption in fund-raising is that if the cause is just and worthwhile, the organization's internal staff personnel should be willing to provide substantial support, in a material fashion, to the fund-raising effort by significantly contributing to the effort themselves. If the organization cannot convince its "own people" to contribute to its cause, why would an "outsider" feel compelled to make a contribution? That is why it is important to have the data as to what percentage of one's own internal staff contributes to the program. Having this information available, combined with the knowledge of the average contribution of the organization's internal constituencies, can go a long way to convince outside individuals and organizations that those individuals closest to the athletic organization itself, those who are working in and benefiting from the sports organization itself, hold the athletic program in high esteem.

■ Principle 66 ■
In seeking contributions, look first to one's own internal staff.

Prior to attempting to institute a full blown external fund-raising campaign or major project, one should examine other sources of income, particularly those sources of money internal to the sports organization. It is suggested that only after the internal sources of funding are exhausted should one focus on outside fund-raising efforts.

Generally speaking, there are four ways to be able to increase the athletic program's purchasing power. These four avenues are listed below in terms of priority, that is, in the order of importance within the sports program.

■ Principle 67 ■
Exhaust internal avenues of generating support prior to instituting external fund-raising projects.

The first method of increasing the program's fiscal resources is through wise fiscal management of resources currently available to the sports program. Every dollar saved is, in reality, a dollar earned. This is no trite statement. It is a significant fact. One must be frugal in the management of resources and in purchasing practices. For every dollar saved, through whatever methods utilized, there is a corresponding reduction in the need to raise money. In other words, one can raise money by saving money.

The second method or tactic that should be pursued in terms of obtaining additional fiscal resources revolves around the justification of additional funding from the sponsoring organization. In a school setting, this involves convincing the school administrators or the school board of the need for a bigger piece of the proverbial pie, the school budget. The ability to convince the ''powers that be'' of the need for such additional funds can greatly reduce the need for outside fund-raising activities.

The third tactic revolves around the internal fund-raising through profit centers organized and managed by the sports staff. To the extent that these profit centers (tickets, concessions, parking, etc.) are successful in generating significant amounts of money to the athletic program, there is a corresponding reduction in the need to raise additional funds outside the school or athletic arena.

There are times, however, when there is a demonstrated need for additional monies *in spite of* effective and efficient fiscal management in the day-to-day operation of the sports program. In some instances money is needed *in addition to* the financial support provided through the sponsoring organization. Even internal fund-raising efforts that might have been instituted are not sufficient to meet all of the program's needs. When all of the above methods fail to generate needed funds, then the fourth and final avenue for generating sufficient fiscal support for an athletic program, the **formal, external fund-raising effort** is not only warranted but required.

▄ Principle 68 ▄
Obtain input and approval prior to initiating promotional and fund-raising activities—
''Spread the blame/responsibility.''

The administrative concept of seeking counsel and prior approval for fund-raising activities is important for two very pragmatic reasons: (1) to gather potentially helpful ideas and suggestions and, (2) should anything go wrong, to distribute the fallout or negative consequences. This is sometimes referred to as the ''spreading the blame/responsibility syndrome.''

Far too often, would-be fund-raisers are in too great a hurry to carry out their plan of attack. The result is that they find themselves out on a limb, all alone. Those in authority, who should be passing ultimate judgment on the suitability of such activities and who are held to be ultimately responsible, are not consulted. This lack of consultation, this lack of securing approval can become a major stumbling block for the fund-raiser.

▄ Principle 69 ▄
Don't interfere with overall fund-raising efforts of the central organization or administration (recognize the pecking order of one's own group or entity).

It is important not to have one's fund-raising activities interfere (or be perceived to interfere) with the overall fund-raising efforts of the central organization or administration. This is especially relevant in schools. Most school systems and many colleges and universities have policies that restrict fund-raising efforts to those activities that have been approved by and are coordinated through a designated administrative office (McIntyre & Anderson, 1987).

There does exist a pecking order within any organization in terms of who will be encouraged or allowed to be involved in specific fund-raising activities. Recognizing this pecking order or hierarchy eliminates many headaches for the athletic fund-raising practitioner. The pecking order in terms of fund-raising importance within public schools might include fund-raising efforts on behalf of or by the school board, the superintendent or the principal, various department chairpersons, the band, various music groups, numerous athletic teams, the school newspaper, the year book, numerous organizations, special class trips, etc. The list could go on and on.

There must be an established procedure or system for requesting permission to engage in fund-raising and promotional activity. There should be set criteria against which all requests to raise funds may be judged. Additionally, there must be priorities established that guide the approval process. Finally, there must be a clear understanding of exactly who will be the individual (or individuals) who will have the power to actually authorize the go-ahead of any specific fund-raising proposal.

Of course, great care must be taken to insure that there are provisions for equal treatment and protection of all sports in terms of compliance with both the letter and intent of Title IX, if applicable. Toward this end, it is advisable to involve members of the central administrative staff. In high schools those individuals might be the vice principal, principal, and perhaps the superintendent. In college the dean, the vice president and even the president might be involved in reviewing and approving the establishment of criteria and procedures.

Frequently, such criteria and procedures are included within the Athletic Handbook of Policies, Procedures, and Practices. One specific educational institution has the policy that stipulates requests for sport fund-raising activities be first submitted in writing to the Athletic Director for initial review and possible approval (Stier, 1988). The information included within the formal request to engage in raising monies includes:

■ **Principle 70** ■
Establish criteria by which proposed fund-raising activities can be evaluated for suitability.

1. How the money would be generated, with details
2. How much money is needed
3. The time involved
4. Who will be contacted in the quest for money
5. The method for accounting of the funds generated
6. For what purpose(s) the money will be used

Following approval at this departmental level, the request is channeled ''upstairs'' to the next appropriate administrative level for review and approval or rejection. The final approval, however, is reserved for the chief executive officer or designee who will decide whether or not the specific request has merit or not and can be permitted to be implemented.

At each of the levels of review, the appropriate administrator or staff member may provide written statements relating to the reasons why the request is rejected or written statements that stipulate under what circumstances the fund-raising project can be initiated. There are two significant advantages of such a review process. First, the coaches or boosters who desire to engage in fund-raising activities have valuable input and guidance from other administrators, some of which are experienced fund-raisers within the institution. Second, the central administrators are aware of the specifics of the request to raise funds and are able to pass judgment on its merits, taking care that such activity would not interfere with the *big fund-raising picture* of the total institution or organization.

An example of such a request form utilized by coaches to receive permission from the central administration of a university is provided in Appendix D. This form is used in the review process so that a number of central administrators, athletic and nonathletic, will be able to review the request and to render a decision as to its suitability for the institution.

▪ Principle 71 ▪
Fund-raising and promotional efforts must be compatible with community and institutional standards.

One of the first questions that should be raised in any consideration of a fund-raising project or promotional activity is whether such activity would meet the standards for the community in which the event(s) will be held. For example, in some communities gambling activities might be not only frowned upon by the various constituencies (on religious or moral grounds) but might also have legal limitations. The importance of considering the educational, ethical, traditional, religious, and social code should not be minimized in evaluating the suitability and acceptability of any proposed activity or event.

Of course, the determination of what is appropriate and what is not appropriate will vary in light of what type of sport program is involved. It will also vary as among various sections of the country and from community to community in the same state. What may be suitable, in terms of raising monies or promotional events for the university located in New York City might be totally inappropriate for a midget football program in a small farming community located in the south.

Some examples will suffice. The question of accepting tobacco (cigarettes, cigars and chewing tobacco) advertisement for the athletic program or for inclusion on athletic schedule cards is very controversial. On the one hand, athletic programs are attempting (or so they say) to educate students-athletes on the evils of stimulants and depressants (misuse, abuse, and use of drugs). On the other hand, many of these same sport programs are accepting advertisements from companies that produce, market and sell cigarettes, cigars, and/or chewing tobacco. The same scenario can be drawn in respect to the area of alcohol. Is it appropriate on one hand to take money, services, and products from these corporations and businesses, while on the other hand discouraging the use of these products of these businesses among the athletes?

Various individual institutions as well as national organizations, including the NCAA, have initiated a dialogue concerning the appropriateness of accepting advertisements for alcohol and/or tobacco products in various tournament publications (Advertising, 1989). Similarly, there are ever increasing concerns being expressed in athletic circles in terms of any type of advertisements for sporting events from the alcohol and/or cigarette industries. The final word has not been heard on this controversial subject.

What is evident, however, is that should such advertisements become *persona non grata,* it will be more difficult to generate monies to replace these lost revenues. This is because advertisement monies and contributions toward sports at many levels from the alcohol and tobacco industries have been significant in terms of total dollars. Should these dollars disappear, the challenge for the sports fund-raisers will be to replace these contributions (in terms of actual dollars, goods, and services) with similar support from other sources. It has become almost too easy for athletic administrators to supplement their athletic budgets by tapping the almost bottomless pot of gold held out by the tobacco and alcohol corporations.

Restrictive Philosophies

Fund-raisers must remain cognizant of *any restrictive philosophies* or policies existing within their organization or school that might have an effect on their plans. These restraints may take the form of internal or external restrictions.

Clearinghouse for Fund-Raising Activities. In some schools and organizations, coaches and/or athletes must first go through some sort of a clearinghouse prior to proceeding with fund-raising activities. In some communities, there is an unwritten agreement or understanding between the school and the Merchants Association that individual merchants will not be "hit" with repeated requests for money by numerous groups from the school. For example, band boosters, individual coaches, athletic boosters, representatives from student government, the school paper, or the school radio or television station, or from individual student organizations within the school. Rather, these schools attempt to coordinate or regulate all such fund-raising efforts so that the individual merchants will have only a few *official* requests from representatives of the school. Such an arrangement goes a long way toward creating a positive, professional image on behalf of the school in the eyes of the community.

This prevents a situation in which ten different groups attempt to sell Christmas ornaments during the month of December or have ten car washes during the first week of school. Such overkill can be prevented if all potential plans have prior approval through one central office or clearinghouse, such as the athletic director or the director of development. In an organization of any size, such as a school, there always remains a need for coordination of *all* fund-raising activities, as well as an understanding of what is appropriate in light of the history, the philosophy, and the existing circumstances within the organization and the community.

Picking up "Nickels," "Quarters," or "Dollars." Another type of overkill is exemplified when a coach or sports booster approaches local businesses to raise so-called "nickels" for a particular sport, followed by the chief athletic administrator hitting the same local businesses for "quarters" for the overall athletic program. These efforts are then followed by the development officer, the principal, or the president approaching the same businesses for the "big bucks"—only to find the community businesses most unreceptive to repeated requests for funds from the same organization. Community people and businesses can become "tapped out" (figuratively and literally) by repeated requests for money.

Limitating Who May Be Solicited. There may be specific individuals, groups, or organizations placed "off limits" as potential donors for sport fund-raisers. This is frequently done so that these donors are not repeatedly approached by representatives of the same organization. Rather, they are reserved for visits or solicitations by the representatives of the higher administration—the heavy hitters.

On the other hand, there is always the possibility that the athletic fund-raiser may initially face a negative response on behalf of the central administration, but through persuasive arguments, may make a case to have the specific sport fund-raising effort approved. This was the case at a well-known university (NCAA Division I), located in the Midwest. The university administrative hierarchy—institutional fund-raisers—balked and complained to the president that the athletic staff had approached a national beer distributor, located in their state, for corporate sponsorship, trade outs,

■ **Principle 72** ■
Always be cognizant of any restrictions pertaining to fund-raising activities.

and numerous other fund-raising activities. The potential consequences involved hundreds of thousands of dollars going to the athletic department over the next three to five years, with the promise of much more to come.

The university development people advanced the argument that **they** were *going* to approach the same prospect (beer distributor) in the future and that this prospect rightly belonged to the overall university development apparatus. As such, they argued, this prospect should be off limits to the athletic fund-raising staff.

The athletic director countered that position by advancing the argument that the university, as well as the beer distributor, had both been in existence for many, many decades and, up to that point in time, the university development staff *had failed to even ask* the beer distributor for any money. Thus, it was argued, the beer distributor should be considered "fair game." It was the athletic director who was able, in the short span of several months, to conclude a sizeable and long-term financial arrangement with the company: a multi-year arrangement that would result in literally hundreds of thousands of dollars in actual cash plus an equal amount of contributions in the form of equipment and supplies, services, including radio and television time, accruing to the athletic program on an annual basis. In this particular case, the argument advanced by the athletic department prevailed.

▬ Principle 73 ▬
Contributors like to give for tangible purposes and to successful programs.

It is far easier to obtain contributions for tangible purposes—building, facilities, equipment, awards, etc.—than for intangible purposes such as utilities or postage. Similarly, donors are more likely to contribute when their gift(s) can have a long-lasting impact on the program. Obtaining money for uniforms, lasting 4 to 6 years, is usually easier than attempting to gather funds to pay for the current year's phone bill. This is the reason buildings have names of the donors on the side of the structures. It is more difficult to locate a plaque stating that Mr. Smith contributed to paying the electric bill at the high school in a certain year.

▬ Principle 74 ▬
Don't waste efforts or time on nickel and dime fund-raising projects.

One has to be choosy in selecting which fund-raising projects and which promotional activities to undertake. Promotional activities and special events are designed to raise money, increase attendance, improve image, and provide recognition to team members, coaches, boosters, and sponsors.

One must concentrate on those fund-raising activities that will generate the greatest number of dollars, services, and products from donors. There must be meaningful outcomes in light of the *total* resources expended. Spending too many resources on fund-raising activities that generate few dollars, or on promotional activities that are only marginally successful, is foolish. Since time and effort is finite, the activities undertaken must be not only successful but meaningful in terms of actual dollar value received in cash, services, or products. Athletic administrators must learn to place a dollar value on the time and effort of their staff and then use both effectively and efficiently in promotional and fund-raising efforts. It is necessary to set priorities in terms of where to place resources and efforts for the maximum impact, whether that impact is money or public exposure.

Generally speaking, the number of special fund-raising projects should be limited to those that will generate at least 10% to 15% of the annual net donations needed. Thus, seven to ten distinct fund-raising activities during any twelve months period should be the maximum number of projects attempted. Ideally, the number should be much less, with the dollar value per project much greater.

The second time around is always easier. This is especially true if careful and accurate records were kept of the activities previously implemented. The key is to maintain written documentation of previous fund-raising attempts. This documentation serves as a guide for the future so that successful efforts may be replicated, while unsuccessful ones can be eliminated from further consideration. Much time and effort can be saved by repeating what proved to be successful in the past, since the initial planning, work, and evaluating have already taken place.

Another reason why a repeat project is often easier to implement, especially if the previous experience was successful, is that members of the public or various constituencies have an expectation of what the repeat activity will be like, and, if it was a satisfying experience the first time, there is a predisposition to participate the second time around. Frequently, word-of-mouth advertisement helps to publicize the positive nature of the event or project. One of the best forms of advertising and motivating others to be more receptive to participate in a fund-raising project is old-fashioned word of mouth.

■ Principle 75 ■
Repeat successful fund-raising activities are easier to complete than new ones and take less time and effort.

Soliciting and Getting Potential Donors to Actually Contribute—Getting the Job Done

Prospective contributors, whether individuals or persons representing organizations or businesses, like to hear about the positive consequences that will result from the successful conclusion of the solicitation. Thus, the emphasis should be on the positive, that is, the meeting of the programmatic needs that will be possible with the contributions sought. Negativism or the veiled threat that dire consequences will result should there be insufficient contributions only reinforces a negative image of the sport area. The solicitation should be upbeat. There should be sound justification based on the value of the sport activity and how the existence of the program or sport will meet the needs of the participants, the sport programs as well as the overall goals of the sponsoring organization.

■ Principle 76 ■
Emphasize the positive aspects resulting from the fund-raising drive or project rather than the negative consequences, should the attempt fail.

Numerous companies like Kodak and Xerox, as well as a whole host of other large and small companies throughout the United States, have created national matching gift programs. These programs provide funds to match donations made by these firms' employees to nonprofit organizations with certain restrictions and specified dollar limitations. Some companies even provide more than a one-to-one match, while others match contributions by retirees, outside directors, and even spouses in addition to employees.

■ Principle 77 ■
Take advantage of national matching gift programs.

Altogether, there are well over 1,000 companies in the United States that match employee contributions to specific not-for-profit entities (7 Answers, 1990). Schools and colleges as well as other nonprofit sport organizations should explore this rich potential source of additional funds by checking which companies have such programs and disseminating the information to prospective donors.

Since 1954, when corporate matching of employee contributions was initially introduced on a national scale, over $1.2 billion dollars have been donated in this country through matching gifts to schools (including sports programs), cultural groups, public radio and television, hospitals, health, social service groups, civic organizations, and the United Way (7 Ways to Double, 1991).

Sport fund-raisers can take advantage of the matching gift programs by soliciting funds from individuals who work for the companies and making them aware of the doubling effect their contributions will have through the matching gift program of their employer. The *first step* is to become aware of such companies. The *second step* is to become aware of potential contributors who work for these businesses. And, of course, the *third step* is to convince these individuals to actually donate to one's program.

The Council for Advancement and Support of Education (CASE, Suite 400, 11 Dupont Circle, Washington, DC 20036) serves as the National Clearinghouse for Corporate Matching Gift Information and publishes numerous pamphlets, leaflets, and books on the topic of matching gift programs. One such series of publications, *Double Your Dollars* (1990), lists nearly 1,100 companies that participate in the matching gift program for institutions of higher education.

Altogether, CASE publishes four different leaflets listing companies possessing matching gift programs for (1) higher education, (2) elementary and secondary schools, (3) nonprofit cultural organizations, and (4) hospitals, health, and other organizations. **Appendix E** contains a partial list of corporations that match employee contributions to higher education. Some of these companies also have matching gift programs in place for other cultural and community service nonprofit organizations.

▩ Principle 78 ▩
Maintain an open door policy in all that one does.

Although it may seem obvious, this statement is worth repeating again, and again, and again. It is imperative that one possesses integrity. A person's word is indeed one's bond, or should be. This is especially true in the area of fund-raising. Maintaining the highest ethical standards, exhibiting complete honesty, as well as an openness in all that one does, helps create that all important positive image, which, in turn, helps to establish and sustain credibility.

One way to facilitate the cooperative nature of working relationships is to assume a completely open and honest position in everything that one does. The one sure method of creating suspicion, apprehension, distrust, and doubt is to attempt to deny access to someone for any purpose. The fiscal books and all records should be *open* to all, literally. Maintaining an *open* door policy, holding meetings *open* to all, and being willing to respond directly to any and all questions, are positive elements in the creation of a positive image and reputation. This holds true for public and private schools as well as for youth sport teams and recreational organizations.

Although this degree of openness might seem, at first glance perhaps, as boarding on the inane, in reality, it is a sound judgment. Conducting one's activities in such an obvious nonsecretive fashion, assuming such an open posture, and projecting an honest image leads to building credibility and trust, which in turn can form the basis or foundation for a positive and lasting relationship and a more productive fund-raising effort on a continuous or periodic basis.

▩ Principle 79 ▩
People "buy" ideas from those they trust or those in whom they have confidence.

The one indispensable quality that each person has is one's credibility, one's truthfulness, if you will. This credibility (or integrity) is absolutely essential for long-term success in sport fund-raising. Without it, one is doomed to fail. Building this trust, establishing this credibility, reinforcing this confidence, is the continual challenge and task of those involved in the institution, program, or organization. One must work for the long haul. There are no quick fixes in terms of building a deserved reputation of high integrity. In this same vein, one should not be a flash in the pan but one who is in the program for the long term, earning the respect of others by one's honest and forthright actions and decisions.

The worst-case scenario would be when those involved in the promotion and fund-raising activities are viewed with distrust and suspicion and having a lack of integrity. The end result will be an inappropriate promotional effort and a failed fund-raising attempt.

The **hot button** is the major motivating factor that causes the *potential* contributor to become an *actual* contributor. One method is to create a sense of urgency on behalf of both the sport program and the prospective donor. This may be accomplished by establishing specific dates (deadlines) for securing specific sums of money, or by establishing financial goals to reach within a certain period of time.

Find out what turns the individual on. What motivates the person to action? What are the needs of the person that can be satisfied by contributing to the sports program? This type of information is essential. This data must be ascertained and acted upon if one is to be successful in motivating someone to action, that is, deciding to actually contribute in some fashion to the sports program.

> ▨ **Principle 80** ▨
> *Find the* hot button(s) *of the potential prospect.*

In attempting to determine what motivates contributors, it is prudent to use sensitivity, awareness, empathy, intelligence, and respect in search of the prospective donors' needs. Various publics will have different characteristics, wants, and needs (Moore and Gray, 1990).

A key element in obtaining a commitment from a prospect is determining what will make the person willing to act *now* in a manner beneficial to the sport program. *When there is a match or fit between the needs of the prospective donor and the benefits derived from contributing to the sport program, the end result is usually a contribution of some fashion.*

> ▨ **Principle 81** ▨
> *Identify and match needs of donors and constituencies with the program benefits provided by the organization.*

When asked to market a need, it is wise to point out the *benefits* that will accrue to the sport program and/or to the donor. This is commonly referred to as selling the "sizzle as well as the steak." It is the benefits—those that accrue to the sports program and those that accrue to the benefactor—that can be the motivating, attracting factors resulting in tangible assistance.

For example, when selling season tickets (the "steak") it is wise to promote the excitement and enjoyment ("sizzle") of the games. One sells tickets—admission to athletic contests. However, the enjoyment and pride that the purchaser will experience by attending the games and by wearing the complimentary hat and jacket (both possessing the school's color logo) given "free" to those purchasers of season tickets comprise the benefits, that is, the "sizzle." Mere admission to the games is considered the "steak." The "sizzle" is the accompanying excitement, the enjoyment, the comradely, and the pride one takes in the team during game day and by wearing the athletic program's stylish apparel.

> ▨ **Principle 82** ▨
> *Sell the sizzle—as well as the steak.*

▦ **Principle 83** ▦
For fund-raising projects, investigate the use of a feasibility study

The purpose of a feasibility study (conducting market research) is to investigate whether or not the fund-raising project or activity will be successful—prior to actually committing the full resources and effort of the organization behind the project. It is nothing more than a way to test a fund-raising program (service or product) to determine its potential. It is a means to diminish the downside risk in any one endeavor, through market or consumer researcher on a limited population (Frank, 1989). It is a trial effort.

Such research can assist the fund-raiser by (1) surveying fans to determine what will help attract more of them to the sporting events, (2) developing a spectator or an audience profile so that it is possible to provide a more effective presentation to attract sponsors as well as advertisers, (3) measuring the potential effectiveness and/or actual effectiveness of a specific promotional campaign, and (4) assisting in fine-tuning various marketing strategies.

A feasibility study should reveal characteristics of the community in which the project is to be conducted, as well as any special considerations that could affect the program, for example, competition from other sources—schools, service clubs, charities, etc. Feasibility studies are not the exclusive domain of large athletic programs in major universities. On the contrary, small colleges as well as high schools and youth sport programs can take advantage of this strategic planning tool. There are several ways to accomplish this. College or university athletic departments have only to go across campus and request assistance from the department of business or marketing within the same institution. There are numerous marketing classes conducted on college campuses throughout the country. The students in these programs are frequently looking for projects to participate in for college credit.

The potential fund-raiser or promoter should contact the professor of such a marketing course and request assistance from selected students in the marketing class in terms of conducting a feasibility study. This study would not only assist the potential fund-raiser but would provide very valuable assistance and further hands-on experience to the students. Since the students would most likely be juniors or seniors and would be working closely with their professor, the likelihood of a meaningful and helpful feasibility study is enhanced.

Another way to secure a feasibility study is to solicit assistance (in the form of a contribution) from professionals who are involved in marketing and in conducting survey research. What better way to be able to obtain a feasibility study than to go to the recognized experts, those who conduct such studies for a living, and request such assistance as a donation.

Sometimes coaches and fund-raisers find themselves in graduate school taking classes in administration, business, or marketing. What better opportunity for the would-be fund-raiser to kill two birds at one time than to conduct a feasibility study as part of the graduate class assignment as well as to reap the tangible benefits such a study would provide. The point of the matter is that fund-raisers and promoters should not shy away from utilizing the feasibility study as a meaningful tool. It can have a significant impact on many fund-raising projects.

Of course, it is not necessary to conduct a feasibility study or to do market research each time one wants to initiate a fund-raising project. It is useful and worthwhile if one is to be involved in a single, major fundraising activity that will consume a significant amount of the organization's resources (time, money, effort, etc.).

Most feasibility studies are miniature attempts of the "real thing." The feasibility study is followed by an assessment of success and failure and can involve face-to-face interviews with selected members of the constituency, sometimes coupled with actual requests for contributions from selected members of the constituency. Such requests can be by means of actual face-to-face meetings, mailings, or phone calls.

The process of identifying characteristics of prospects (segmentation) should be systematic and done by professionals familiar in marketing research techniques or social science research. Such expert assistance should be sought if the potential fund-raiser lacks such expertise. In a college setting, the easiest way to obtain descriptors (age, sex, annual income, occupation, education, etc.) of any given segment of the population is to ask students in advertising and marketing classes or a marketing professor to undertake this research as part of the class project (hopefully at no cost). The fund-raiser can also search for the information at the local library, the Chamber of Commerce, and at the town hall or municipal building. "By pooling the obtained information, a fund-raiser can obtain a picture of the total life-style pattern of prospective donors so that soliciting can be accurately targeted and motivating/cultivating techniques appropriately developed and scripted" (Buell, 1984, p. 616).

A specific, separate fund-raising project should be conducted within a specific time frame. Generally speaking, the effort should be 4 to 6 weeks in duration. This is recommended because in fund-raising activities that last longer than 6 weeks, it becomes very difficult to maintain and sustain the high level of energy needed for successful completion of the project. Also, it becomes too easy to put the work off until a later time. Most of the work will be completed within the last 30 days prior to the event anyway, human nature being what it is today.

Principle 84
Keep the duration of any specific fund-raising project to a limited, specified time period.

In any fund-raising activity, the athletic program should seek to spread the risk and minimize the actual involvement, while still sharing meaningfully in the income generated. That is, secure others as partners to assume some of the risk, as well as garner some of the rewards, so that both the effort, as well as the downside risk or exposure, are minimized (McKenzie, 1985).

Also, never begrudge others from reaping a reasonable profit when they cobroker a fund-raising effort. As long as the sport program obtains the benefits sought, what matter does it make what the so-called partner(s) gain?

For example, teams can enter into an agreement with a service club for the club's members to sell general admission tickets. The service club might net 25% to 35% of whatever the service club is able to sell in the way of tickets. The motivating factor on behalf of the service club is the potential profit from selling the tickets. The sport program will benefit as well through the 65% to 75% profit from the sale of tickets—with no effort and little down-side risk on behalf of the athletic program.

Principle 85
Spread the risk, minimize the responsibility, and share the benefits.

Fund-raisers would do well to adhere to the *KISS* philosophy when considering the advantages of simplicity of a fundraising activity. The *KISS* philosophy (*keep it short and simple*) holds true for most promotional and fund-raising efforts. Simple

Principle 86
Utilize the KISS philosophy—Keep it short and simple.

fund-raising and promotional activities are often the most successful. Short time frames are ideal.

The intricacies involved in complicated, dragged-out projects often take away from the ultimate objectives with the process becoming the central issue rather than the actual objective, that is, raising money for the sport program. Besides, overkill via overcomplication can doom a potential fund-raising effort before it ever gets off the ground. In fund-raising, less is sometimes best.

■ **Principle 87** ■
Strike when the iron is hot.

An accepted principle in fund-raising is to "strike when the iron is hot." This simply means that the timing of the fund-raising activity is *everything*. Witness the successful marketing of such timely items as the pet rock, cabbage patch dolls, and the sensational hoola hoops. Timing is crucial if the effort is to take advantage of a real *or* perceived need, a conducive climate or a receptive atmosphere.

A classic instance in which a college failed to act when timing was of the essence involved the winner of the $2,000 top prize in an athletic raffle. The winner, one of the community's leading business leaders, indicated to the athletic booster club that he was going to donate the $2,000 back to the organization. He indicated that when the President of the college arrived at his place of business to have their photo taken together (commemorating the winning of the $2,000 jackpot) that he would hand the check back to the President, with the stipulation that the money go back into the coffers of the athletic support group (ASG).

Due to an oversight, however, the president was not asked to visit the businessman. After a few months, this jackpot winner, in a conversation with a member of the support group, mentioned that he had given his wife the money as he thought that the college did not want the $2,000 since they had not bothered to contact him after he won the grand prize to make arrangements for the photo session. In this instance, the failure to follow up cost dearly, both in terms of public relations and in terms of hard, cold cash.

■ **Principle 88** ■
Know where the majority of funds are coming from prior to announcing a general fund drive.

In announcing a goal to the general public for any major fund-raising activity, it is advisable to already have a sizable amount collected (or committed in advance). The reason for this is that with proper planning one should know who the prospective givers are, and these individuals and organizations should have already been approached and have committed themselves. Thus, shortly after the announcement of the major fund drive, the organizers can truthfully announce that one-third of the goal has already been reached. Again, this is a great motivator and generates even greater enthusiasm and support for the fund drive.

Prior to announcing the dollar goal, the 10 major donors and the next 100 largest donors should have been contacted and donations actually received or the pledge obtained. Having these gifts in hand is important so that specific amounts of current contributions can be publicly announced at strategic intervals during the campaign.

■ **Principle 89** ■
Nothing breeds success like success.

Successful fund-raising activities indeed spawn additional successful projects. The reputation an organization earns through putting on successful fund-raising projects only enhances its future efforts in generating additional monies through other promotional and money-making activities. The successful atmosphere surrounding individual fund-raising projects lends credence to these same or other projects being repeated in the future. Again, success breeds success. Success brings an expectation of success, and expectation of success facilitates future efforts.

The worst possible scenario in the world of fund-raising is to actually attempt to raise funds but to fail and to be viewed by the publics as having failed. Members of the community often take a dim view of failure on behalf of those involved in fund-raising for athletic causes. Granted, not every attempt at fund-raising will be a howling success. However, it is better not to even attempt to raise funds unless one is fairly confident of at least breaking even and not causing an embarrassment to the sports program and the sponsoring organization.

■ Principle 90 ■
Failure at fund-raising efforts creates significant hindrances for future attempts to raise money.

Nothing turns off constituencies and members of the public more than a poorly orchestrated fund-raising effort. This is especially true if it is perceived that the major reason for the failure of the effort is the incompetency or lack of expertise of the athletic staff. It becomes too easy to make that jump from the feeling of inadequacy of the athletic staff in generating monies to the opinion that the athletic staff might be inadequate and/or incompetent in their other areas of responsibility. Hence, becoming involved in raising money for sports is not something one should jump into without careful thought.

Don't be afraid to attempt various fund-raising projects. Don't let the prospects of running a fund-raiser discourage you from even beginning to research the possibility. Far too often people tend to make too much of a big deal about organizing and running a fund-raiser. They make it too complicated and intricate. As a result, the process becomes more difficult than it needs to be, and experience turns off many individuals from becoming involved in the project. Naturally, the fundraising process ceases to be fun but instead is a chore.

■ Principle 91 ■
One needn't be a rocket scientist to be a successful fund-raiser.

What it takes to be a success in generating resources is a confidence coupled with a sufficient knowledge base. That is why a thorough study of the various principles outlined in this publication is essential. The knowledge base that accompanies the mastery of the principles will go a long way to helping anyone become a more effective and efficient fund-raiser.

The practice of sprinkling so-called "ringers" within a crowd of prospective contributors is a time-proven success strategy. One example of the use of ringers will suffice, however, the concept has limitless possibilities within the world of fund-raising.

■ Principle 92 ■
Use strategically placed "ringers" to motivate others to action in meetings that are organized for the purpose of raising money.

The athletic staff planned a semiformal dinner gathering of individuals who might be interested in becoming initial members of the school's booster club. Prior to the dinner festivities, the athletic director visited with several key community leaders as well as the superintendent and the principal. After the dinner, the athletic director was involved in delivering the pitch about the advantages of securing memberships within the newly created booster club and explaining the various levels of membership within the club.

When the athletic director announced that memberships were now going to be sold, the community leaders, including the superintendent and the principal, were most visible and vocal in their demonstration of support for the booster club. In fact, these individuals were the first group of people rising from their respective tables, which were situated throughout the large dining hall, to head toward the front of the room where the memberships were to be sold. These community leaders (these ringers), by their actions and their visible support, motivated others within the large room to likewise join these leaders in rising from their respective tables to head toward the membership tables to secure their respective memberships.

People tend to follow the actions of others who act in a specific manner, especially those whom they respect and/or those of the same or higher social strata. Humans have been likened to a flock of sheep, unflattering but perhaps all too true, when it comes to being motivated to act when in a crowd. Like the group of cattle following the leader to some destination, people also tend to follow the action of others, especially if these other individuals have influence within the community or possess power or prestige. Thus, the use of ringers to help motivate others to a specific course of action can be, if utilized properly, effective and efficient.

■ Principle 93 ■
Don't become overextended.

One of the common faults of inexperienced, as well as experienced fund-raisers and promoters, is attempting to do too much in terms of available time and resources. Trying to do too much can result in the significant lessening of quality of what is undertaken. This attempt to "be all things to all people" has scuttled many a would-be successful fund-raiser. Priorities need to be established so that tasks that are "doable" with a minimum quality level can be undertaken.

An example of this can best be illustrated by explaining the strategic planning process one school experienced. The newly organized booster organization decided at an early organizational meeting to follow the tactic of assuming responsibility for a few fund-raising projects, but doing them in a correct and first-rate fashion. The first goal was to initiate a major membership drive for the purpose of generating three types of support: (1) moral support, (2) financial support, and (3) physical (personnel) support. Only after the initial membership drive was successful and there was the confidence that the membership drive would be successful on an annual basis, was there an effort to examine other means for generating additional dollars for the sport program.

The next project assumed was a major golf tournament in the spring of each year. After two years of an ever successful golf tournament—which created significant financial support and positive public relations—the booster organization launched a major, annual, fund-raising project, a project that grossed $10,000 in its initial year. After this project had experienced a history of success and all details were worked out, the boosters then turned their attention to yet another annual fund-raiser.

After five years, this booster organization had four major, annual fund-raising activities that generated thousands and thousands of dollars. The key to this success story rested in the organization's leadership: individuals who insisted that quality rather than quantity, that substance rather than fluff, would be stressed in terms of all of the fund-raising and promotional activities.

■ Principle 94 ■
The public is fickle—they frequently overlook past successes but rarely forget (forgive failures.

When fund-raising activities lack the minimal quality level that would be expected, in any respect, it is the sports public that seems to remember the faults. Indeed, the sports public has a rather short memory when it comes to successes, but a long memory for failures. In fact, the sport public can be extremely unforgiving. This is evidenced by the philosophy, "What have you done for me lately?" It seems that it only takes one error or failure to overshadow the benefits from 100 successes. Since there is a tendency for the public to freely criticize errors and since errors are more likely to occur when sport personnel are stretched too thin in terms of their capabilities, it seems only logical to see to it that one has sufficient time to complete tasks, as well as accessibility to appropriate tools or resources,

It is very important to match appropriate solutions with specific problems, needs or objectives. *Overkill,* in terms of inappropriate allocation of resources, is a wasteful management error. For example, a printed high school basketball brochure need not consist of 64 (or 32, or even 16) pages of four-color, very high quality, glossy paper. Perhaps an 8-or 4-page brochure (organized, illustrated, and printed in a first class fashion) might meet the needs of a secondary school program and more closely match the resources of the athletic department.

Another example involves the case of the athletic director attempting to sell, door to door, $50 advertisements for a sport program. This is a chronic waste of skilled manpower. This is not a task that requires the time and effort of a highly trained, educated, and experienced sports administrator. There is a definite need to set *suitable priorities* and to elect *appropriate courses of action,* as well as *resources,* geared to accomplish *specific and appropriate results.* Only in this way can one anticipate success within the fund-raising arena. One does not need a Mercedes to drive to the grocery store when a Ford will do the trick and consume a lot less in terms of total resources.

■ **Principle 95** ■
Don't kill a fly with a sledge hammer.

Asking for the Money or a Donation

The cardinal sin in sales or fund-raising is to fail to ask for the donation or money or whatever it is that is being sought or solicited. An example will suffice. In a study of college graduates, 26% of all respondents who have been to college indicated they have made some sort of donation to the undergraduate school they attended (Lindenmann, 1983, p. 18). However, of those respondents who said they *had not made a donation,* 25% said that they had not been asked. It is difficult to get the money if one does not ask for it. Naturally, there are skills and tactics and techniques to be utilized in ''asking'' for the contributions so that it does not seem so obvious. However, the fact remains, one has to ask for the donation if one is to receive it.

In soliciting cash contributions, be specific, or nearly so. That is, ask the prospective donor for a specific amount if you have a reasonable knowledge of what that individual can afford to contribute. On the other hand, it might be appropriate, for a variety of reasons, to provide to the potential contributor with various options, levels, or ranges at which a contribution can be made. In this way, the individual donor has the option of choosing the most appropriate level at which to make a contribution. The more options or levels of contributions available, the greater the potential donor response.

■ **Principle 96** ■
In asking for money, specify an amount or an amount within a specific range.

■ Principle 97 ■
Provide a vehicle or means by which potential contributors can actually consummate the giving of a contribution.

Naturally, one needs to ask for the money. However, merely asking for the contribution is not all there is to it. The means must be provided for the potential contributor to actually consummate the giving of that which is to be contributed. This is true whether money, objects of value, or services are being contributed. People tend to shrug off appeals to action if a means of action is not provided and readily available. This means providing an *immediate* opportunity for the contributor to act, to do something, to give something to someone, to sign something, to mail something back in a stamped envelope, to drop a contribution into some receptacle, etc.

■ Principle 98 ■
Don't be bashful—be assertive when seeking contributions.

Don't be afraid not to take "No" for an answer, but also be smart enough to accept "No" when further attempts might result in negative feelings and a poor image. One should not be a *hard sell* promoter or salesperson. There may be other more appropriate opportunities for future sales, so don't burn any bridges. Instead, cultivate the individual or the organization for future solicitations. However, keep the person or group somehow involved in the meantime through the use of mailing lists. That is, send newsletters, conduct phone calls, personal contacts, involve them in special promotional activities, as well as periodic free tickets to special events, etc.

■ Principle 99 ■
Overcome the FEAR of objections to requests for contributions through a thorough knowledge of the "product" or "service" and the available "benefits."

One must be trained in overcoming objections to the sales pitch or presentation and request for contributions and support. One should never *fear* rejection by prospects. Most important of all, rejection should never be taken personally. Rejection, or the refusal to "buy" or to contribute or to become involved on behalf of prospects are merely some of the possible consequences of the total sales and promotional processes. There is no inherent implication that either the fund-raising project or the salesperson are not of value or worth.

Objections raised may be the result of skepticism or ignorance or just natural reluctance to making any type of commitment. One of the key ingredients in salesmanship (asking for money) is being able to meet and overcome objections by prospects. Overcoming objections can be facilitated by (1) knowledge and confidence in the product or service one is "selling," (2) persistence, (3) possession of a positive attitude, (4) overall confidence in one's ability or position, and (5) being professional in the sales approach, including the actual "closing" of the sale (asking for the money).

■Principle 100■
If in doubt, allow the donor (or legal counsel) to determine whether or not a specific contribution qualifies as a tax deductible donation.

Too many coaches, athletic administrators, and booster club members claim that all so-called donations or payments are tax deductible when, in reality, this is not always the case. To qualify for tax deductibility, contributions to booster club organizations or to a sport program need to meet very specific and rigid requirements. The buying of Christmas ornaments by well-meaning supporters or fans from team members does not qualify for a tax deduction. One cardinal rule boosters need to follow in the solicitation of all funds, when there is any question as to whether or not any donation is tax deductible, is to indicate to the donor that the determination of whether or not the contribution is tax deductible is up to the donor (and the donor's legal counsel).

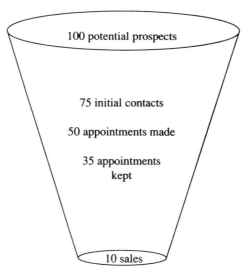

Figure 8.1 The funnel concept of fund-raising.

The Funnel Concept of Prospecting and Selling

A fundamental concept in the sales or solicitation profession revolves around the **funnel concept of prospecting.** This concept indicates that for every ten sales actually consummated, it might be necessary to have 35 appointments. In order to secure 35 appointments it may be necessary to schedule 50 appointments. Working backward, in order to schedule 50 appointments, 75 people may have to be asked for actual appointments. Finally, in order to actually contact 75 people to ask for these appointments, one could be involved in attempting to reach 100 potential prospects.

Of course, the numbers may vary, but the principle remains the same: start with a much larger number of prospects, say 100, to actually reach 75 individuals in order to set up 50 appointments so that 35 appointments will be kept. Out of these 35 appointments, *perhaps* 10 actual "sales" will be consummated. Thus, if one wanted to conclude 10 sales, the concept is to start with 100 potential prospects. If 20 sales becomes the goal, then the potential prospects one must face number 200 (see fig. 8.1).

There is a real need to *carefully* select, train, evaluate, and motivate solicitors. Not just every Tom, Dick, or Harry **or** any Mary, Jane, or Sue can become effective solicitors. This is especially true when it comes to soliciting large sums of money or major contributions.

In addition to carefully selecting, screening, and training potential solicitors, the assigning of specific solicitors to particular potential donors is of the utmost importance. Generally speaking, significant donations are more easily obtained from prospects if approached by solicitors who have given a larger amount than they are asking, who know the donors from whom they are seeking money and who are at the same or higher social or economic standing or prestige.

In planning to seek funds or assistance from a prospective donor, it is often wise to use the "paired" approach; that is, *pairing* the fund-raiser with a known friend or associate of the prospect. Thus, the solicitor is able to take advantage of the association

▬Principle 101▬
Choose solicitors very carefully—and train them.

between the friend or associate of the prospect to hopefully gain instant respectability and acceptance in the eyes of the prospective donor.

Similarly, the ''paired'' approach is useful when attempting to train future solicitors. In this instance, novice solicitors are paired with an experienced fund-raiser on actual calls to prospects. Thus, experienced and skilled workers are able to provide the all-important on-the-job training and support mechanism for the neophyte which is so necessary within the world of fund-raising.

▬Principle 102▬
Continually expand the prospect pool—never put all the "eggs" in one basket.

Always have additional prospective donors ''waiting in the wings'' to be contacted should the current prospects not result in contributions. To achieve this goal, fund-raisers should employ the technique of ''snowballing'' when seeking additional prospects whom they may solicit. Specifically, this means asking those satisfied with the sport program or who otherwise have an interest in the welfare of the program (booster club members, friends of the sport program, contributors, parents, etc.) for referrals, that is, names of 3 to 5 individuals to add to the so-called ''prospect list.'' This is an established practice in the general sales profession, a common tactic in the prospecting process. The end result is a continual expansion of the number of possible contacts who can be approached for solicitation purposes.

▬Principle 103▬
Provide for an equitable exchange for contributions made by donors.

Sports programs should attempt to provide donors a fair, but generous and appropriate, slate of benefits in exchange for contributions made to the program. The major challenge facing sports promoters is the determination of the value, in the form of benefits, that should be returned to donors in exchange for the contributions made by them.

Athletic programs in colleges and secondary schools generally tend to return to donors, in the form of various benefits, somewhere in the neighborhood of 5% to 10% of the actual value of the donation. Such benefits might include, but not be limited to, tickets, premiums, special privileges, etc. In such a situation, if a contributor donated a steer worth around $800, the donor might receive approximately $40 to $80 worth of so-called benefits in return.

Self-Promotion

▬Principle 104▬
Don't forget to "toot" one's own "horn."

There is an old proverb that is most applicable in the fund-raising and promotional arenas. It goes like this. If a tree falls in a forest and if there is no one there to hear it, does it make any noise? The answer, in terms of promotion and fund-raising, is a resounding NO. Unless the constituencies are aware of the positive aspects of the sport programs, most of one's efforts fall on deaf ears.

It is therefore essential that those involved in the sports arena take great pains to spread the good word to all constituencies in terms of the positive elements of the sports programs. However, not only must a continuing and conscientious effort be made to make others aware of the advantages and achievements of one's sports program, but great care must be taken lest the attempt to spread the good word be viewed in a negative, self-serving, and destructive manner. Of course, it goes without saying that the self-promotional and public relations effort be based on absolute truth and accuracy.

References

Advertising. (1989, May 3). *NCAA news,* Vol. 26, 18, p. 5.

Bronzan, R. T. (1984, May). Fund-raising today demands better ideas. *Athletic Business, 8* (5), 12–18.

Buell, V. (1984). *Marketing management : A strategic planning approach.* New York: McGraw-Hill Book Co.

Double your dollars. (1990). Council for Advancement and Support of Education (CASE).

Frank, N. (1989, March). Consumer research—A valuable tool for sports marketers. *Team Marketing Report,* p. 6.

Lindenmann, W. (1983). Who makes donations? National survey provides need data. *Caser Currents, 9* (2), 18–19.

McIntyre, M. & Anderson, J. (1987, January). Development—an old word with a new meaning. *Journal of Physical Education, Recreation and Dance, 58* (1), 72–75.

McKenzie, W. (1985, August). 10 Rules for fund-raisers. *Athletic Business. 9* (8), 20–25.

McMillen, Liz. (September 5, 1990). A study to determine the cost of raising a dollar finds that average college spends just 16 cents. *The Chronicle of Higher Education, XXXVII* (1), A31.

Moore, Deborah, B. and Gray, Dianna, P. (1990). Marketing—The blueprint for successful physical education, *Journal of Physical Education, Recreation and Dance, 61* (1), 23–26.

7 Answers about the program that works 365 days a year to sustain our traditions of academic excellence. (1990). The Florida State University Foundation, Tallahassee, Florida.

7 ways to double your dollars. (1991). Council for Advancement and Support of Education (CASE).

Stier, Jr., W. F. (1988). *Policies, procedures and practices in intercollegiate athletics.* (2nd ed.). Brockport, New York: State University of New York, Brockport. (ERIC Document Reproduction Service No. ED301558).

Corporate sponsorship at the State University of New York College at Brockport. (Courtesy of State University of New York College at Brockport/photo by James Dusen)

Techniques and Tactics of Fund-Raising

9

Four Models of Fund-Raising

According to a 1989 survey conducted by the magazine *Athletic Director* (Wegs, 1990), 69 percent of all secondary schools nationwide resorted to some type of outside fund-raising to supplement their sport budgets. In fact, between 20 percent and 50 percent of these athletic programs' budgets were generated via outside fund-raising campaigns of one kind or another.

When thinking of becoming involved in fund-raising, it is often useful to attempt to classify fund-raising activities and efforts into distinct categories. Chapter One of this book categorized such fund-raising efforts into four general methods for generating financial support for the sport program. These four methods include:

1. Single person (face-to-face) cultivation and appeals.
2. Corporate sponsorships.
3. Profit centers.
4. Special fund-raising projects, promotional tactics and ideas.

The first three categories of generating revenues will be discussed in detail within this chapter. The fourth, *special fund-raising projects, promotional tactics and ideas*, will be addressed in chapter ten.

There are four generally accepted means by which individuals may be approached in the solicitation of money, services, and products, either on a *straight contribution* (solicitation basis) or on a *purchase* ("supermarket" basis) (see chapter eight). These include (1) person-to-person (face-to-face) solicitation, (2) door-to-door appeals, (3) direct mail, and (4) the use of the telephone.

Single Person (Face-to-Face) Cultivation and Appeals for Resources

Person-to-Person Solicitation or Single Person Cultivation

The eyeball-to-eyeball or person-to-person solicitation is frequently referred to as the door-to-door approach for grown-ups. This approach is a flat-out request for contributions for a worthy cause. It is a person-to-person contact on the street, at civic club luncheons or in the office. By far, this is one of the most productive and efficient means of gathering resources that can be used.

SMU Mustang Club members: A. Kenneth Page, SMU president; David Lott, fund drive chairman; Forrest Gregg, SMU athletic director; and Lamar Hunt, Mustang Club president. (Courtesy of Southern Methodist University/ photo by Jim Bradley)

▬Principle 105▬

Establish convenient categories of "giving" to facilitate contributions.

It is frequently helpful to establish donor classifications as part of a planned giving campaign ($100, $250, $500, $1,000, $5,000, etc.) through such easily distinguishable names as the Gold Club, Silver Club, the President's Club, The Varsity Club, the Coach's Club, etc.

Often, it is necessary to conduct some good old-fashioned research about the prospect prior to contacting the prospective donor. This can be cut short by taking advantage of other people's knowledge (common contacts, centers of influence) of the potential contributor. The immediate goal is to be able to properly cultivate, educate, and share pertinent information about the sport organization with the prospect with the aim of converting the prospect into a donor.

Alumni Outreach Efforts—Endowment Outreach Efforts

Both *alumni outreach* and *endowment outreach efforts* are very common at the college level and are becoming more acceptable on the private secondary school level. In terms of endowment outreach efforts, these are attempts to generate funds, grants, and long-term commitments from businesses, graduates, "friends," and other individuals and groups. The interest generated from these endowment funds are then utilized annually for general operating purposes and/or capital expenditures. Such efforts are an attempt to insure fiscal longevity and responsibility for the entity being supported.

Cultivating Prospective Major Donors—Big Ticket Donors

In working within the sport world in promotion and fund-raising, it is necessary to recognize that many of the people we come in contact with are successful business people (both men and women). As such, these women and men expect proper (professional, first class) business relationships and interactions. Similarly, there are expectations that those involved in fund-raising and promotional efforts will demonstrate specific competencies. That is, they must demonstrate professionalism at all times in their representation of the sport arena.

Solicitors must be willing and able to fully discuss with the prospect the needs and strengths of the organization, the institution, the program, as well as how the money will benefit the program and the participants. This is extremely important in dealing with big ticket donors. Needless to say, use of common business etiquette is an absolute must. This involves basic politeness in terms of meetings, telephone usage, written communication, office management, etc.

In attempting to solicit large sums of money, avoid cold calls whenever possible. Instead, contacts or *Centers of Influence* should be utilized to pave the way and to open the doors to potential contributors and supporters, whether they be individuals or corporations. The concept of utilizing third party *Centers of Influence* to gain access to individuals and organizations (as potential contributors and donors) is a valid one. In the area of high finance and big time donations, it is absolutely essential that cold calls be avoided at all costs. The time and effort it takes to cultivate third party *Centers of Influence,* for the purpose of gaining access in a receptive atmosphere to heavy hitters (contributors), is well worth it when one considers the potential ultimate payoff, that is, large and significant contributions of money, goods and/or services.

■■Principle 106■■
Avoid cold calls like the plague in soliciting big dollars.

When dealing with the so-called big ticket donors, one needs to be assertive in actually *asking* for money, *and* for a sufficient amount, *and* for a specific purpose. In attempting to decide how much to ask, it is better to ask for too much than for too little (don't insult the prospect). Nothing insults a potential donor, especially a heavy hitter, *than asking for too little money.*

Knowing your prospect, doing one's homework prior to approaching a prospect in terms of the needs of the prospect, the desires of the prospect, the limitations of the prospect, and the prejudices of the prospects, prevents this embarrassing situation from developing. Often, the fund-raiser is unsure about the amount of money the potential donor might feel comfortable in contributing. In this case, one might present a range of possible donations or involvements from which the potential donor might select the most appropriate. This gives the potential donor the opportunity to select the most suitable degree of involvement with the fund-raising and/or promotional activity.

■■Principle 107■■
Don't insult your prospect by asking for too little.

Door-to-Door Solicitation and/or Selling

Literally almost anything can be sold on a door-to-door basis. Like the sale of Girl Scout cookies, which earn millions of dollars annually for this national organization, sport organizations can reap sizable rewards for a well thought-out and planned program of door-to-door solicitation and/or selling. There are numerous companies that produce a wide variety of candies and other goodies that can be sold as part of a fund-raising program. Appendix F contains a partial list of similar companies that provide a variety of products that might fit a sports organization's portfolio for fund-raising.

One such company is *Mrs. Sittler's Candies.* Located in the state of Illinois, the company has reportedly sold, on an annual basis, over 125,000 pounds of chocolate-covered candies and peanut brittle. For the most part, this candy and peanut brittle is marketed and sold through the efforts of various scout groups, school organizations, and little league athletic groups (Drotning, 1981). Nestle-Beich, a subsidiary of Nestle Foods located in Bloomington, Illinois, is one of this country's largest manufacturers and sellers of candy for the fund-raising market. The total fund-raising candy market in the United States is extensive, approaching three-fourths of a billion dollars annually, according to Paul Fine, vice-president for marketing for Nestle-Beich (personal communication, P. Fine, May 28, 1992). A company that claims to be the largest nationwide fund-raising organization working with schools and youth groups in this country is QSP, Inc., a subsidiary of The Reader's Digest Association, Inc. QSP, Inc. has provided over $85 million in profits to various groups, organizations, and individuals in a single year through the sale of both edible and nonedible items (The Nation's Leading, 1990).

Yet another fund-raising company is Benchmark Products, located in Mansfield, Ohio. This firm sells a wide range of quality edible and nonedible products on a wholesale basis to sponsoring groups (many of which are athletic teams as well as other school-sponsored groups). These groups then resell the items on either a take-order basis or on a point-of-sale type program. The **take-order** selling program involves having athletes or other individuals approach prospective purchasers with a catalogue and taking orders for the items. Later, when merchandise is delivered to the athletic fund-raising coordinator, the items are hand delivered to the buyers. The **point-of-sale** program involves the seller actually having samples of the merchandise, selling the items, and collecting the money, on a door-to-door or point-of-sale basis.

Of course there are numerous similar companies manufacturing and/or selling candy as part of a fund-raising effort throughout the United States. The trend in recent years is for fund-raising product companies to diversify and expand their product line. As a result, these companies are able to provide on a wholesale basis not only candy but also other edible products, such as cookies, as well as a whole host of nonedible products to local fund-raising groups to be sold to the general public for a profit.

Using such programs and products from any number of these national and regional companies can generate sizable profits, depending on the number of participants taking part in the selling campaign and their effectiveness in obtaining multiple sales per purchaser.

Such solicitations can be either on a cold call basis or as a follow-up to a previous contact made by mail, by an earlier phone call, exposure to media, or by a personal contact. Previous knowledge on behalf of the potential contributor as to the worthiness of the cause and the benefits that will accrue to the sport program significantly increases the potential for success. This emphasizes the need for sufficient publicity and public exposure.

Depending upon the specific situation, such as the item being marketed, the sponsoring organization, the purpose for the solicitation, local conditions, etc., such appeals can result in approximately 25% to 50% of those persons contacted actually making some type of contribution. Naturally, the cause must be worthy and a good case (justification) must be made for the potential prospect to actually make a contribution and/or a purchase of an item or service being marketed by the athletic program. In the case of marketing items for sale, it is imperative that an appropriate product (good quality for the price) be secured to sell to the publics.

Students are frequently utilized to sell products and services on a door-to-door basis. Two concerns administrators should be aware of in respect to student sales are (1) the safety factor and (2) the liability exposure for the sport organization and organizers that might result if accidents befall students engaged in selling, especially door-to-door. The health and safety of the individual student is always of paramount importance and must never be compromised.

Factors to consider include, but are not limited to, weather conditions, the time of day the students are expected to sell, the available adult supervision for the youngster, and the area in which the students will attempt to market their wares. For younger participants, their efforts, while they are actually involved in the selling process, must be adequately monitored by adults to insure that the welfare of the student is not jeopardized in any fashion. Naturally, one must be cognizant of various community laws that restrict or prohibit door-to-door sales, regardless of the purpose.

Parents and sport organizers must be reminded that the use of student sales can quickly wear out their welcome within a community if the practice of using students is inappropriately implemented or becomes overused. There is a danger of too much of a good thing in three respects. *First,* there is a danger of the people in the community, the prospective contributors or purchasers, being inundated with so many requests for funds that there is a negative reaction by these individuals and groups. These individuals and businesses become tired and irritated with repeated requests for financial support of the sports organization, regardless of the apparent worthiness of the project.

The *second* area of concern involves the student sellers and their families. Fund-raising efforts can also become overused from this perspective. Just as the people being asked to contribute or buy something from the students can react negatively to repeated requests, so too can the students themselves and their families. Sometimes this reaction can be very vocal and violent. On the youth sport level as well as in the junior and senior high schools, parents and their children can easily become resentful of the time commitment expected by the athletic program in the soliciting of funds and/or selling items on behalf of the sports program. Too much of anything can become old very quickly. The consequence can be bitterness or jealously on behalf of the families of the student solicitors.

This is especially true if there are a number of athletes within a family and each of them becomes involved in selling merchandise or soliciting funds within the community. If other organizations also expect these same students to participate in similar door-to-door canvassing in hopes of generating monies, the problem is exacerbated further. There

▬Principle 108▬

Don't wear out your welcome with various constituencies through too frequent and bothersome door-to-door solicitations.

is indeed a limit as to the number of sales parents and the local businesses can endorse (or endure). A community can quickly become saturated with door-to-door canvassing (even for worthy causes).

The *third* area of concern centers around the practice of having students on the high school and college levels involved in selling merchandise as part of a fund-raising project. This type of situation needs to be closely monitored. All too frequently these students (especially athletes) approach coaches and teachers within the institution in an effort to market whatever it is that they are selling. The consequence may very well be the creation of ill will toward the athletic program. Many athletic departments have a policy prohibiting students from approaching staff members within the school in order to prevent just that type of negative fallout.

A final warning concerns the issuing of *quotas* to students or groups of students. These quotas often place inordinate pressure on the youngsters as well as their families. The consequences can often negate, in terms of public relations, any benefits that might result from the actual generation of monies for the sport project.

Direct Mail Appeals

A direct mail solicitation for funds clearly states the purpose(s) of the campaign as well as how the money to be raised will be used for the benefit of the sport program. The written communication is a ''sales piece'' representing you and the sport program. As such, special care must be paid to the outside envelope, the enclosed cover letter, the contents (brochure, etc.), the response piece, and the return envelope. All must be coordinated and each must be professionally prepared, superbly written, and expertly printed.

Some general guidelines helpful in making a direct mail appeal successful include (Yiannakis and Braunstein, 1983, p. 83):

1. The appeal should ask for a specific figure.
2. The requested amount should be in round figures ($25, $50, $100, etc.).
3. The communication should provide for a convenient means of responding (self-addressed, stamped reply envelope).
4. The request for funds should include opportunities to make contributions in cash, pledges, gifts in kind, deferred giving, endowment contributions, memorial giving, as well as for designated purposes.

One of the biggest challenges involved in a direct mail appeal is creating an effective fund-raising letter. Kuniholm (1990) suggests six characteristics for such a letter. These include:

1. Create an eye-catching opening paragraph.
2. Include a statement designed to convince the would-be donor to read the rest of the solicitation letter.
3. State how a specific problem can be solved through a donation or contribution.
4. Provide information that will clearly make the reader aware of the purpose of the letter, that is, solicitation of a contribution so that the reader is not confused as to the true nature of the letter.

5. Identify the reader's interests, concerns, or priorities (as they relate to the solicitor's program or activities).

6. Explain a notable event or activity that has recently taken place in your organization or program.

Additionally, an effective fund-raising or solicitation letter should certainly include a personalized greeting ("Dear Philip" or "Dear Joanne"). And, of course, a handwritten note as a "P.S." at the end of the letter puts the finishing touch on the personalization effort with the direct mail appeal (McDermott-Griggs & Card, 1992).

In terms of returns on investment, the typical rate of return or yield for direct mail appeals may range in some instances from less than 1% to 4%. Thus, unless there is a very large mailing list, it might not be worth the effort to initiate such an appeal. One way to increase the likelihood of significant returns in a direct mail campaign is to use a culled, qualified list of prospects (White, 1991). Such a list can be purchased from professional "list brokers," as well as developed internally within one's own program. For example, a list of "hot prospects" consisting of previous contributors might significantly increase the yield or return as much as 50 percent.

Sometimes direct mail requests can be "piggybacked" with other written communications to various constituencies. For example, bank statements might include an enclosure from a local sport group seeking funds or contributions from the bank's customers for the worthy purpose. The advantages are obvious and numerous. In this situation, the bank provides the bulk of the work, pays the expense of the initial mailing, and provides the population to be solicited. The sport program might be asked to provide the insert, if even that, thus taking advantage of the bank's mailing via the piggyback concept.

When attempting to arrange this type of piggyback arrangement, it is not unusual for 2 to 4 months to pass before all of the details are worked out to everyone's satisfaction. Even once an agreement has been reached it is necessary to allocate some 2 to 4 weeks "lead time" in terms of providing the necessary printed information to the organization that has agreed to accept and distribute your insert. The point to remember is that this type of arrangement is not something that can be accomplished overnight. It takes time and a significant amount of planning, but the results can often be well worth the effort, especially when one considers the amount of money saved through such an arrangement and the extent of distribution achieved.

Telephone Solicitation

Appeals for support via the telephone can be very productive provided there is adequate planning, supervision, and follow-up of the activities. In fact, many athletic administrators and coaches feel that when properly run, phon-a-thons are the quickest and easiest way to raise dollars and increase your donor base (Ritrievi, 1989).

The key is the proper use of volunteers as callers or solicitors. Parents, athletes, coaches, booster club members, alumni, school officials, as well as influential community members, all make potentially effective and efficient solicitors. Whether students, alumni, or others are staffing the phones, always have supervisors and refreshments available during the phon-a-thon activity.

Naturally, adequate facilities with a sufficient number of telephones are absolutely essential. It is best if there are sufficient phones in one general location so that the phone marathon can be properly monitored by trained leaders. The number of phones will determine the number of solicitors needed for the phonathon. If you are limited on the number of phones available, callers/solicitors can work in shifts.

A key component to a successful phonathon is providing appropriate and timely orientation and training for each caller. While the team of callers is being confirmed and the availability of phones secured, it is necessary to complete research into potential prospects and to develop a prospect list, with names and phone numbers of those who will be called. The list might include alumni, former athletes, vendors, supporters, etc. Advance publicity can be of immense assistance in getting the word out to the potential prospects that the telephone solicitation will take place. Also, it is fruitful to coordinate or match the solicitors with those potential prospects with whom they might have something in common.

For example, athletic coaches might be paired to call former athletes whom they had coached. Highly successful, well-known business people would be assigned to call other business executives. Potential alumni donors and former players might be divided or classified by the decade in which they attended—1940s, 1950s, 1960s, 1970s, 1980s, etc. Another common tactic is to plan for two separate and distinct phone campaigns each year—one for the renewal of previous donors and the other for soliciting new donors.

Each caller should be provided cards or lists with names, addresses, and telephone numbers, along with an adequate supply of pens or pencils, stationery, athletic department envelopes, return envelopes, and pledge cards. In addition to the pledge cards, *detailed directions* are provided in terms of what to say (a "script") when the prospect initially comes to the phone (introduction to the cause), how to respond to objections (overcoming hurdles), suggestions as to ways of closing (asking for the money), and instructions on completing the paper work following the conclusion of the phone call (adequate follow-up). Adequate follow-up is essential regardless of whether or not the prospect actually makes a pledge because one needs to make plans for subsequent phonathons.

The script might contain information similar to:

"Hello, this is _____. I am a student-athlete on the football team at ABC high school. This evening the athletic department is conducting a phonathon to raise money for the football program. In addition to myself, there are a number of other students, coaches, and alumni calling former players, general alumni, and supporters in an effort to raise money for _____. We would like to have you help our athletic program by contributing a *gift* of $50.00."

It is essential that the caller can adequately explain how the funds raised will be utilized—whether for equipment, recruiting, special trips, scholarships, etc.

If the potential contributor has previously donated, the caller should know this fact and should mention the previous gift and thank the person. When there are so-called "giving categories," the solicitor should asked for an amount greater than the donor had given previously. If the potential donor is unable or unwilling to contribute at a specific level, the caller should not be afraid or embarrassed to ask why. Also, the caller should ask for a contribution at the next lower level. As a last resort, one should ask for some nominal gift so that the individual ends up giving something to the athletic program.

Frequently, neophyte solicitors are allowed to watch more experienced brethren as part of the formal training process. These beginning solicitors are frequently encouraged to participate in role playing, with input and evaluations provided by experienced solicitors, prior to actually making the initial calls. Again, adequate and timely education and training coupled with actual practice become the watch words.

In terms of the date and time of the actual calls, there are two common tactics. The *first* approach is to have the calls made during a specific time period on certain dates. For example, for 4 hours on a Saturday and a Sunday afternoon, and from a central location where all of the telephone solicitors can make their contacts. The *second* alternative is to have the calls made on an individual basis. In this situation the telephone solicitors are given the names to call, along with other pertinent information and directions, and are allowed to make the calls at times and sites convenient to them— for example, anytime during a 2 to 3 week period.

In the latter instance, there is less immediate supervision and less personal support provided to the solicitor. These two disadvantages have to be weighed against the flexibility enjoyed by the solicitors and in terms of the opportunities to actually *reach* prospective donors and contributors via the telephone at differing times.

Corporate Sponsorships

In today's climate of ever increasing costs for sports, more and more athletic administrators are looking at the world of corporate sponsorships to help alleviate the enormous economic crunch being experienced at all levels. Across the board, from the very largest university sport program to the junior high school athletic program, administrators are experiencing a shrinking of the purchasing dollar. Only within the past decade has the corporate sponsorship route of fund-raising really been examined in seeking significant monies. The big-time collegiate and university sport programs are currently blazing the trail in amateur sports, and the efforts are beginning to trickle down to the smaller colleges and even the high schools and youth sport levels.

There has been a long history of businesses and corporations using sports for promotional purposes. In 1852, the New England railroad sponsored a competition in the sport of crew between Yale and Harvard. Before 1900, trains and streetcars had a close association with baseball with so-called "baseball trains" bringing numerous fans to games. After the turn of the century, Gillette began to utilize boxing to market the sale of razor blades. Coca-Cola was the first to associate itself with the Olympics by sending cases of coke on the trip transporting the US team to the 1928 Olympics held in Amsterdam. Of course, the 1984 Olympics in California cemented the relationship between the corporate world and sports when Coca-Cola paid some $3 million dollars for the privilege of being billed as the "official soft drink" of the Los Angeles Olympics. As the result of the extensive corporate sport sponsorship at the Los Angeles Games—generating over $230 million in profit—the 1984 Olympics has been nick named the "corporate Olympics" (Brooks, 1990).

Today, corporations and businesses recognize that having products associated with sports and sport activities and personalities can generate sizable increases in sales, resulting in mega-profits. There is a definite business relationship between the sports entity and the corporate entity in any corporate sponsorship. In recent years such relationships can be big business involving large dollar amounts. Even as late as the mid-1970s, General Motors turned down the opportunity, for only $2,000, of gaining the title sponsorship of the New York City marathon. In 1989 the same sponsorship was secured by Mercedes-Benz for a mere quarter-of-a-million dollars (Ferguson, 1990).

At the local level, food and beverage companies are prime prospects for any athletic program. This is because their corporate parents frequently provide monies in their budgets to support the local markets. Thus, it behooves the coach or athletic administrator to work with the local arm of national food and beverage corporations in the solicitation of corporate dollars through sport sponsorships. It is estimated that one-third of the NCAA Division I-A schools are actively involved in some kind of *local* corporate sponsorships (Berg, 1989).

In 1989 over 4,000 companies formed a funding pool for corporate sponsors, an increase of 150 over the previous year and a gain of 3,700 from 1982. Of the $2.55 billion dollars available in special events marketing and funding available from corporate sponsors, some 65% of those funds were earmarked for sports. To keep the growth of corporate sponsorship in its proper perspective it is interesting to note that in 1982 only 10 corporations had event-marketing departments. Today, over 400 corporations have such departments or divisions (Wegs, 1990).

Brooks (1989) cited three basic concepts in the successful sale of any product or service. First, corporations are involved in communication, and it is sports and sport personalities that can provide the medium. Second, in today's society, sports provide a mechanism whereby corporations may gain access to various and differing segments of consumers. Third, sports enable marketers to attach an image to products or services that differentiate the products or services from others in the marketplace. Thus, sport sponsorship may be thought of as the selling of rights from a sports organization to a corporation or business whereby the business may utilize any of the images and symbols associated with the sport for the benefit of the business.

Two universities that have been in the forefront of soliciting significant corporate sponsorships for their collegiate athletic programs are the University of Denver (Krupa, 1988) and the San Diego State University (SDSU). Diane Wendt, associate athletic director at DU, has been most successful in putting together a corporate sponsorship program involving 16 major donors, both local and national.

At the Division IA level, Fred Miller, the athletic director at SDSU, has likewise been in the forefront of corporate sponsorship in an attempt to subsidize the athletic department's financial resources. Through an innovative corporate sponsorship program, the Aztecs grossed $1.2 million dollars in 1988 and 1989 from sponsorships such as Coca-Cola, Texaco, and Dodge (Special Report, 1989). By 1991, SDSU's sponsorship involvement included Avis, Texaco, Chrysler-Dodge, Volkswagon, USAir, Mariott Hotels, and State Farm Insurance. Sponsorship of one San Diego State University football game ranged from $10,000 to $16,000 while a single basketball sponsorship cost between $4,000 and $8,000 (Goldberg, 1991).

With some 85% to 95% of the nation's biggest athletic programs running in the red, corporate sponsorships are being viewed as a viable method of blunting the financial crunch facing our nation's university sports programs. In fact, in 1990, Miller proposed that 23 out of the 105 or so NCAA, Division IA institutions enter into a corporate sponsorship consortium to attract national sports for both football and basketball at these big-time sport schools.

Diet Pepsi Women's Walk, for University of Nebraska at Omaha women's athletic department. One thousand women raised $80,000. (Courtesy of University of Nebraska at Omaha Women's Athletics/photo by Jim Bradley)

Even sport conferences have been actively engaged in soliciting the corporate sponsorship dollar. The Southeastern Conference is considered by many to be the leader in entering into corporate sponsorship agreements on a conferencewide basis. Dr. Harvey Schiller, who took over the conference commissioners job in 1986, has generated millions of dollars for the SEC and, in doing so, has placed the SEC in the forefront of conference marketing. Maxwell House, Gillette, Pepsi, Golden Flake, 10K Isotonic Drink, and Ruby Tuesday Restaurants have contributed an estimated $200,000 each in rights fees just to become an SEC corporate sponsor. Additionally, each company was required to spend an additional $1 million on other promotional events (Couzens, 1990).

One of the reasons why so many corporations and businesses are seeking to become involved in corporate sponsorships with colleges, universities, and even secondary athletic programs is that they have been priced out of the arena by the NFL, NBA, and the MLB. Another reason is because businesses and corporations are keenly aware that such association with sports in general, specific sports programs, and individual sports personalities can be good for business in terms of increased awareness of products and, most importantly, greater sales of products and services. It boils down to money, period. It is estimated that corporate sponsorship of a team or specific sport contests has the potential for improving the way in which fans view the sponsoring company's products by nearly 20%.

Even on the secondary level, corporate sponsorships have been very successful. In fact, the state of California has been most successful in tapping the rich and fruitful sponsorship arena. The California Interscholastic Federation and its Southern Section, in particular, have been true leaders, if not pioneers, in the world of soliciting for corporate sponsorships on the interscholastic level. As early as 1976, the Southern Section of the California Interscholastic Federation successfully negotiated a corporate sponsorship package with Dr. Pepper in an effort to supplement its athletic awards program.

From this initial effort, the payoff in 1989 amounted to over $1.6 million dollars flowing into the high school coffers from statewide sponsorship agreements with such giants as Coca-Cola and Reebok for the support of the state high school championships over a three year period (Bring on the Sponsors, May 1989, p. 8). The state's year-end competitions now carry names such as "CFI/Reebok Track & Field Championships."

In 1990 it was reported that corporations in Alaska and Minnesota helped to underwrite state high school championships. Some $500,000 was provided to the Alaska School Activities Association by only four companies in that state. In Minnesota, the State High School League received $275,000 from a bank holding company (Corporate Sponsors, 1990).

Television has begun to play a large part in sport sponsorship, even on the secondary level. In September 1989, two high schools in the greater Cleveland area played in the first televised contest of what was to be a weekly high school sports cable television package. The game attracted more than 8,000 fans to the stadium. However, the total TV viewing audience was estimated at more than 8.5 million with some half-a-million people in the state of Ohio itself (Brewington, 1989).

Dealing with high school sports on the national level, *SportsChannel American,* a joint venture of NBC and Cablevision, a cable sports network, signed what was expected to be a multi-year television deal with the National Federation of State High School Associations to begin in September of 1989. The agreement initially called for the televising of 25 contests (both boys and girls sports). However, the venture was cancelled in the early fall of 1991.

Of course, the television coverage of high school state championships in such sports as football and basketball is nothing new. States like Indiana, California, Minnesota, Texas, and Florida have been active in this regard for some years. In fact, some $540,000 was earned from the televising of the Minnesota state high school ice hockey tournament.

Television on the college and university level has involved big dollars for many years. However, while only 1% of the collegiate athletic programs are at the level of the super powers, such as Notre Dame with its historic 5–year television package with NBC, the other 99% of collegiate athletic programs are left to attempt to pursue corporate tie-ins commensurate with their level of competition.

How Corporate Sponsorships Work

In exchange for money and services given to sports organizations and schools by sponsors, the schools and athletic programs enter into a reciprocal agreement or arrangement for provision of a variety of benefits (Schmader, 1989). Such reciprocal arrangements often call for a variety of benefits. Some of these can include special arena and stadium signage highlighting the sponsor and the sponsor's products, general or specific advertising and inclusion in ads within game programs, title sponsorship recognition, publicity, photo opportunity with coaches and athletic administrators, mention in the advertisements that appear in the local media, public address announcements, scoreboard messages, customer/client relationship enhancement, employee moral enhancement through free tickets for employees, securing block tickets for donation from the sponsoring organization to charities, direct sales or sampling opportunities before, during, and subsequent to athletic contests, and the list can go on and on and on.

In terms of determining what the benefits might be worth to a potential sponsor, Jackson (1988, p. 18) suggests to look at the going rate (dollar value) of other sponsorships for similar events being marketed in the area. When comparisons are possible and suitable, one needs to be willing to negotiate and be even somewhat arbitrary. Being flexible in this area of establishing the final cost to the sponsor, as well as creating the components of the benefit package for the potential sponsor, is a must.

In today's market place, it is highly advisable, if not essential, to be able to provide the potential sponsor with adequate data about the sport program's ability to reach specific target market consumers. Irwin and Stotlar (1991) emphasized that corporations need to know the return value derived through both (1) the number of exposures generated and (2) the number of exposure recipients. Thus, coaches and athletic administrators must be able to conduct meaningful and fruitful research in terms of the types of individuals who attend the sporting events and their purchasing habits and capacities.

Additional information sponsors are interested in securing include age, gender, income levels, and home addresses of contest patrons. This information falls under the category of patron demographics research. Psychographic market research deals with the attitudes, opinions, and life-styles (revealing interests, values, and activities) of those attending the sporting events.

Another area of data or information that can be helpful for sponsors is information that indicates the cost-effectiveness of the advertisement or association. A study by Stotlar and Johnson (1989) revealed that spectators at college stadiums were able to successfully recollect the advertisements on scoreboards located in the stadium or arena upon leaving the facility. In fact, nearly 70% were able to identify the advertisements, with 77% remembering in football stadiums and 62% in basketball arenas. Plus, nearly one-third of the products purchased at the stadiums and arenas were bought *as a direct result* of stadium advertising. The conclusion of this investigation was that stadium and arena advertising (frequently included as part of a corporate sponsorship package) can indeed be effective.

Since it is of the utmost importance for the sport administrator to have access to this data in approaching potential sponsors, it is necessary to conduct survey research of fans and patrons. The crux of the matter is that sport marketers and administrators must be armed with appropriate information and hard data prior to attempting to convince corporations and businesses that it is to their benefit to become corporate sponsors.

Soliciting Large Organizations, Businesses, or Industries

The larger the organization, business, or industry, the greater the likelihood that the final decisions as to which worthy cause will receive specific donations will be removed from the local level, that is from the responsibility of the local manager or administration. Conversely, it is the smaller organizations and businesses that are able to have decisions relating to contributions made at the local level, without significant delays.

There are four questions to answer when considering approaching businesses, corporations, and industry. These are:

1. What type and amount of assistance should be sought (cash, "people" support, services, or other assistance, such as introductions to third party potential donors)?
2. What kind of information do you seek to find out about these potential donors?
3. What kind of information do you provide to the potential donors?
4. Who in the organization should initially be contacted in the solicitation effort?

It is necessary to do one's homework before approaching big ticket donors directly on an individual basis. It is helpful to understand the type of activities that might be looked on favorably by the potential donor. Additionally, what type of contributions have been made previously by the donor to other charitable causes? For what purposes? In what amounts?

There should be an attempt to match what the sports program or activity is attempting to accomplish with what the potential donor wants to support and has supported in the past. This can be accomplished by a thorough examination of the donor's beliefs and feelings toward the type of program one is involved in and the achievements of the sports program. This researching of information pertaining to potential donors can be facilitated by seeking information from mutual friends (centers of influence), gathering information from the local library, and from the local chamber of commerce.

■■**Principle 109**■■

Create a compatible match between the needs of the sport program and the interests of the corporation or business.

Attempt to make a match between the corporation or business whose social image is compatibly aligned with your program. For example, companies that create or market products for women might be receptive to women's sports programs. Similarly, corporations that perpetuate the sport image (soft drink companies) might be receptive to supporting the sport teams within your organization. Manufacturers of weight equipment or football equipment may be potential advertisers for and/or contributors to football programs. Corporations marketing tennis equipment might be more willing to contribute to tennis programs than to become involved in financially supporting baseball teams.

The objective is to develop a plan that matches the sport program (and/or its goals) with the sponsor, that is, to help reach the goals of the sponsor, as well as the goals of the sport activity or organization. To do this, it is necessary to correctly assess the general goals and purposes of the potential donors, whether they are individuals or businesses, so that a correct match between the donor and the requesting organization can be made.

This two-way match between the potential sponsor and the sports entity also involves consideration of local and national mores, customs, and expectations in which the sports organization finds itself. One example that involved a major university ended in a failed attempt with a potential corporate sponsorship. In this situation, the university attempted to enter into an agreement with a major gambling casino in Atlantic City, New Jersey.

The proposed corporate sponsorship, when announced by the publicity departments of the university and the casino, raised an uproar, both nationally and locally. There was widespread concern raised among alumni and others associated with sport and the institution. The school and the athletic administrators took a beating in the local and national press. The proposed sponsorship soon became a very hot potato. As a result, the proposed sponsorship never came to fruition. Both the university and the casino recognized that the negative, national publicity over the suitability and appropriateness of a so-called "marriage" between amateur sport and a gambling casino was detrimental to the interests of both the university and to the casino. The decision was made to cut the university's losses (negative publicity) and to back off from the planned "marriage."

This is a good example of a corporate sponsorship match that did not meet the needs of either the university or the casino. In fact, it did the opposite. The negative publicity associated with the questioning of the appropriateness of such a tie-in between a university sports team and a gambling casino caused negative publicity and brought a potential negative image to the eyes of the public. In the end, both the casino and the athletic entity elected to back off and not consummate the relationship, thus, supposedly preserving the gulf between sport and the world of gambling.

Principle 110
Successful corporate sponsorships must involve a suitable image on behalf of the corporation or business.

Whatever the need of the potential sponsor is, meet that need, if possible. If a company, a potential sponsor, needs more foot traffic, then establish a sponsorship program that includes a coupon that must be redeemed in the store since this will be very attractive to the prospective sponsor. The *first* step is to find out what the sponsor needs. The *second* step is to meet or fill that need. In attempting to find out what these potential needs might be, observe and seek input from a variety of individuals. Above all, don't be afraid to ask the potential sponsors what their needs are and then attempt to work out a special, individualized deal with each sponsor. Be flexible. Be imaginative. Be creative. Be willing to negotiate.

Principle 111
Find the sponsor's specific need and fill it.

Packaging and Imagery

In attempting to sell a corporate sponsorship program, the packaging of the actual sponsorship plan itself is very, very important. Similarly, the manner or fashion in which the plan or proposal is presented is equally important for positive results. That is, the plan outlining the proposed strategies, the activities, the efforts, etc., must be created, packaged, and presented in such a fashion as to place the most favorable light on the plan. The individuals who have responsibility for making the decision (or recommending the decision to higher authorities) regarding the extent of the corporation's involvement in the sponsorship plan should be favorably impressed with the presentation and the packaging of the plan as well as the plan itself. Professionalism is the watchword here.

The packaging of the proposal and the manner in which it is communicated can have a direct relationship on successfully communicating a positive and accurate

Principle 112
The packaging is almost as important as the content in the creation of a proposal for sport sponsorship.

image of the sport program to potential sponsors. The ultimate goal is to successfully explain the purpose(s) and the needs of the sports program as well as the components or factors affecting the sponsorship plan to representatives of corporations, businesses, and industry so that intelligent decisions can be made, hopefully in favor of the sports program.

▬Principle 113▬

Don't let a brochure be a substitute for a knowledgeable person-to-person contact.

Although it is essential in many instances that a first-class pamphlet, kit, or printed brochure be created for use by solicitors when dealing with prospective donors, it must be remembered that a promotional or informational brochure is only a tool to be used in conjunction with a professionally trained (volunteer or staff personnel) solicitor. The brochure should not be created with the intention that the piece be the only contact a prospective donor will have with the program. The brochure is not a substitute for a professional person-to-person contact by a trained, experienced solicitor who is well versed with the specifics of the sport organization and the skills of salesmanship. Brochures and pamphlets are important, but one should not rely on them exclusively to sell the concept or the program. The major purposes of the brochure or pamphlet are threefold:

1. To provide written communication that will provide insight into the program, the needs, the accomplishments of the athletic operation, the proposed plans, etc.
2. To provide answers to frequently asked questions in an honest and forthright fashion, *in advance*.
3. To address potential objections or controversial, negative aspects or questions, in advance.

The content of the solicitation kit (information or promotion package) should consist of a clear statement as to the organization's *mission statement*, as well as a "brag sheet" on the athletic program (Stier, 1990). A copy of the athletic mission statement at the State University of New York College at Brockport, is included within Appendix G. Additionally, one or more of the following could be included as part of the solicitation kit:

1. Background information about the organization and its activities, a rationale for its existence, as well as the stated objectives and goals.
2. A one-page prioritized list of specific needs.
3. Gift range table—money, equipment, time, and other resources.
4. An invitation to become affiliated with the organization, present and future.
5. Summary of justification for support that can include a list of values and benefits of the program and the accomplishments to the participants, schools, the community, and to the business sector, etc. Also, what specific benefits will accrue to the contributing corporation or individual.
6. Background about the solicitor(s).
7. List of officers and prominent members of organization (and their achievements).
8. Description of the roles of the coaches and other staff.
9. List of top contributors—individual and corporate (with range of gifts).

10. Photos, press clippings, brochures, and pamphlets on the organization and the sports programs.
11. Explanation of the organization's academic and athletic programs and services provided to various publics.
12. Financial efficiency of your organization (how much it costs to raise "X" number of dollars).
13. The percentage that the soliciting organization's own *people* have contributed (coaches, etc.).

When attempting to establish a sponsorship with a business or corporation, attempt to meet the needs of both the potential corporate sponsor and the sport program. Some helpful hints regarding the creating of an equitable exchange agreement with a corporate sponsor are listed below. The three key concepts to keep in the forefront in the area of corporate sponsorships are: (1) do everything with class, first rate, (2) satisfy the corporate sponsor fully, and (3) don't give away the store.

▬Principle 114▬
Have an equitable exchange process—don't give away the store.

Helpful Hints in the Creation of a Corporate Sponsorship Proposal

1. Put the proposal in writing in a concise, clear, accurate, and neat package.
2. Make the proposal specific. Include exactly what the program is, what is required, what it will do, and what might it do in terms of the sponsor's sales and exposure.
3. Price the sponsorship program in a realistic way on the basis of what the market will bear. Be prepared to justify the price.
4. Keep the price the same for all companies. Don't charge one company a smaller amount for the same benefit package than the large company just because the latter has more money. The concept remains that the fee structure should match the benefits and all sponsors should pay the same fee in order to receive the identical benefits.
5. Start small at first. Don't go after IBM at the national level but start with the local companies in town. Develop a successful track record—nothing sells like a track record (success).
6. Realize the program limitations and where the program exists in terms of the pecking order within the general geographic area (pro teams, major universities, colleges, high schools [big and small], youth teams and recreational organizations, as well as corporation and business teams and activities).
7. Don't promise what can't absolutely be delivered. The name of the sponsor can be displayed within the facility, but there can't always be a guarantee that 1,000 people will redeem coupons or that there will be special TV coverage for an event (unless you have the TV contract in hand).
8. It is a matter of matching or creating the right **fit** between the sport program and the potential sponsor. There must be a matching of needs and resources on behalf of the sport organization and the sponsor.
9. Always go the extra mile. Always do more and give more than expected.

10. Make sure the sponsor is continually kept abreast of what is being done and how successful the program was (how many people were involved, etc.). The creation and sharing of a final written and personal report (with appropriate expressions of appreciation) to the sponsor's representative tops off the whole effort and sets the stage for possible future involvements with the sponsor.

11. At the conclusion of the event or arrangement, don't neglect to send all participants a letter thanking them for their participation in the name of the sponsor and the sports program.

Types of Corporate Sponsorships/Partnerships

There is a variety of different types of sponsorship or partnership arrangements that can be established between the sports program and a company or corporation. In exchange for entering into a sponsorship arrangement or agreement, sponsors can be given different names or designations such as "title sponsor" or "presenting sponsor" or a "team sponsor" or an "event" or "game sponsor."

Tradeouts. Tradeouts work well because they don't cost the sport program money in terms of hard, cold cash. Cash flow is not hindered through the use of tradeouts. In fact, just the opposite. The cash flow of a sports organization is enhanced through the use of tradeouts. It is important to remember that a tradeout doesn't cost the sports program cash. Instead, the athletic program provides services for something that is in turn of value to the sports program (Moore & McGarey, 1986). In a media tradeout agreement, the program offers items or services to the media that the athletic administrator has placed a cash value on. These services are put together in a package format with different cash values. For example, tickets, program advertisements, booster club memberships or public address announcements may be exchanged in return for media time on the station.

Of course, tradeouts can work equally effectively with all types of organizations including, but not limited to, the following:

1. Radio stations
2. Television stations
3. Printing houses
4. Grocery stores
5. Hardware stores
6. Equipment manufacturers
7. Newspapers

Gifts-in-Kind. *Gifts-in-kind* can involve any gift that the sports program can utilize and aids in off-setting the athletic budget. The list of possible gifts is almost endless. For example, donations could take the form of equipment and facility donations, program advertising, tickets, free motel rooms, sport banquets being underwritten, free advertising in the media or on billboards or buses, donated trophies or awards, sponsorship of a recruiting film or videotape, sponsorship of a radio or TV program or series, etc.

Such items are a blessing in that, depending on what they are, the gifts can either be converted to cash or sometimes used themselves in the operation of the sport program. For example, gifts of beef, pork, various commodities, air time, ticket printing, stationery, stocks, bonds, club memberships, etc., can be used by the sport program per se for the purpose for which they were intended, or these gifts could be used as prizes in other fund-raising activities in an effort to generate other resources. They could also be bartered for other items that are needed by the athletic program.

The advantages accruing to the donor rest in the fact that such contributions of noncash gifts, from inventory items as well as used clothing and equipment, can reduce taxes owed by the donor as well as creating positive public relations for the contributor, whether an individual or a company. In some instances, such contributions of noncash items also enable the contributor to make larger donations than might otherwise be impossible.

For example, corporations, under existing IRS rules and regulations, are allowed to deduct overhead costs plus 50% of the markup for the items they donate to "qualified charities serving the ill, needy, or infants." For example, in the case where a corporation had an equipment item that had cost $2,000 and retailed for $3,000, the corporation would be allowed to claim a deduction of $2,500.00 (the cost plus 50% of the markup) upon donating the item to the charity (Guttman, 1992).

There are numerous examples of large corporations making significant contributions of gifts-in-kind or noncash items to sport-related groups. Kodak, headquartered in Rochester, New York, contributed videotapes and photo films to Boys Clubs and Girls Clubs. Glacier, a bottler of spring water in California, has donated thousands of dollars worth of spring water to bike-a-thons and skateboarding contests.

One word of caution in dealing with gifts-in-kind. The determination of what is fair market value of the noncash items donated to the charity remains the responsibility of the individual or corporation making the actual donation. It is never the responsibility of the fund-raising entity to be involved in the appraisal of any donated item. Rather, the nonprofit organization should merely document that a particular item was actually donated, provide a receipt and a sincere "thank-you" and leave it at that. Attempting to serve as an appraiser only "muddies the water."

Profit Centers

Profit centers are those areas or aspects of a sport program that have the capability or potential for generation of a positive cash flow (income), a genuine profit, for the sport program.

Types of Profit Centers

Depending on the type of athletic program, the skill of the available leadership, the level at which the sport program operates, the size of its following, the basis of its support, and its competitive success—as well as many other factors—there are generally nine areas that may be considered potential *profit centers*. These areas are:

1. Ticket sales
2. Concessions
3. Program sales
4. Merchandise, product sales

5. Parking fees
6. User fees for facilities and services
7. Vending machines—profit sharing
8. Luxury box seating
9. Parking condos

■■Principle 115■■

Increasing attendance at contests directly increases potential for other profit centers.

Many of the profit centers depend upon traffic patterns in order to have sufficient numbers of people to take advantage of the availability of the items or services for sale. For example, unless there are people in attendance at games, the likelihood of much money being generated from ticket sales, parking privileges, as well as the sale of merchandise and concessions, is minimal. Therefore, it is essential to do those things that will result in attracting more people to games if it is the objective to increase money generated from the various profit centers that can exist at game sites.

■■Principle 116■■

Think twice before encouraging spectator attendance if the team is not something of which to be proud.

If the athletic team is not winning, or if the team's performance is truly an embarrassment, one might think twice before going out on a limb and exerting extraordinary effort and resources in encouraging spectator attendance. Frequently a spectator's first impression is truly a lasting impression. There is only one opportunity to make a first impression. This is not just a catchy phrase but is an important factor to consider.

There must be something worthwhile to promote and to attract the interest of the public. If spectators, especially first-time visitors, don't like what they see, they just won't come back. They don't come back even when the team improves. On the other hand, if the team is somewhat competitive and exciting to the spectators, the time is ripe to begin to promote and place special emphasis on getting people to attend the contests. Success does breed success.

■■Principle 117■■

Scheduling of opponents can have a major impact on promotional efforts and the profitability of profit centers.

Scheduling of opponents can be an effective method of controlling the potential for promotional activities. Likewise, the scheduling of specific opponents can have a direct impact, either positive or negative, on the profitability of various athletic profit centers, such as tickets, concessions, parking, sale of merchandise, etc.

What if part of the home schedule consists of a number of "bunnies" coupled with some very attractive home contests? In this situation in which only a part of the home schedule is competitive, there are generally two avenues to pursue. First, one can create a "mini home schedule" that can be promoted as a **super** home schedule while downplaying the "bunnies" or mismatches. The second avenue open to the sport ticket promoter is to attempt to combine some of the team's strong or natural rivalries *with* the "bunnies" in ticket combinations and promotional packages. In this way, potential ticket purchasers are required to buy tickets to both contests, thereby increasing the likelihood of greater attendance (and possible increase in the profit centers) at some of the less competitive contests.

In promoting the availability of one's various profit centers, it is a good principle to consistently emphasize the fact that the proceeds (profits) go to support a worthy cause (the sport program). This awareness campaign can be coupled with the publicity generated in support of the actual items for sale. This can be effective whether the items are tickets, concessions, parking space, merchandise, or programs. One method of inexpensively promoting such items, as well as the charitable cause, is to send flyers to parents, alumni, and businesses advertising a few of the items or services and informing them where they may be purchased. Additionally, obtaining permission from local grocery stores and other retail businesses to insert the flyers into shopping bags or on the back of cash register receipts is an excellent method for mass distribution to the general public.

How can a sport program take advantage of some of these inherent profit centers that might exist within its domain? There are no simple answers to this all-inclusive question. Depending upon the specific circumstances that exist for each athletic program and sport team, evaluate ideas and suggestions that have been utilized in other athletic arenas for possible use in one's own situation. However, the following information and suggestions regarding each of these nine categories of profit centers will reveal many common concepts applicable for almost any athletic program.

■Principle 118■
Always publicize the fact that the proceeds from profit centers go to the sport program (a positive selling point) and publicize the items that are for sale.

Ticket Sales

Establishing a Plan of Attack in the Structuring of the Ticket Operation.
The first task at hand is to establish realistic ticket prices. There needs to be flexibility in terms of ticket prices for various age groups. There is also a need for diversity in the promotional activities involving tickets to sporting events. The question, "what type of fringe benefits should accrue to the different ticket purchasers," such as preferred seating, reduced prices, special gifts, unique entertainment, etc., needs to be answered.

In marketing athletic tickets, that is, establishing a ticket selling campaign, one must determine who the prospective purchasers are, the starting and closing dates of the sales effort, and the appropriate sales techniques. For example, will the marketing campaign involve use of the U.S. mail, door-to-door solicitation, use of the phone, assistance from booster club members via person to person solicitation, or some combination of all of these?

There seems to be little crossover between men's and women's fans within the same school or sports program. It seems that fans tend to form rather strong allegiances, and they will follow one sport but not all of the sports within an athletic program. This is an important concept when attempting to market tickets to women's sporting events. Rick Klatt, the Director of Sports Promotion for both women and men at the University of Iowa, was quoted as saying that "People go to men's games because other people are there and people go to women's games because they want to be there" (Lamphear & Frankel, 1990, p. 28).

Thus, when attempting to move tickets to women's sporting events the promoters need to realize that it is not necessary to attempt to compete with the men's programs for the same spectators. Rather, the promoters for the women's programs should attempt to identify and reach those potential spectators who can be influenced to support the women's programs and teams because of the quality of those activities.

Decisions Relating to the Method(s) of Marketing Tickets and the Pricing of Tickets

Other factors to consider in terms of the ticket operation includes the actual pricing of tickets as well as special marketing and promotional strategies of the sport activity or contest. One promotional tactic involves the availability of special types of tickets (a tiered system). For example, there may be special tickets for reserved seating or preferred seating, and special packages can be made available for season tickets holders. Finally, teams can provide combination (coupon) ticket packages for multiple numbers of games in the same sport or involving multiple sports.

Whether or not to have advance ticket sales is an important decision. There are several advantages of being able to sell game tickets in advance of the actual date of the contest. Generally speaking, ticket managers provide for advance ticket sales in order to:

1. Serve as an insurance policy against a losing team, a poor-drawing visitor, or bad weather (outdoor teams)
2. Create a positive cash flow prior to the start of the season
3. Create enthusiasm in the community for upcoming season
4. Inform the community of needs of program
5. Inform the public of the existence of the entertainment value of the sports activity

Principle 119

Empty seats cost money in terms of lost revenue— attempt to put such seats to good use.

A great deal of the promotional activities associated with sports programs involves attempts at increasing attendance. Such efforts can be implemented around special activities (programs, events), which are attractive to the general public, as well as around reduced or special-price incentives that serve as the carrot or an attracting factor. Whatever specific tactics are used, the objectives include (1) maintaining the support of fans and spectators, (2) introducing potential new spectators to the program, (3) increasing attendance, and (4) putting the potential empty seats to some productive use, now and sometime in the future.

One shouldn't be afraid to discount or give tickets away. People who come as spectators often do purchase concessions. These same people also tend to purchase merchandise if appropriate items are for sale. Of course, such individuals might come back and be paying customers sometime in the future. A recent study reported by Friedman (1989) revealed that discounted game tickets are the most effective way to influence fans to attend a professional or college sporting event. This technique might also have similar, practical results at the high school level.

There are innumerable promotional plans that can be used to promote athletic attendance at sporting events. These tactics, which have proven successful at different times within a variety of athletic programs, revolve around three general courses of action:

1. Establishment of special or group **rates** (discounted) or free admission.
2. The use of **free** tickets.
3. Promotional activities associated with the **marketing** of tickets to specific segments of the community.

The examples provided below under each of these three categories are not **all** inclusive. In reality, one is limited only by one's imagination and by what **one** can learn from others who are in similar situations who have implemented successful promotional programs dealing with ticket promotions.

Establishment of Special or Group Rates (Discounted) or Free Admission.

1. Customer appreciation day/night in which a sponsor buys tickets (often **at** discounted prices) and that are given away to the customers of the sponsors.
2. Family (immediate family) ticket discounts to provide for the needs of **those** with large families (an attempt to attract youngsters to the contests).
3. Free or reduced tickets to everyone whose last name is SMITH or JONES or whose last name begins with a specific letter, etc.
4. Free or reduced prices when accompanied by a full ticket purchaser (even if the "guest" happens to be a stuffed animal or cardboard figure).
5. Kids' night (children free with accompanying parent).
6. Availability of discount prices for specific games (for off nights).
7. Discount ticket (coupons) books for families.
8. Guest night—2 tickets for the price of 1 or 3 tickets for the price of 2.
9. Coupon discount with the purchase of a ticket.
10. Group sales at a discount—discounted tickets to youth-oriented organizations such as youth sport groups; to service clubs like the Lions club, Kiwanis, and Elks; to specific corporations or groups such as the phone company, gas company, electric company, board of realtors, labor unions, etc.
11. Merchants are given tickets (coupon book) at a discount to use as they see fit.
12. Provide merchants with 20 game tickets for every $20.00 of contributions to the sport program.

The Use of Free Tickets.

1. Tie in with local businesses to give tickets away to special populations.
2. Give tickets away via the community Welcome Wagon to new individuals and families in town—an excellent method of introducing the sports program to newcomers in town.
3. Free tickets to worthy causes such as hospitals, scout groups, etc.

Promotional Activities Associated with the Marketing of Tickets.

1. Offer local groups the opportunity to sell tickets for a percentage of their gross sales.
2. Ask every vendor who sells to your school to buy 2 season tickets and/or 250 general admission tickets to your games.
3. Sell advertisers a package deal including sponsorship of a game, plus game tickets and an ad in the program and/or signage within a sport facility.
4. Arrange for community groups (youth hockey club, little league, midget football) or businesses to sell tickets and receive a cut of sales price (20% for example).

5. Sell tickets to a game accompanied by a free (or reduced) ticket to the local theater or bowling alley or golf course.
6. For every ticket a person buys to the theater, bowling alley, or golf course, the purchaser receives a free or reduced priced ticket to one of the selected sport contests.

■■■**Principle 120**■■■

Take advantage of the individuals who attend the contests— Build a prospect list from the names of those individuals who purchase or inquire about tickets.

Use your ticket sales and phone or written inquiries to help create a list of backers and supporters by building a mailing prospect list. Then use the list to further promote the sport program by mailing newsletters, ticket information, as well as a whole host of special promotional materials. The names and mailing addresses of individuals who have attended a sporting event or who are potential supporters are very important in terms of future communication attempts. They are also important in terms of future purchases of tickets and sport paraphernalia.

The mailing prospect list can be built through a variety of means. *One* method is to encourage spectators to complete a short questionnaire, designed to obtain such pertinent information, at an athletic contest. This questionnaire can also be used in a contest, for example, a raffle for prizes, thus insuring that more people will complete the form. *Another* tactic is to just ask spectators to complete an opinion survey in an effort for the athletic organization to be able to better meet their needs.

A *third* method is to simply provide a means by which spectators can drop in a business card, or just sign their names and addresses on a preprinted form, and drop it into a box provided for that purpose. The athletic administrators can then mail to these individuals a carefully designed form soliciting information. A *fourth* technique is to simply record the names and address of any individual who orders tickets to contests or who contacts the athletic office for information, for any reason whatsoever.

The ultimate objective is to obtain a current list of individuals who might be interested in the sports program and teams. Great efforts should go into maintaining an up-to-date listing of those who are prime candidates as sports spectators, fans, and supporters.

Concessions

■■■**Principle 121**■■■

Don't be penny wise and pound foolish—Operate concessions to make money.

The overriding consideration when contemplating involvement in the area of concessions is whether or not the end results are worth the effort and resources that must be put into the total concession operation. If the paid athletic staff are involved in the concessions arena, then the cost of their released time must be accounted for and factored into the total cost of the concessions operation. However, if volunteers are responsible for the general operation of concessions, then there are no real, significant costs, in terms of salaries for staffing the concessions area.

Whether the athletic concession area is staffed by salaried athletic personnel or by volunteers, it is the total financial, promotional, and public relations effort that must be taken into consideration. If such financial, promotional, and public relations *benefits* of the concession activity do not justify the time and effort required for the management and supervision of the concessions area, **then it would behoove the sport organizers or boosters not to become actively involved with concessions.** The major justification for maintaining a concession operation is to generate a profit, both in terms of money and in respect to positive public relations, for the sports program.

There are specific considerations to be examined in reviewing the prospect of being involved in any type of concession operation. These include:

Operational Aspects of Running Concessions—Points to Consider. One of the first decisions to be made involves the determination of the menu itself. What will be the mainstay of today's menu? What will sell? What will produce the greatest profit? What snacks will be provided?

Particular attention needs to be paid to low-cost food items as well as items that provide a high net profit with as little work as possible. The degree of skill required in the preparation of items must be taken into consideration. Items like cold drinks, cotton candy, popcorn, snow cones, hot dogs, nachos, and the like, are not time intensive in their preparation and enjoy a high profit margin for the concession operation. Special attention, especially in today's world of health and food consciousness, must be paid to the ingredients (salt and cholesterol) in the food that is for sale.

However, the concession operators need to be aware of local ordinances that have a direct impact on their operation. Some municipal laws require that packaged snacks require a vending license in order to be sold. Hot dogs and nachos, in some locales, are included under restaurant codes and the operation of the concession stand must meet the local code standards. Foods cooked in grease, such as hamburgers and french fries, might require the sponsoring organization to follow strict restaurant *and* fire codes that could include venting hoods, fire extinguishers, specific amount of square footage in the cooking area, etc. (Cohen, 1992).

In recent years concession menus have become more and more complex and extensive. As a result, cashiers have a challenge in adequately performing their responsibilities. More and more, concession operators have replaced "cigar box" cash boxes and have instead invested in electronic cash registers or at least basic adding machines. One of the reasons behind this shift toward a wider menu selection has been the demand by potential customers. Today, the typical sports concession stand may have 20 to 30 items while only 10 years ago the average concession operation might have offered only a basic menu of soft drinks, beer (if allowed), popcorn, hot dogs, hamburgers, and candy (Ferguson, 1990).

Once the menu has been determined, the appropriate pricing of each menu item must be made. The goal is to make a reasonable profit. This means that the profit margins (money remaining after cost of sales and merchandise is deducted) must be high enough to warrant the involvement (time and effort) in concessions. Running a concessions stand is not a get-rich scheme. It takes hard work, dedication, advance planning, and an understanding of marketing to the public. Patience also is a great asset.

Monitoring the concession operation is a major challenge. There are many factors to pay close attention to if the concession stand is to be successful. One of the major areas that must be constantly monitored is the supervision and training of workers. The National Association of Concessionaires, as well as area restaurant associations and various concessionaire suppliers, have training aids and advice to assist the new and experienced workers (Bigelow, 1989).

Proper selection of staff and adequate training are two important factors in insuring honesty of the concessionaire workers, both those who volunteer and those on salary. Close supervision and established work rules will go a long way to prevent skimming of profits by those individuals working in the concession stand. The maintaining of cleanliness is yet another major challenge. How the concession operation is viewed by the public in terms of cleanliness will determine, for the most part, how successful the operation will be. No one will want to purchase food items at a site that is not clean. No one wants to be served by an attendant who has dirty hands.

Today the watchwords are *service* and *quality*. If the concession stand cannot meet the ever increasing standards in terms of expectations of the customers, the result will be an ineffectual and inefficient operation. The result will be lost profits and negative public relations.

The establishing and following of proper accounting procedures are essential ingredients of any concession stand. Hiring, training, motivating and keeping qualified, friendly workers is another difficult task for the managers of the concession stand. Ordering and storing an adequate supply of all items, food and drink items as well as nonfood items, must be done well enough in advance to insure that the items are on hand for the actual athletic event. Nothing could be worse than for the day of the athletic contest to arrive and for the concession workers not to have the proper items to sell.

There are four essentials necessary for any concession stand to be successful. *First,* there must be appropriate items to sell. *Second,* there must be adequately trained and professional salespeople to work the concession stand (including the various machines). *Third,* there must be people at the event who desire to purchase (are motivated to act) the items for sale. *Finally,* there is the task of assessing and evaluating (on a continuous basis) the total concession operation.

The need to act upon the evaluation of the various aspects of the concession stand is mandatory. Evaluation of the operation of a concession stand is facilitated by the maintenance of good and accurate records of all that is done in the concession operation. This is so that those successful efforts can be retained and repeated while changing and improving those areas needing a facelift.

Essentially, everything connected with the concession area should be evaluated in light of what is working well and what can be improved in the future. Here, as always, hindsight is a valuable tool. As the concession stand continues to operate and the workers gain experience and a feel for the total operation, the concession area will hopefully be more productive and successful.

Picking Concession Food and Drink Items—Points to Consider. In selecting the food and drink items to comprise the menu, it behooves the forward thinking promoters to answer the following questions (Cohen, 1991). What would the operators of the concession stand enjoy buying and eating themselves if they were spectators? What items are easy to market and advertise? What would be enjoyable selling? Which items are easy to prepare, handle, and actually sell? Which items have a built-in high profit margin? What brands are well-known by the public and are viewed as quality items? What products have a natural appeal to the majority of people within the general geographic target area? What products can be stored without undue problems and difficulties (spoilage)? What items are easy to clean up within the facility where the food and drink are consumed? What food items can be easily and profitably marketed and sold before and during as well as after the athletic contest/event?

Generally speaking, some of the highest profits within the concession area are generated by cold drinks (90%), cotton candy (90%), popcorn (85%), nachos (90%), sno-cones (95%) and hotdogs (50% to 60%) (Cohen, 1992). It is not uncommon for hot dogs to generate half of a stand's total profit. Even pizza (heated in a micro-wave) has become a staple in some areas of the country.

Determining Pricing Schedule and Cost of Sales—Points to Consider. In determining the profit margins, cost of sales, and overhead, a good rule of thumb is that income, minus the cost of merchandise, but prior to deducting other expenses, should not fall below 65%. In the world of athletic concessions, mark-ups in the area of 65% to 85% gross profit are quite legitimate.

It is also wise to ask the vendor for suggestions as to the sale cost that might be appropriate in a particular area. In essence, the law of supply and demand (what items customarily sell for in your area) is often a criteria for determining the price one can charge for any given item. Pricing must be competitive. That is, items can be sold for what the market will bear without gouging the prospective customer.

In determining *net profit,* one has to consider the amount of money that remains after *all* expenses are deducted. Generally speaking, a concession operation should be generating at least at a 55% to 60% net profit.

To achieve this, items that have a low cost to the concessionaire, items that are not complicated to prepare, items that have a high profit margin (low cost versus high sales price, such as popcorn), and items that are popular with the public should form the basis of inventory for the concession operation. A concession stand operated by volunteers, parents or boosters, which involves no cost for personnel, naturally enhances the net profit potential for the concession operation.

Popcorn, the old reliable concession stand staple, still meets all of the criteria for a great food component for any concession stand. Popcorn is something most people like and accept. It is a food item that is healthy and attractive for the consumer while being relatively inexpensive for the concessionaire. It is also easy to prepare. In short, the profit on popcorn is relatively high considering the initial cost of the item and the time and effort in its preparation for consumption (Herzog, 1990). The gross profit for popcorn generally runs as high as 85% over the cost of the popcorn itself and the serving container, usually a bag or cup (Cohen, 1992).

Promoting the Concession Area—Points to Consider. The following sugges-tions are generally considered to be wise advice for the concessionaire in the effort to promote profitability of the operation.

1. Use point of purchase display posters and printed advertisements (obtained from supplier) as they make your product more attractive.
2. Use value pricing and advertise that fact via display and advertising. That is, offer several sizes (small, medium, and large) in some items and lower the cost per ounce of the large offerings. This encourages the customer to ''trade up.'' There is definitely a trend for larger containers to be sold today.
3. Use professional menu board (vendors can provide these as well).
4. Have a ''special'' on the menu. Once customers are attracted to the concessions area, they frequently purchase other items.

▬Principle 122▬

Popcorn is still a great food snack for a concession stand.

5. Train your staff in selling—have them ask customers if they would prefer a specific item. Have them make suggestions as to possible purchases by the customer (Cohen, 1992).
6. Provide an incentive bonus for salespeople.
7. Advertise during, before, and after game. Send people into the stands, if permitted.
8. Use the PA system to advertise before, during, and after the sport event. Also provide for specials periodically (and for a specific period of time, 10–15 minutes), the so-called ''Zayre 15–minute In-Store Special'' concept.
9. Keep all display items filled. Drink dispensers should be kept 75% full so as to attract attention and motivate the purchaser to action.
10. Secure an animated beverage dispenser and keep it where it can be seen. Similarly, place the hot dog rotisserie in a visible spot where customers will see it (and smell the food). Vendors are only too happy to assist in the marketing of their products. Take advantage of their experience and expertise.
11. Have an active, clean, and attractive concession stand, one that will attract attention.
12. Have all food handlers use plastic gloves and have the concession area very, very clean. *Also, never allow concession workers to eat or to engage in horseplay while in the concession stand.*
13. Food should *never* be served at the wrong temperature. Food that should be hot must be hot. Food that should be cold must be cold. Nothing is worse than a cold hot dog or a warm soft drink or stale popcorn.
14. Change products and add new items regularly.
15. Provide a suggestion box for customers to provide ideas on how to improve the concession stand.

Gross Profit Potential for Various Food Items—Points to Consider. The following list provides general information on gross profit ranges for various food items that are common components for a concession stand inventory (Briggs & Duffy, 1987, p. 47).

Food Item	*Percent of Gross Profit*
French waffles	90%
Popcorn	75%–85%
Sno-cones	80%
Foamy drinks	80%
Frosty freeze drinks	80%
Slush drinks	80%
Iced tea	80%
French fries	75%
Donuts	75%
Corn dogs	75%
Nachos	70%
Candied apples	70%
Hot chocolate	70%

Food Item	Percent of Gross Profit
Shaved ice cones	75%
Cotton candy	75%
Carbonated drinks	65%
Ice cream	65%
Hot dogs	65%
BBQ sandwiches	65%
Coffee	60%

Program Sales and Other Printed Pieces

Team programs can be sources of sizable profits for the sport program, depending upon a number of factors such as the printing costs, the cost of sales of such items, and, finally, how the printed piece is financed, that is, whether or not advertisements are included within the printed piece in an effort to offset the cost of the item. In the production of an athletic pprogram, or for any printed piece for that matter, there are several decisions that must be made prior to the actual printing of the piece.

The *first decision* to make in terms of printed pieces for sport programs revolves around the determination of the actual purpose(s) of the items. In addition to the traditional printed athletic program, other printed items might include team calendars, schedule cards, media guides, recruiting brochures, highlight flyers, etc.

Another decision to face is the actual makeup or composition of the printed items. For example, a decision has to be made in terms of the number of pages involved, the size of the pages, the quality of the paper, the number of color inks (if more than black), the actual number of pieces printed, the number of photographs, and whether or not professional typesetting is used in printing the publication piece. And, of course, how many of the items need to be printed, that is, the actual press run *and* when the printed items are needed. It is important to keep in mind that the cost per printed piece decreases as the total number of pieces printed is increased.

A *third decision* to make is whether or not to use ads within the printed piece. If ads are to be included, what shall be the going price of the ads for a full page, a half page, a third of a page, a quarter page, an eighth page, as well as the front and back covers and the inside of the front and back covers? How much can reasonably be expected to be raised through the sale of ads, and what percentage of the total printed space shall be devoted to advertisements?

A *fourth decision* hinges on how the advertisements shall be solicited. That is, will members of the coaching staff seek paid advertisements? What about the athletes themselves? What role shall the booster organization or parents play in the sale of advertisements for the printed athletic program? Will outside professional "head-hunters" whose professional job it is to raise money through the sale of advertisements be sought and hired to perform this task?

A *fifth decision* hinges on whether or not the printed item will be given away or sold. If it is to be sold, for what price? Through what mechanism will the printed piece be distributed? Will the printed item(s) be distributed at games as well as through other means (mail, etc.)? Will the piece be made available by hawkers before and during the contest? Will the programs be available at the ticket counter and at the ticket taking area? Can the items left over also be used for recruitment purposes at a later time for those programs that are involved in the student recruitment process?

Athletic printed programs, as well as other printed items, can be successful in promoting the image of the sport program to the general public. Additionally, such items as team calendars and game programs or souvenir programs can be structured in such a way as to provide sizable profit to the athletic organization. The profit potential essentially hinges on the factors of (1) selling advertisements and (2) selling the printed program or calendar, or whatever the printed item might be, for a specific price to the sports fans, either at athletic contests or through sales within the community.

Merchandise, Product Sales

Another profit center revolves around the selling of merchandise related to the athletic team or sponsoring organization. In attempting to arrive at a reasonable sales operation of merchandise there are five essential areas that must be addressed. These include (1) selecting the merchandise, (2) pricing of the merchandise, (3) ordering correct merchandise at an appropriate time, (4) marketing strategy for the items, and (5) accounting for the funds as well as any remaining or left-over inventory.

The entire area of licensing has grown to a point where not only the professional teams are able to garner large amounts of money, but numerous colleges and universities are also taking advantage of the opportunity to license their logos on any number of merchandise items. While college and universities might not be able to match the 1990 $1 billion dollar income from merchandise advertising and licensing of professional teams, there are substantial profits out there waiting for an astute, knowledgeable sport marketing person (Revenue Opportunities, 1991).

Selecting Merchandise. What can be sold? What is marketable for any given athletic program? What do people want to buy? These are critical questions indeed. To answer the question—WHAT can be sold?—the answer is ALMOST ANYTHING. For example, t-shirts, ties, sweatshirts, book bags, shirts, jackets, pants, shorts, bumper stickers, sports calendars, sales, ad books (selling ads to businesses), caps, glasses, cups, etc. Literally scores of advertisements from vendors will cross the desk of any athletic director during the course of a school year, illustrating literally hundreds, if not thousands, of items that can be sold through merchandising and marketing efforts. Additionally, consideration should be given to the quality of the items, the wholesale cost to the organization, the potential selling price, the net profit, and the available support of the sales force.

In summary, items or products selected to be sold should be useful, sometimes unique, and a better value or at least equal value than what people normally purchase from a local merchant. If a particular product or item can't stand up to such scrutiny, perhaps the wisest strategy of the sport promoter would be to pass on the item and to look at other possible merchandise to resell and promote.

Naturally, the more visible and popular the sport entity is, the more attractive their merchandise is to the general public and to fans and supporters. Merchandise possessing the team's logo from Syracuse University has more appeal to a larger audience than a team's logo from a medium size high school. This does not mean that the high school cannot successfully market and sell various items of merchandise. To the contrary. Small schools and small athletic organizations can still successfully select merchandise that can be sold to appropriate constituencies in sufficient volume to create a meaningful net profit.

Use of Team Mascots, Logos, and Colors. In planning to select and/or create various items to sell, it is important to utilize one's school or club colors as well as logo on the merchandise. (For examples of logos, see appendix J.) Create an identity with the athletic team or organization through the use of a team *mascot, logo,* and *colors* on all merchandise sold. It is important to remember that the logo, mascot, and/or symbol that is representative of the sport entity be professionally created and expertly utilized on all items of apparel for sale or distribution.

In 1991 the Chicago White Sox became baseball's equivalent to the National Hockey League's Los Angeles Kings and the National Football League Los Angeles Raiders in terms of the popularity of the team's merchandise purchased by the general public. In 1990 the Chicago White Sox changed their team's uniform colors to silver, black, and white. As a result, the sale of team merchandise jumped dramatically from eighteenth place in major league team merchandise (1990) to the top spot among all baseball teams in 1991. This was the largest single season improvement of any baseball team in league history. In fact, Chicago's sales accounted for almost 12 percent of all baseball league merchandise sold in that year (USA Today, 1992).

It may indeed be worth the time and effort to have one's athletic logo or symbol protected under the trademark regulations. This prevents others from utilizing, without permission, another organization's unique logo or symbol which has been appropriately registered (Irwin, 1991).

Licensing of Sports Logos, Symbols, and Names. Schools and sports organizations can make significant monies by authorizing, for a specific fee, other organizations, companies, and individuals to become a licensed producer and/or seller of a wide variety of goods bearing a team's or school's trademark. Licensing enables the holder of the trademark to retain quality control of the merchandise bearing the trademark, to enjoy expanded market opportunities, and to realize significant potential royalties from the sale of merchandise bearing the protected trademark.

Licensing has been recognized for more than two hundred years in this country. However, most of the dramatic growth in licensing in the world of sports is a much more recent phenomenon. In point of fact, the sale of licensed athletic products has exploded tremendously during the past twenty years. Sale of all licensed products in this country grew from a mere $17.6 billion in retail sales by the end of the 1970s to more than $60 billion by the start of the 1990s (Parkhouse, 1991).

Almost anything can be licensed. Licensing of athletic logos, characters, sayings, slogans, symbols, and names is made possible because of the Federal Trademark Act of 1946, popularly known as the Lanham Act. Subsequently, this act was revised in 1989 with the passage of the Trademark Law Revision Act. *Indicia* is the term used to describe the trademarks, the names, the symbols, and the designs that have come to be associated with the holder of a trademark. Securing the protection of a federal registered trademark protects the school or sports organization against unauthorized use of the registered trademark, called a trademark infringement.

Once registered, only the owner of the trademark may use the items so protected unless the owner expressly authorizes other individuals or organizations, through a licensing agreement, to use the trademark. Usually the licensing agreement calls for a payment of a fee in exchange for the right to use the protected symbol, name, or logo, in an approved fashion (Wong & Barr, 1991).

The popularity of licensed athletic merchandise is such in the 1990s that many schools and athletic programs, not only the very largest NCAA Division I institutions, can enjoy rather meaningful financial and public relations benefits from the securing of protected trademarks of logos, names, and symbols and subsequently licensing the use of such trademarks to responsible vendors and manufacturers.

A school or sports entity may retain and renew its trademark registration in perpetuity as long as the trademark remains in use, continues to be identified with the school or sports organization and is not abandoned. In the past, courts have ruled that abandonment has taken place when a trademark has lost all significance as an indication of its origin or when the holders of the trademark have failed to protect their exclusive use of the trademark.

There are several national organizations in the United States that assist athletic groups in marketing their logos and sport symbols as well as protecting these identifying indicia under the appropriate federal and state copyright and trademark laws. Some of these organizations are the Collegiate Licensing, Co., the University Licensing Program, and the Merchandising Rights Agency, LTP. (see Appendix H). Additionally, there are several professional organizations dealing with the licensing business such as the Association of Collegiate Licensing Administrators (ACLA) and the Licensing Industry Merchandisers' Association (LIMA).

Licensing of sport merchandise has become big business on the college and professional sports scene. In fact, sports licensing in 1965 was relegated to such items as baseball caps, towels, and some small NFL football statues (called ''Bobble Heads''). Former NFL Commissioner Pete Rozelle is credited with founding the billion-dollar industry of licensing and marketing NFL trademarks (Sports Marketing, 1990). In 1988 however, sales of such licensed merchandise by the major sports leagues and universities were estimated to be more than *$2.65 billion* (Special Report, 1988, p. 14).

A Success Story. When the San Jose Sharks led the National Hockey League in team sales of sports-related gear in its first year of play (1991–1992) with some $30 million in sales many were shocked. In fact the Sharks were considered to be at the same level as the Los Angeles Raiders, Chicago Bulls, and the Chicago White Sox as the most popular professional merchandise in 1992. How could a new team generate that much in sales of its merchandise and athletic gear in its initial year of league competition?

How this came about is a good example of careful marketing and research into what the public, the customers, wanted in the way of logos, mascots, team colors, and athletic apparel. Extensive market research was utilized in surveying segments of the public's preferences in terms of art work, color combinations, styles of jerseys, various team names, etc. A contest to select the team's name resulted in the selection of Sharks. Further research revealed that this name scored high with adults wanting to purchase products for children as well as with young people who were interested in a logo or mascot with which to identify within a sporting setting (Hiestand, 1992).

All of this research was instrumental in enabling the management of the Sharks to develop an excellent public relations campaign and a highly productive and profitable merchandise operation as well. It was the foresightedness, the planning and the research that made it all possible. The end result was a theme that was easily identifiable and products that were highly desirable. This translated into financial profit and publicity gains for the team.

In 1992 the Sharks' management operated a full-blown national mail-order operation and had also opened the first of what they hoped might be as many as six retail stores to help market and sell the team's merchandise. Naturally, national television exposure had been obtained via paid advertisements and through the team's activities on the ice (Hiestand, 1992).

Pricing of the Merchandise. A wise decision in the pricing of the merchandise is essential. Actually there are two goals in terms of marketing any merchandise. The first goal is to make a profit. That is certainly expected. However, the second motive or objective is to obtain an ever increasing exposure of one's program within the community and among the various constituencies. Thus, it does no good to price the merchandise so high that only a limited number of items are actually sold. It is better to sell a larger number of items at a lesser profit per item and gain additional exposure via the distribution of the various merchandise to a wider population. A 40% to 50% net profit on the sale of general sports merchandise is not unreasonable.

Ordering an Adequate Amount of Correct Merchandise on Time. The twin sins of any sport promoter dealing with merchandise include: (1) not being able to secure the correct items for sale from the wholesaler, and (2) ordering an incorrect number (either too many or too few) of the items. Failing to order on time is indeed an almost unforgivable cardinal sin for the sport merchandiser. One simply must be able to make a decision and execute a commitment in a timely manner for the purchase of whatever items the organization wishes to sell. There is no hard and fast rule when it comes to ordering merchandise, but individual vendors will be able to provide the sport organizers with rather specific time requirements for particular items. The basic concept is to plan well enough in advance of the date when the merchandise is needed, thus insuring that there is sufficient time to have the item(s) shipped.

Naturally, items that are in stock and are generic in nature can be provided in less time than items that must be custommade. For example, generic sweatshirts can be obtained in a much quicker turnaround time than can sweatshirts that must be screened or embroidered with the name and logo of the particular athletic team.

The number of items ordered rests upon a number of factors, including the best judgment as to how many can be moved (sold) once the items are on hand as well as whether or not any items will be presold. That is, will the money for a specific number of sweatshirts be collected prior to the placement of the order of sweatshirts? Or, will the athletic organization purchase the items and hold them in inventory while attempting to sell them? Preselling and collecting the money prior to placing the order greatly diminishes the risk of ordering an incorrect number of items or items with incorrect sizes.

▬Principle 123▬

Preselling merchandise greatly reduces the risk of leftover items and financial exposure.

Marketing Strategies for the Merchandise. How will the items to be sold be marketed? That is, how will they be advertised and sold? Will youngsters sell the items door-to-door? Can they be sold through the school store? Can they be sold at games? Will parents of the athletes be asked to purchase and/or sell such items? Who will train the sales force? Who will manage the record keeping of the sales operation? These questions must be answered in light of the resources and limitations that exist within a particular athletic organization.

Parking

Depending on the demand, charging for parking can prove to be a most effective way in generating a significant source of income for the athletic organization or group. Of course, there are some essential ingredients that must be present in order for parking to become a money maker. *First,* spectators must desire (need) to find a site to park their vehicles; *second,* there must be an absence of free parking spaces (lack of competition); and, *lastly,* there must be suitable and safe parking spaces (adequate supply) available that can be cordoned off and used as a parking lot(s) for an appropriate time and for an affordable price.

The use of available parking spaces for additional income is not the exclusive purview of big-time athletic programs. Rather, schools of all sizes at every level of competition can rent out parking spaces for any type of event that attracts large crowds and where available and free parking space is somewhat limited.

User Fees for Facilities and Services

Anytime an athletic operation has control of the indoor or outdoor facilities, in terms of scheduling the use of such facilities, and has the authority and responsibility for renting the facilities (gyms, pools, fields, weight rooms, etc.) to outside groups or entities for specific fees, there is potential for raising sizable monies for the athletic program. The athletic department might rent out part of the facility to any number of outside organizations such as church groups, other schools, professional, and semi-professional teams, square dance clubs, youth sport teams, etc. The list is literally endless.

The concept is simple. An outside entity pays for the use of the athletic facility while agreeing to provide an umbrella insurance policy, as well as adequate supervisory and security personnel coupled with an agreement to make repairs for any and all damage caused by the group.

Another way to make money through the use of facilities is to conduct sport camps or clinics, or to rent the athletic facilities to an individual or group who in turn would conduct such programs. There are various types of sport clinics, as well as summer athletic camps, that can be fairly easily organized and can be equally popular and profitable. In the latter category, any number of sports (baseball, ice hockey, football, soccer, basketball, swimming, etc.), as well as cheerleading camps and camps organized for the training of student athletic trainers, may be established and planned for the school's facility. Other types of camps that utilize sports facility can also be conducted. For example, weight loss camps and camps for older people have proven to be both successful and popular on college campuses.

In the area of sport camps and clinics as well as with the use or rental of facilities, there are two avenues that may be pursued. First, the athletic department can organize and run the camp or clinic itself. In this scenario, the organization does not have to pay for the use of a facility and can save the cost of what would have been the rental fee. The second option is to simply rent out the facility, in exchange for a straight fee or for a percentage of the *gross* profits, to an outside organization. In this scenario, it is the outside entity that will take responsibility for organizing and implementing the sport camp or clinic. In this second option, there is less risk involved to the organization owning the facility that is being rented out, but also less profit.

Vending Machines

Vending machines, those silent and inactive sales devices, can be a boon to the treasury of any sport organization. Usually placed in schools and within and around athletic facilities, vending machines provide a profit-sharing opportunity with the owner of the machines. The major questions to be answered revolve around the exact percentage of the gross sales that accrue to the athletic organization, the location of the machines, and the contents within the machines. There is usually no work involved for the school where the vending machines will be placed as all licenses and permits are obtained by the owners of the machines. The only responsibility of the school or the athletic team is to provide a specific location for the machines.

The contents of vending machines today can include almost anything. Items such as coffee, soups, milk, candy, soft drinks, sandwiches, ice cream, hot chocolate, pastry, gum, and fruit are all popular items that can be sold through the vending machines. Of course, items such as cigarettes, which can also be sold via such machines, must be evaluated very carefully in terms of appropriateness within an athletic or educational atmosphere or arena. Even including candy and other snack foods in vending machines can come under criticism and can result in negative publicity for the school or the athletic organization within some communities.

Luxury Box Seating

Typically, luxury box seating is thought of as being the exclusive property of professional athletic teams with their large stadiums and sports complexes. However, the idea of so-called luxury or preferred seating arrangements can be utilized by many schools and athletic programs. The concept is simple. Special seating, on a season long basis, is set aside for the exclusive use of patrons willing to pay for the privilege of having access to strategic seating (super view of the athletic action) and the "extras" or special amenities that often accompany the executive or luxury seating accommodations, such as the availability of special foods and drinks as well as privacy. Renting the use of these executive or luxury seating accommodations can result in significant income to the sponsoring organization.

Parking Condos

A more recent phenomenon in terms of generating income is the use of so-called parking condos. Adjacent to large stadiums or field houses are built two-story, covered structures utilized to provide both safe and convenient parking for vehicles (cars, vans, and buses) as well as facilities for meals and relaxation before, during, and after athletic contests. Essentially, these structures, which might be owned privately or by the school itself, provide opportunities for rather sophisticated tailgate parties and secure parking of vehicles by fans willing to rent such facilities on a single season or multiple season basis.

Such parking condos may be rented for $800 to $1,200 per season. Of course, the attraction of the parking condos rests not only in the availability of exclusive, convenient, and secure parking for individual's vehicles but also in the fact that the two story structure contains so-called party rooms that the "owners" of the parking condos can utilize on game day for elaborate pregame and postgame gatherings for either intimate personal get-togethers or for business gatherings. Of course, those who have leased the condos may take advantage of the party facility and the parking space throughout the calendar year (Regan, 1992).

References

✔Berg, R. (1989, September). The money game. *Athletic Business,* pp. 28, 30–34, 36, 38, 40.

Bigelow, C. (1989, January). Spicing up your concession profits. *Athletic Business,* pp. 42–45.

Brewington, P. (1989, September 1). TV's focus: What's good in prep sports. *USA Today,* p. 2–C.

Briggs, J., Jr. & Duffy, J. (1987). *The official soccer fund-raiser's guide.* North Palm Beach, Florida: Soccer Industry Council of America.

Bring on the sponsor. (1989, May). *Athletic Business,* pp. 8–10.

✔Brooks, C. (1990, October). Sponsorship: Strictly business. *Athletic Business,* pp. 59–62.

Cohen, A. (1991, May). Concessions come of age. *Athletic Business,* pp. 61, 62, 64.

Cohen, A. (1992, January). Cooking up concessions. *Athletic Business,* pp. 35–36, 38.

Corporate sponsors in Alaska, Minnesota. (1990, October). *Athletic Director,* p. 12.

Couzens, G. S. (1990, January). Doctor's orders. *SportsTravel. 2* (1), 53–58.

Drotning, P. (1981). *500 ways for small charities to raise money.* Hartsdale, New York: Public Service Materials Center, Inc.

Ferguson, M. (ed.). (1990, September). Ringing up concessions. *Athletic Business,* pp. 63–66.

Ferguson, M. (ed). (1990, October). Sports Marketing. *Athletic Business,* p. 26.

Friedman, A., (ed.). (1989). Consumers indicate discounted tickets (1989, March). *Team Marketing Report,* p. 5.

✔Goldberg, M. (1991). Brought to you by. *College Athletic Magazine (CAM). III* (3), 4–5.

✔Guttman, M. (1992, March 16). It pays to be in-kind. *Sports Illustrated.* special advertising section.

Herzog, B. Snack to the future. (1990). *College Athletic Magazine* (CAM), *II* (5), 33–36.

Hiestand, M. (1992, January 23). Research helps Sharks get sizable bite of gear sales. *USA Today.* p. 9–C.

Irwin, R. (1991). A license to profit. *College Athletic Magazine* (CAM). *III* (1), 18–21.

Irwin, R. and Stotlar, D. (1991). Putting up the numbers. *College Athletic Management* (CAM), *III* (5), 5.

Jackson. B. (1988, September). An event marketing primer—Part II. *Athletic Business,* pp. 18–19.

Krupa, G. (1988, April 1). Promise and pitfalls of sponsorship. *Sports Inc.,* pp. 19–21.

Kuniholm, R. (1990, January). Direct mail that delivers: How to write effective fund-raising letters. *Case Currents,* 31–35.

Lamphear, M. P. & Frankel, E. (1990). Filling the seats. *College Athletic Management* (CAM), *II* (3), 27–29.

McDermott-Griggs, S. & Card, J. (1992). Creating a successful fund-raising letter. *Journal of Physical Education, Recreation and Dance, 63* (1), 57–59.

Moore, M. & McGarey, E. (1986, August). No money down—marketing athletics on a limited budget. *Athletic Business,* pp. 64–67.

The Nation's Leading Youth Fund-raising Company. (1990). Ridgefield, CT: Reader's Digest.

Palmisano, M. (1988, October). Merchandising can mean added revenue for you. *Athletic Purchasing & Facility,* pp. 28–31.

Parkhouse, B. (ed.). (1991). *The management of sport—Its foundation and application.* St. Louis, Missouri: Mosby Year Book.

Regan, T. H. (1992, May). *Parking Condos.* Unpublished Manuscript. Columbia, S.C.: University of South Carolina, Department of Sport Administration.

Revenue opportunities—corporate sponsorships, licensing, merchandising and broadcasting. (1991, January/February). *Athletic Director,* pp. 14, 27.

Ritrievi, C. (1989, October). Dialing for Donors. *College Athletic Management* (*CAM*), *I* (10), 56–57.

Schmader, S. (1989, May). The elusive event pricing formula. *Athletic Business,* p. 18.

Special report. (1989, January 9). *Sports Inc.,* pp. 27–28.

Special report: Licensing. (1988, December 5), *Sports Inc.,* pp. 6–7, 14.

Sports Marketing (sort of). (1990, August). *Athletic Business,* pp. 13.

Stier, Jr., W. F. (1990, August). ADs walk fine line on promotions. *Athletic Administration,* pp. 18–19, 21.

Stotlar, D. K. and Johnson, D. A. (1989, September). Stadium ads get a boost. *Athletic Business,* pp. 49–51.

USA Today, (1992, January 1). p. 1–C.

Wegs, M. (1990, April). Corporate Sponsors—A New Athletic Partnership Unfolds. *Athletic Director,* pp. 18–21, 38.

Wegs, M. (1990, April). Successful capital campaigns. *Athletic Director,* pp. 22–23, 25.

White, J. (1991). The direct route. *College Athletic Management* (CAM). *III* (1), 40–43.

Wong, G. M. & Barr, C. (1991, June). Sports licensing gets a boost from Carolina case. *Athletic Business,* pp. 18, 21.

Yiannakis, A. and Braunstein, S. (1983). *The Complete guide to successful fund-raising.* North Palm Beach: American Sports Education Institute.

Tailgating at a Mississippi State University baseball game. (Courtesy of Mississippi State University)

Special Fund-Raising Projects, Promotional Tactics, and Ideas

10

A variety of promotional activities and special events may be planned and implemented to raise money for athletics, to promote a sport program, to increase attendance, to improve an image, and to provide recognition for team members, coaches, boosters, and sponsors. The critical factor is to find what is acceptable within the community and what will generate sufficient funds in light of the expenditure of resources (downside risks). Naturally, the same caveat regarding saturation of the community with an excess amount of activities holds true for school-sponsored events, just as it does for the door-to-door sales projects cited earlier.

While many activities involve little time and money, others involve significant amounts of both. Additionally, many of the ideas and projects presented in this chapter have the potential for significant success, both in terms of generating monies *and* in promoting individual sport activities. However, the actual benefits, including revenue generated, can vary for each of these projects or activities depending on individual circumstances.

There are five questions any person who is contemplating becoming involved in raising money for a sports program must be able to answer prior to actually initiating a project. The answers to these five questions will go a long way in determining whether the fund-raising effort is justified, as well as aiding those involved in the shaping of the campaign or project itself, so as to increase the likelihood of eventual success. These questions include:

1. What is the complexity (degree of difficulty) of the project? Is it very simple or complex?
2. What expenditure of effort and what resources will be necessary to complete the project?
3. How much time involvement is at stake?
4. What is the degree of exposure, that is, what are downside risks of the effort(s)?
5. What are the potential positive consequences or the gain in terms of money, other resources, and positive public relations?

▰Principle 124▰

Combine (piggyback) fund-raising and promotional events with other attractive and popular activities.

The concept of combining a fund-raising or promotional event with another activity is a well accepted principle. An example is piggybacking the date and timing of a reverse raffle to coincide with an evening of viewing the televised national (NCAA Division I) basketball championship game on a big screen television. This enables the organizers of the reverse raffle to use the attractiveness and to tap the popularity of the basketball championship game so that the desirability of the reverse raffle (held just prior to the game and during half-time) would be enhanced. See chapter 11 for details on organizing a successful reverse raffle.

Another example of the piggyback technique is obtaining permission from the electric company (or gas company or refuse company) to be allowed to insert advertisement or promotional materials about one's sports program in the monthly statements from the business or corporation. This piggyback approach enables almost every household to receive the mailing containing the sports promotional materials with little effort or cost to the sports program. The only cost to the sport entity is the expense for the printing of the promotional materials, and frequently even that can be absorbed by the business making the actual mailing.

A third example of the piggybacking concept involves combining two separate promotional and fund-raising projects. For example, the combining of an *auction* with a *craft show*, both held within the same facility and at the same time. In this attempt, the principle of synergism comes into play. That is, the attractiveness of both activities is greater than either single activity standing alone. See chapter 11 for details on the combination craft/auction concept.

On the following pages is a listing and description of some of the more popular and successful fund-raising and promotional ideas that are applicable for the sport scene (see fig. 10.1). Most of these activities, with slight adaptations, are applicable at almost any sport level. For convenience sake, these fund-raising and promotional ideas and projects included within this section have been arbitrarily classified within the following five categories:

1. Sales
2. Gambling and contests of chance with prizes
3. Specific fund-raising and promotional projects
4. Game day and half-time activities
5. Banquets and luncheon activities

Sales

The sale of any number of items and services is a traditional means of attempting to raise monies for sport purposes. *Almost anything* can be sold in almost any setting. Items such as books, plants, pizzas, candles, light bulbs, seasonal candy, bakery items, trash bags, household cleaners, flowers, calendars, and coupon books are just a few of the numerous *items* that can be sold by door-to-door or group sales. Sales of these and other items are also possible while sitting in a mall, on a sidewalk, or in a department store. Sales may be consummated prior to, during, and/or after athletic contests or special events, during school hours, etc.

Many of the strategies involving the *sale of items or services* can be linked with other *special projects, game day and half-time activities,* as well as with *banquet and*

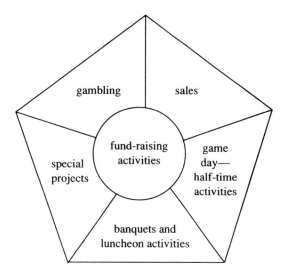

luncheon-type activities. Sales can be affiliated with special holidays, such as Valentine's Day, Christmas, Thanksgiving, Easter, and the 4th of July. Space itself for advertising may be sold within the sport facility, as well as within the sport publications and over the airways during, before, and following athletic contests. Additional items that can be marketed and sold include, but are certainly not limited to, sales of souvenir sport publications, team programs, sport booklets, team photos, as well as various sport merchandise. For detailed coverage of the area of *merchandise* and *product sales*, refer to chapter 9.

Gambling and Contests of Chance with Prizes

The two major stumbling blocks to successfully employing games of chance as a means for generating additional funds for a sports program rests upon (1) local and statewide legal restrictions and (2) the local mores of the community that determines acceptable levels of behavior by organizations such as sports programs. If these two obstacles can be overcome, there are several very effective fund-raising projects based on games of chance. Some of the more productive contests of chance are outlined below.

50/50 Drawing. Frequently utilized at sport contests or gatherings, the 50/50 drawing is very simple, takes little effort or time, and has a downside risk of zero. Specifically, this technique involves the selling of tickets (for example, $1.00). Half of all of the monies raised from the sale of tickets is given away via a drawing of some type with the remaining half of the money reverting to the coffers of the athletic program. If a single drawing would result in some 500 tickets being sold, the actual amount of money given away will be $250 (either to a single winner or split among multiple recipients), with the remaining $250 going to the sports program.

Over a number of games throughout a season, this can be a sizable amount of money for athletics. Additionally, the excitement of the drawing and the possibility of positive public relations and publicity enhances the effectiveness of this specific project. Winners can be publicized in the local paper or in school or athletic publications, as well as via the public address system at subsequent drawings.

Raffle. A raffle is a lottery in which a number of individuals purchase chances to win a prize or prizes. Anything that can be sold can be raffled—wood, automobiles, trips, wine and cheese at Christmas, cash, savings bonds, free weekends at a hotel, items of food (beef, turkeys), game balls, athletic equipment, vehicles, etc.

The raffle project can be either very simple or very complex, depending upon the structure of the raffle itself. Usually the raffle is time consuming in its organization and planning respects and has significant downside risks in terms of effort expended and the negative consequences of failure. Many raffles are organized so that the actual raffle activity takes place with another type of activity (piggyback), either a dinner or luncheon. Usually, the items to be raffled off, as well as other resources needed for the raffle, will be donated by various contributors. However, this necessitates that these potential contributors be contacted and donations be successfully solicited in a timely fashion.

In many situations in which money is part of the raffle winnings, the money to be given away is generated from the sale of raffle tickets. Thus a risk associated with this type of raffle is the need to sell a sufficient number of tickets to cover the expenses of the raffle itself, including any cash awards to be distributed. This means the use of a suitable sales force and adequate publicity for the raffle.

Finally, the downside risk is notable in that the failure of the raffle project not only means the loss of time and effort spent on the project but also creates negative publicity toward the sponsoring organization and upon the sports program itself. The general public takes due notice of any such failure. Hence, it is important that such projects become successful. It would be better not to have attempted the raffle than to try to pull it off only to fall on one's face, in full view of the public and various sport constituencies (Briggs and Duffy, 1987).

Reverse Raffle. The reverse raffle is a variation of the time-proven raffle project, in which the winning tickets pulled from the so-called bowl are those pulled last, in reverse order of the regular raffle. In a reverse raffle, with some 200 tickets sold and with five prizes the first 195 tickets pulled would receive nothing. The 196th ticket would receive the 5th prize, the 197th ticket pulled would receive the 4th prize, the 198th ticket would earn the 3rd prize, the 199th ticket garners the 2nd prize, while the GRAND PRIZE would be reserved for the 200th or last ticket pulled.

The advantage of the reverse raffle, in addition to its uniqueness, is that the excitement generated through the awarding of prizes in reverse order is significant. Every ticket purchaser will have his/her ticket actually pulled. When the number of tickets remaining becomes smaller and smaller there tends to be greater excitement among all in attendance. Finally, when there are just a handful of tickets remaining, all eyes are on the bowl and the final drawing of the winning tickets. Contrast this to the regular raffle in which the 5 winners are declared after the first five tickets are pulled.

The reverse raffle works best when there are 200 or less tickets to be selected from the bowl. With a potential of some 5000 winning tickets, it would be foolish to attempt a reverse raffle. There would not be sufficient time to pull all 4999 tickets before reaching the grand prize—the people in the audience would have long ago fallen asleep or left for home.

Pseudo Give-A-Way. This contest is ostensibly a raffle but without the actual selling of tickets. Rather the item to be given away will be given to the holder of a ticket stub sometime during the contest, most preferably at half-time. There is nothing for the potential winner to buy other than a ticket to the athletic contest. Usually, the items to be given away are donated for this purpose. Naturally, suitable publicity for the event and appropriate credit to the individual or organization responsible for donating the item or items is required. In some states and communities, this pseudo give-a-way falls under the gambling classification and must be treated as such by meeting all of the requirements, including record keeping and truth-in-advertising regulations.

Lottery/Sweepstakes and Sport Pools. Lotteries and sport pools provide opportunities to generate both small and large sums of money depending upon the structure of the lottery or sport pool, as well as upon the successful efforts of the marketing team behind such a program. Frequently, the determination of winners for lotteries or sweepstakes of sports programs are the actual numbers of state lottery winners (either in one's own state or in an adjacent state). However, any method of selecting numbers, which will be determined in the future, will suffice. Sport pools, those associated with professional contests, are most popular during the championship contests—the Super Bowl, the World Series, the Stanley Cup Finals, the NBA Championship, etc. Again, the use of sport pools, like the lottery or sweepstakes, can result in financial gain by the amateur sport program with a minimum of risk, save the effort to sell tickets for the pool or the lottery.

Casino Nights. The so-called casino nights are modeled after the casinos in Las Vegas and Atlantic City. Casino nights provide opportunities for a wide array of gambling games from *craps* to *black jack* to *roulette* to *poker* to *baccarat* to *backgammon,* etc. Dealers can be athletic staff, as well as members of the boosters organizations, who have undergone an indoctrination in terms of the various rules and regulations of various games. The gambling is not conducted with actual cash. Rather, cash is exchanged at the ''bank'' for play money, which in turn is used at the various gambling tables. Prizes, which are donated to the charitable event, may be exchanged at the end of the evening's festivities with the play money won at the various gambling tables. Whether a cover charge is in effect or not is up to the organizers of the event.

Sometimes a professional card manipulator/teacher can be hired to provide both demonstrations and lessons to participants on how to play the different gambling games and to perform various card tricks. This lends an atmosphere of professionalism to the evening's festivities and enables all in attendance to have an authoritarian source to answer any questions that may arise. Of course, such an experience is also great entertainment.

Bingo. One of the most popular games of chance in the United States and Canada today, bingo is a game in which players place markers on a card with a pattern of numbered squares as the numbers are drawn and subsequently announced by the caller. This game has significant potential for both public relations and monetary benefits accruing to the sports program on a recurring or isolated basis. Whether the bingo games are organized and sponsored exclusively by the sport organization or are co-sponsored by another organization, the potential for significant profits are very real. Naturally, local and state laws must be adhered to with appropriate licenses or permits obtained. One potential problem might be the competition provided by various church groups and professional bingo organizations in some communities. A company that claims to be the *largest distributor* in North America of bingo and other fund-raising supplies, equipment, and related merchandise is Bazaar & Novelty, Toronto, Canada.

▬Principle 125▬

When planning special promotional and fund-raising events, take advantage of the numerous holidays and/or special school events for special themes.

National holidays (Christmas, New Year's Eve, Halloween, President's Day, Thanksgiving, Independence Day, Labor Day, Memorial Day, Valentine's Day, Easter), seasonal activities, and special school events, such as Homecoming Weekend, Midnight Merry Madness, Alumni Day, Parents Day, etc., provide natural opportunities for special promotional and fund-raising events. Such athletic projects as a Christmas tournament, Octoberfest, Winter Sports Special, Spring or Fall Golf Outing, Fall Homecoming Weekend, etc., lend themselves to being repeated on an annual basis coinciding with the annual holiday, season, or special event. Of course, repeated fund-raising events are easier to implement in succeeding years and tend to become more successful as they are repeated annually.

▬Principle 126▬

Breakdown tasks into their basic components—Assign tasks to individuals on the basis of both interest and ability.

Whenever an organization is attempting to plan and implement an involved fund-raising or promotional project, there is always a need for a well-thought-out division of labor among the people working the event. Generally speaking, there is a need to address specifically a number of different areas or tasks. The responsibility for these areas may fall to one individual or may be assigned to committees. The point is that careful thought needs to be given, in most cases, to each of these categories whenever a fund-raising project is being planned.

A typical administrative or organizational structure includes an overall *project chairperson* for the fund-raising event, whose responsibility it is to coordinate and supervise the entire operation and to serve as the motivating force, the spark plug for the event. Working with the project chairperson might be any number of committees, each with a chairperson, assigned to address a separate and distinct aspect of the project. Again, it is the responsibility of the overall project chairperson to coordinate the efforts of all of the various committee chairpersons and their specific committee members.

Some fund-raising efforts will necessitate, merely by the very nature of the activities involved, more committees than others. However the work or tasks are assigned, it is important to break down the work to be done in an organized and logical fashion, keeping in mind the talents and time available from the individuals who will actually be doing the work.

Remembering the age-old principle that it is easier said than done, the **objective** is to assign tasks to actual doers, individuals who are interested in **completing** assigned tasks successfully, on time, rather than assigning tasks to people **who mean** well but who are unable to produce when called upon. Possible breakdown **of** specific responsibilities for fund-raising projects by individual committees include:

1. Site selection
2. Theme or topic
3. Publicity and promotion
4. Ticket, program, and invitation
5. Exhibitor or participant solicitation
6. Equipment and supplies
7. Finance
8. Decoration
9. Refreshments and hospitality
10. Trouble shooting (on-site)
11. Prize or gift
12. Security
13. Cleanup
14. Post event roundup and assessment

Specific Fund-Raising and Promotional Projects

The following are special activities that are social, recreational, educational, or athletic in nature and are planned and implemented for the purpose of raising funds and/or promoting the sports program.

1. **Athletic contests** scheduled against a variety of opponents, such as varsity against alumni or against students, media versus athletic staff, faculty versus general students, members of various community organizations versus one another, and All-Star games are just a few of the possible match-ups that comprise marketable contests and generate sizable gate receipts. These contests may be held as ''stand-alone'' events or may be associated with a regular sporting contest by serving as a preliminary game to a varsity or regular season sport event. Income can result from a charge for spectator admission as well as entrance fees for teams. Also, sale of refreshments and souvenirs can contribute significantly to the fund-raising aspects of this activity.

2. **Coaches clinics and workshops** dealing with coaching strategies for any number of sports may be sponsored by the booster group or by the sport organization itself, with the profits going toward the athletic program.

3. **Youth sport camps or clinics** may be very attractive and profitable, especially if the needed facilities (practice facilities and dormitory space) may be secured without costing the sponsoring organization an arm and a leg. Cheerleading camps and athletic training (sports medicine) clinics are also a possibility. In fact, any type of sport related camp or clinic can be feasible if there is (a) a demonstrated need for such a camp, (b) available facilities at

an affordable cost, and (c) capable and available staff willing to work at the camp or clinic.

4. **Fun nights** are all-night (12 to 24 hours) gatherings staged within the athletic facilities and that are supervised by school or athletic staff. During the hours of the Fun Night, numerous physical activities, games, and contests are played by the participants who have paid a sum to the athletic program for the opportunity to partake in the Fun Night.

5. **Team and individual athlete photos** may be obtained on a donated or reduced cost basis and displayed in a prominent place within the school, as well as sold to parents and friends of athletes.

6. **Flea markets and consignment sales** involve resale of donated merchandise or items placed on consignment. These sales are frequently held in conjunction with a regular athletic event or standing alone as an event in itself. The profit is generated through the sale of the donated items or from a percentage of the sales price in the situation involving items left on consignment.

7. **Car washes** are a perennial fund-raising project and merely require access to water, a high traffic location, and many, many individuals willing to use elbow grease to wash (and perhaps wax as well) all sorts of vehicles.

8. **Free car washes** are a variation in that the car washes are *FREE* and all the driver has to do is simply drive in and have the car washed without any charge whatsoever. The profit comes from the advanced planning in which the organizers of the *free car wash* obtain pledges, ranging from 10¢ to $1.00 *per athlete, per car washed.*

   With 20 to 40 youngsters soliciting such pledges, it doesn't take long for a sizable amount of money to be generated, as long as the cars keep driving up for the *free car wash*. An example will suffice. Assuming that each of 30 athletes have a pledge of 20¢ for each car washed; each car that drives through the wash generates $6.00 in revenue. If 100 to 200 cars are washed on a Saturday afternoon (which is not unthinkable when the car wash is free), the profit potential can be in the neighborhood of $600 to $1,200. Not too bad for a Saturday afternoon.

9. **Invitational tournaments sponsored by businesses and corporations,** such as Tip-Off Tournaments or Christmas Tournaments, have major fund-raising potential. Not only can the costs of the tournament be totally or partially underwritten, thus saving the athletic program the need to spend money from its own coffers, but the tournament sponsored by an outside entity can also generate greater gate receipts. There is also the potential for additional financial contributions from the sponsoring businesses and corporations in terms of actual cash or in terms of equipment and supplies for the sport program.

10. **Novelty athletic events** involving specialized programs can have special appeal to the general public. Two examples are the *Harlem Globetrotters in basketball* and the *King and His Court in softball.* The sponsorship of these groups as special fund-raising events for the athletic program can generate significant revenue, over and above expenses, for the sport program as well as

extensive public relations. However, the risk of bringing such groups to the community is high since there is always the danger of insufficient gate receipts to offset the actual cost of putting the program on. This is why it is frequently necessary to obtain a corporate or business partner who will underwrite the expenses of the project, thus protecting the athletic program from any downside risk in terms of financial disaster.

11. **Craft and hobby shows or sales** can be very popular annual or one-time fund-raising projects. With proper advertisement and a suitable high traffic location, such a project as a craft and hobby show/sale can attract a large number of interested participants, both those who display their craft and hobby work (leather work, wood carvings, pottery, jewelry, woven items, etc.), as well as potential purchasers and browsers.

    The sports promoter first must obtain a suitable site, which could be either indoor or outdoor. The site might be inside a gymnasium, ice arena, or track facility. An ideal outdoor site might be a vacant car dealer's lot or adjacent field. Money can be generated in two ways. First, the site is rented ($50 per 10' by 10' stall) to the craft and hobby exhibitors who desire to display their wares for sale. The second source of income is derived from those who attend the show/sale. The one or two-day event attracts both would-be purchasers as well as browsers who may be charged a nominal admission fee of 50¢ to 75¢ per person.

    The net result is that there are two sources of income, from rental spaces *and* from admissions. If there are 100 exhibitors ($5,000 profit) and around 1,000 paid admissions ($500 profit), the sport program stands to reap sizable profits with a minimum of work. The two keys, of course, are (1) locating and attracting a sufficiently large number of exhibitors and (2) having an attraction that would entice a large number of admissions to see the craft and hobby show/sale.

12. **Rummage, white elephant, or garage sales** can be organized in a similar fashion to the craft and hobby shows, in that donated items are offered for sale, with suitable advance advertisement, in a high traffic location. The major distinction, however, is that the items for sale have all been donated by individuals and organizations rather than being on consignment. There can be extensive ''people'' work involved in the solicitation of donated items, as well as in the collection, storage, and preparation of such items for sale. As with the craft and hobby shows, a suitable location and adequate advertisements are absolute essentials.

13. Other types of specific **shows** and **exhibitions,** such as art shows and antique shows, have potential for significant income if sufficient interest can be created on behalf of both exhibitors and potential viewers or purchasers. For this type of show or exhibition there is a need for (1) appropriate advertisement, (2) suitable location, (3) adequate number of quality exhibitors capable of attracting, and (4) a sufficiently large number of people to go through the so-called turnstiles, all of paramount importance in determining the success or failure of such a fund-raising project.

14. **Bazaars, festivals, fairs,** and **carnivals** have all been utilized as successful fund-raising projects for sports programs. Potential profits are generated from the booth fees, entrance fees (if any), and concession sales. Usually **bazaars** are associated with a variety of food items tastefully displayed in booths, as well as a variety of entertainment, such as **music,** and **exhibitions. Festivals** are frequently organized around a particular season in which the event will be implemented or around national holidays, such as Summerfest, Octoberfest, Springfest, and Winterfest. **Fairs** and **carnivals** often involve music, entertainment, games of chance, amusement rides (merry-go-round, ferris wheel), and animal rides. To minimize the downside risk, the tactic of cosponsoring the event with various service clubs or a local fire department or other group while contracting with a professional carnival operator is often wise.

    One of the dangers of sponsoring or cosponsoring such an event is the legal liability and insurance questions. Careful scrutiny of this area with an attorney is highly recommended. However, the carnival operation is as close to a turn-key project as one can get, once a site is located and advertisement plans are confirmed. The remaining task is to agree to the content of the contract for the carnival or fair including the stipulation as to the split of the profits and any additional costs to be borne by the sponsoring agent(s). It is the professional carnival operator who has the responsibility of actually running the carnival or fair attractions. But, the sponsoring sport entity also shares in the responsibility for seeing to it that the event is adequately planned and safely conducted.

15. **Rodeos** are similar to fairs and carnivals in that professional organizers of such events may be secured to conduct the rodeo under the auspices of a sponsoring organization, such as a local athletic program or educational entity. Again, site selection, insurance coverage, advertisement, determination of split of the proceeds, and other areas of exposure for the sport program must be predetermined. However, the professionalism of the actual rodeo is the responsibility of the professional rodeo organizers in whose interest it is to provide a most attractive festivity so that large numbers of paying viewers will be in attendance.

16. **Donkey baseball** is played where all players, except the pitcher and catcher, play the game sitting on donkeys. This is crowd-pleasing entertainment. Two of the leading donkey ball organizations that account for the majority of the donkey baseball contests staged within the United States, are the Buckeye Donkey Ball company and the Crosby Donkey Ball group. See Appendix H for fund-raising-related organizations.

    The sponsoring organization and the donkey ball company may enter into a percentage agreement of the gate receipts, or it is possible to book the touring group for a flat fee. The sport of basketball can also be adapted to the donkey concept and has proven very popular with audiences of all ages. The profit to the sports organization hinges upon attracting a large enough audience (sufficient gate receipts) to the exhibition which will, in turn, provide sizable gate receipts. It is essential that sufficient monies be raised to pay expenses incurred with the cost of the visiting donkey ball organization and the administrative set-up costs, and, of course, still leave enough left over for the profit column that goes to the hometown sport treasury.

17. **Celebrity golf tournaments** as well as **regular golf tournaments** are traditional spring fund-raising events. It seems that almost every athletic department in the country offers some type of golf tournament, either in the spring, summer, or fall months.

    Typically, the golf tournaments revolve around two central themes. The first is the regular golf tournament in which participants are invited, for a fee, to golf in the athletic program's annual golf outing and to enjoy a subsequent barbecue or dinner that may or may not involve some type of distribution of awards. Members of the athletic staff, as well as athletes and members of the community, would all be invited to participate as golfers in the tournament and for the festivities that follow.

    The second version of the golf tournament involves a fee to play in a foursome with a celebrity. The definition of a ''celebrity'' is left up to the organizers of the golfing event. In some cases the celebrities may be coaches or athletic administrators. In other situations, the celebrity might be a famous golfer, famous athlete or political figure or a noteworthy business person. If the field of golfers is highly visible, admission tickets may be appropriate. In addition, the ''holes,'' as well as the ''tees,'' may be ''sold'' to individuals or corporate sponsorships for $100 to $500, whatever the market will bear. This means allowing the purchasers to have a sign next to the green or tee advertising the fact that the contributor has made a donation to the athletic program by ''purchasing'' the tee or green. Obtaining corporate or business sponsorship to partially help or fully underwrite the cost of the golf outing can greatly enhance the potential profit flowing to the athletic program. The type of assistance can vary but usually involves payment of green fees, carts, tournament refreshments, and prizes or awards, as well as the following banquet or dinner.

18. **Card and board games** such as chess, checkers, backgammon, as well as card games such as bridge, canasta, and pinochle, can be very popular components of a fund-raising project when combined with other activities. This is especially true when these activities can be implemented as a family affair including some games for children. Profits can be realized through the sale of refreshments, as well as admission (ticket) fees.

19. **Excursions** to sporting events or places of interest for sightseeing experiences or shopping sprees can be perennial fund-raising successes. Typically, buses are hired to take individuals to away sites for either sight-seeing purposes or combined with seeing sporting events. For example, a local youth football organization might organize a bus trip to a National Football League city to see an NFL football game, coupled with several hours of sight-seeing in the ''big city.''

    Revenue generated for the youth sports program would be the profit generated from the difference between the cost of the bus and game tickets and what the travelers are actually charged. Another variation might be to organize excursions to a team's own away contests involving boosters and fans in a variety of activities, in addition to the actual game. Such experiences might include a side trip to a popular amusement, sight-seeing, or shopping site and/or a tailgate party prior to or following the game.

20. **House tours** or **garden tours** of stately homes in the nearby geographical area are low-risk projects. Once permission is obtained from the owners of the homes or gardens the organization wishes to include on its tour, it is imperative that adequate insurance coverage is obtained, as well as special plans for special decorations, clean-up, and the staffing of the house during open hours. Of course, planning for the worst-case scenario, one must anticipate that it might rain and take suitable protective steps to provide for covering the floors and rugs, etc. Also, contacting the neighbors in terms of securing adequate parking space is a must. One method of alleviating the parking congestion that might develop is to have a central parking site (maybe at the school or the athletic facility) and then provide bus or van transportation from the parking area to the various homes and gardens. The profit comes from the sale (contributions) of tickets that are marketed well in advance.

21. **Fashion Shows** have proven to be popular and profitable annual or biannual events in many communities. With donated garments and volunteer models, fashion shows become profitable through modest admission fees coupled with requests for donations. A wide variety of fashion shows can be staged. Some possibilities include (a) a wedding fashion show, (b) children's fashion show, (c) gents fashion show, (d) 1800s fashion show, or (e) western fashion show.

22. Staging **professional special sporting events** such as "professional" wrestling matches or sponsoring a full contact karate tournament can result in big money profits provided that there exists drawing power for sufficient spectators. Usually the visiting group takes a percentage of the gross income. It is the responsibility of the sponsoring athletic organization to assume the responsibility of guaranteeing a minimum dollar amount of income to the visiting group. Thus, there is a real risk should the spectator turnout be less than expected and there is insufficient income to cover the expenses guaranteed. On the other hand, the popularity of such groups such as these frequently insure a sell-out situation given adequate promotional, marketing, and advertising efforts on behalf of the local sponsoring entity.

23. Establishing "**haunted houses**" for Halloween involves construction work to convert a suitable vacant structure into a scary (but safe) "haunted house" for which a modest admission charge is established. For a period of time prior to Halloween, such a site can be very productive in generating significant income for the sponsoring sports organization. Success can be assured with an abundance of qualified and interested volunteers to build the structure and take it down again following Halloween, adequate supervision of the facility during open hours, and adequate advertising and publicity.

24. Building a **Christmas and Santa Claus workshop** for children is similar to the "haunted house" concept explained above. In this case, the theme around which the structure is built is Christmas and the season of giving. Again,

admission charges, coupled with requests for donations, can result not only in a successful fund-raiser but also go a long way to create a positive image for the sports program.

25. **Ghost dinners** are an intriguing concept. In this situation, invitations for a ''dinner'' are sent to selected individuals specifying a certain date, time, place of the *make-believe, ghost dinner* as well as the amount of contribution requested. *In reality there is no actual dinner,* and the prospective donors are apprised of that fact during the initial communication attempt. Rather, the money is collected from the donor/purchaser as if the dinner was indeed going to be held. In this approach, there is literally no work in terms of actually conducting the dinner but merely the task of communicating (written and verbal) with prospective donors and soliciting the money. Almost all the monies generated becomes profit accruing to the sports program.

26. A similar concept to ghost dinners is the **ghost (stay-at-home)** event, in which an invitation is sent for a predetermined special event (whether it be musical, sporting, political, educational, drama, etc.) asking the recipients to contribute/donate *what it would have cost them* to attend (sitter, parking, dinner, gas, etc.) the specific event. In marketing this type of ghost event the question is asked, ''Why spend the time and effort to actually attend the event?'' Rather, please donate the money to the sports organization and stay home. Again, the downside risk to the soliciting athletic organization is almost nil.

27. **Dances,** based on unusual and fun themes, can be very successful in providing for great entertainment, as well as financial benefits to the sponsoring organization. Possible themes include the ''Big Band Era,'' the ''Roaring Twenties,'' the 60s Dance Marathon,'' the ''50s Rock and Roll,'' ''Country and Western,'' as well as a host of others. Adequate advertisement and publicity, coupled with a suitable site and a popular theme, can generate significant interest on behalf of the general public, not to mention the fans and supporters of the sports program. Admission fees and concessions form the basis of the income generated for the sports program.

28. **Mall promotions** provide excellent opportunities to get the message of the sport organization before the general public. The objective is to secure permission from a manager of a mall to allow a display table to be set up within the mall over a weekend or on a Saturday and/or Sunday afternoon. The mall traffic can be significant over a weekend, providing the sport program with potential exposure to some thousands and thousands of people, if not tens of thousands. The display table should be artfully designed with professionally created graphics. There should be provision to distribute various publications publicizing the athletic program, its purposes, and its scope of operations. Additionally, an automatic slide carousel (with or without sound) showing slides of the team in action can be an eye-attracting component of the total display. Finally, means should be available for collecting names, addresses, and phone numbers of those interested in the program.

29. Combining major **televised athletic events,** such as the Super Bowl, NCAA Basketball Championship, the Kentucky Derby, the Indy 500, various boxing spectacles, and the World Series with a local sport organization's fund-raising project, has proven successful in many, many instances. Utilizing a wide-screen television or multiple televisions with which to watch the national sporting event in combination with a fund-raising project revolving around either a luncheon or dinner, enables the sport entity to draw upon the natural appeal of the national athletic event being televised.

30. The "**selling**" **of part of the sport facility.** This make-believe sale of part of the sport facility can be organized around several variations. The general concept, however, is to "sell" a piece of the facility, a field or a building, to local fans and boosters. The actual item to be "sold" might be a square inch of the football field or part of the field house. Of course, there is no actual sale, but the pseudo sale nevertheless can be enticing to the general public and sport fans if publicized and marketed in an appropriate manner. To "authenticate" the sale of the square inch of a football, softball, or baseball field or a segment of the ice arena, a fake or tongue-in-cheek "certificate of ownership" (suitable for framing) is provided to the proud "purchaser."

31. **Actual selling of discarded parts of athletic facilities** (segments) can be a hidden source of much needed funds. In this case, actual physical items are sold, with accompanying "certificates of ownership." When a facility becomes slated for demolition, the sports administrators arrange to secure the bricks of the old field house and market (sell) each brick for $10.00 to $20.00. Of course, each brick comes with a metal plate attached to it that certifies that the brick was part of the now-demolished sports facility. Another tactic that can be used is to sell sod from the football field that is slated to be removed and replaced with artificial turf.

32. A slight variation of the selling concept cited above is to simply **rent out advertising space** within a facility. In terms of outdoor facilities, the selling of advertisements on the softball and baseball outfield fences can be very lucrative. Similarly, scoreboard advertisements can often pay, either in total or in part, for the actual cost of the scoreboard. Indoor facilities can likewise be used to provide advertisement space for businesses and corporations.

33. **Rental of the athletic facility to outside groups,** when the facility is not being used by the sport organization, can reap big benefits for both athletic-oriented organizations and nonathletic entities. Rental of facilities can provide sizable profits and create additional exposure of the facility and the host athletic program to the outside publics. It is imperative that adequate supervision of the visiting group be provided throughout the use of the facility to insure that no damage is caused. This supervision, plus the requirement that the visiting renters provide adequate insurance coverage, are two key factors to be addressed that are absolutely essential if the rental is to be worthwhile.

34. **Sponsoring camping, boating, or recreational equipment shows** at the athletic facilities can be productive in exposing a wide range of publics to the school's facilities, as well as provide monetary benefits through the charging

of fees by the exhibitors and the profits from concessions. Insurance factors, as well as proper supervision of the use of the facilities, and adequate cleanup plans, remain important considerations whenever any facility is used by outside groups.

35. **Athletic Hall of Fame** luncheons, brunches, or dinners, honoring past sport greats of the organization, not only can raise sizable monies for the sponsoring group through ticket sales, they are also a great means of generating extensive and immediate publicity, fostering positive and long-lasting public relations.

36. Purchasing and **reselling tickets to various public performances** to the general public can generate sizable profits. For example, tickets for a special event on a specific date are secured at greatly reduced prices to theater shows, sporting events, museums, musicals, etc. Thus, this specific date becomes the team's sponsored event and tickets are resold with that theme to the public under the auspices of the sports organization. The profits are worthwhile considering the amount of work it takes to complete the project. Frequently the tickets to a specific afternoon's or evening's show can be secured at a significant discount (and sometimes free), which enables the sports organization to pocket the difference between the cost of the tickets and the amount that these same tickets can be eventually sold.

37. **Solicitation of equipment and souvenirs** from other organizations, such as pro teams or colleges, for resale or use as giveaways in a wide variety of fund-raising and promotional programs ca be very successful. Almost any item of equipment or apparel can be solicited and used as a promotional tool within some type of project. Some examples frequently used are footballs, jerseys, shirts, shoes, and socks. The key is to make the request or solicitation either in writing or through a mutual friend while stating the charitable purpose for which the solicitation is being made.

38. **Personal appearances by public figures** can enhance any athletic function. This is a variation of the solicitation approach cited above. In this situation, a request is made for personal appearances by highly visible and popular representatives of professional teams, big-time college and university athletic departments, as well as members of political parties or from the corporate or business world. Such personal appearances might be part of a greater overall fund-raising or promotional scheme, such as a fund-raising luncheon or end-of-season athletic team banquet.

39. **Auctions** are a special means of offering a variety of goods for public sale. An auction involves a process of bidding to dispose of accumulations of used, as well as unused, yet serviceable, items for the sport program's benefit. In a **traditional auction,** items are numbered in lots and offered for inspection before the actual bidding begins. At that time, the auctioneer shows each item, describes it with enthusiasm, and encourages competition until someone establishes the highest unchallenged bid or price for it. With valuable goods, one might want to set a bottom bid or minimum price below which the item would not be sold. In such an event, it is helpful to decide ahead of time the actual value of the items.

It is important to have a professional auctioneer to work the auction as it is essential to have authenticity. It is frequently possible to have the professional auctioneer donate his/her services. If not, it is worth the cost to hire a professional to actually do the bid calling at the auction. The initial challenge—the key to the whole auction concept—is to obtain donated items that would be attractive to the public. The second essential component, which is an absolute must, is adequate and timely publicity. The third component is the site location for the auction. Profits result from the sale of the items auctioned off as well as from concessions.

There are numerous decisions to be made regarding the actual format or organization of any auction. In addition to selecting an auctioneer, decisions will have to be made regarding whether or not the auction will be casual (costume or western style), semiformal (business attire), or formal (black tie)? Also, will the auction be for couples or will it be a stag event? Will there be an entrance fee or will free admission be allowed? All of these decisions can be made in light of the community standards, tradition, expectations and goals (Madden, 1989).

Almost anything can be auctioned—inanimate objects, services, as well as individuals. The "people" auction involves the "selling" of individuals for a specific purpose and/or time frame: for example, the auctioning off of the athletic director or other dignitaries for a dinner for two at a local restaurant or the auctioning off of the basketball team to rake leaves on a Saturday afternoon.

Auction items that are usually very popular with the general public and frequently generate profits comparable to or even higher than actual cost include artwork by respected persons, athletic related items, big ticket items (cars, boats, televisions, etc.), computers, jewelry and furs, media advertising package, hotel or motel packages, rare wines and liquors, vacation trips and cruises, uniforms of famous athletes, and activities with famous sports personalities and athletes (Madden, 1989).

40. In a **silent auction,** each item or lot set out is accompanied by a card providing a brief description of the item, indicating the donor and approximate value. Bids are accomplished by indicating a bid amount and signing one's name on the card, raising the price with each successive bid. Frequently, there is a minimum amount that will be accepted for each bid, which avoids the so-called "penny-ante" or nickels and dimes wars. After a specific period of time, bidding is closed, and all cards are collected. The final bidder (highest bid amount) on the card is the purchaser of the item for the amount specified on the card.

41. A **raffle-auction** is a combination of a raffle and a silent auction. Individuals purchase "chances" consisting of two-part tickets, identically numbered for a set price. To make a selection, the purchaser "bidder" drops half of one or more of the tickets purchased into the container adjacent to the desired item. The item to be sold is marked with a minimum bid value. At the conclusion of the raffle-auction, the winning ticket is drawn from each container and the person holding the corresponding number wins the specific item.

"Swim With Mike" is an annual event held on the USC campus, which raises scholarship money to attend undergraduate or graduate school at USC to physically challenged athletes. Money is raised by participants swimming sponsored laps and other donations, both personal and corporate. The "Swim" began in 1981 when former USC All-American Mike Nyeholt was paralyzed in a motorcycle accident. Former teammate Ron Orr decided to organize a swim-a-thon to help pay for Mike's medical expenses and purchase him a fully equipped van. Since then, more than $900,000 has been raised to help 21 students pursue their academic dreams. (Courtesy of University of Southern California "Swim With Mike" Scholarship fund/photo by Long Photography, Inc.)

42. The **blind auction** features blind bidding for items wrapped in paper bags or otherwise disguised so the contents can't be identified. The items may be separated into specific categories such as sporting goods, toys, wearing apparel, crafts, etc. There may be a sign stating the maximum values of the boxes, but the potential bidders are not aware which box contains this great bargain.

43. **Road races (10 K or 5 K race)** have become more popular with the advent of acceptance of the need for fitness among the general public. Obtaining sponsorships from businesses and corporations provide the necessary financial stability at the very onset of the planning segment. Participants can pay an entrance fee and pledges from donors can be obtained for various distances run by individuals. Donated awards provide a professional touch to the event, as does timely publicity, both prior to and subsequent to the race.

44. **"Thons"** are those fund-raising projects in which individuals participate in a wide variety of physical activity usually associated with endurance or skill. Profits are generated from participants paying entry fees and/or having the

participants solicit sponsors who pledge to pay a specific sum based upon the nature of the activity. In a walk-a-thon, the sum pledged (ranging from 5¢ to $1.00 and up) would be per mile walked by the participant. In a swim-a-thon, the sum pledged to the participant would be per lap within a specific time period, 12 hours for example. In a basketball shoot-a-thon, the criteria might be the number of baskets made by the participant within a specific time period. In the lift-a-thon, the pledge is made in terms of the total number of pounds that can be lifted by the participant.

Nearly every physical activity can be converted to the "thon" concept. For example, there are jog-a-thons, run-a-thons, dance-a-thons, serve-a-thons (pledges taken for the number of good serves in volleyball or tennis within a given length of time), game-a-thons (games or contests played over a lengthy period of time such as 12 to 24 hours, in which the number of points or goals scored become the criteria), dunk-a-thons, lift-a-thons, bike-a-thons, cartwheel-a-thons, bowl-a-thons, skate-a-thons. There are even read-a-thons involving the activity of reading books.

The success of any "thon" is dependent upon the successful solicitation of pledges from donors. Pledges may range from a few cents to several dollars per mile, lap, minute, points scored, etc. As an added incentive for the securing of pledges, a variety of awards, based upon the amount of pledges generated, are given to those participants who actually sign up a specific number of pledge sponsors. Sponsors and participants also receive t-shirts, hats, and/or other souvenirs of their involvement in the super event. A great effort should be made to get the general public to watch the "thon" activity as spectators, thereby generating more exposure and support for the fund-raising effort and the sport program the activity is supporting.

In laying the foundation for the solicitation of pledges, it is necessary to create an *information fact sheet* describing the exact nature of the "thon" and how the money raised will be spent. Additionally, a *pledge sheet* to keep a record of the pledges tendered must be created, as well as *tally pledge forms,* which are given to the donors to confirm their commitment to contribute funds based upon the stated criteria.

Of course not all pledges will result in actual cash in hand. Experienced fund-raisers who utilize the pledge technique suggest that if the fund-raising project realizes 75 percent to 90 percent of the pledges initially made, they should consider the effort successful. Following the conclusion of the "thon" activity, two very important tasks remain yet to be completed. The *first* is to appropriately thank all of those who were involved, the participants, the sponsoring donors, as well as the staff who worked at the event or who contributed in any manner to its success, etc. This can help set the tone for next year should the event be repeated. The *second* task is to insure that a strict accounting of all income and expenditures is made and communicated to all constituencies.

45. **Professional fund-raising company selling advertisements** for team calendars, sports programs, and other printed items can generate profits for sport programs. In this situation, the sports program receives free 100 or 200

calendars, programs, schedule cards, etc., to sell, give away, or to display within the community. The company makes it profit from the sale of advertisements minus the cost of producing the printed items.

46. Colleges and universities may set aside ("sell" or lease) buildings and/or portable tents and parking spaces adjacent to major stadiums and gymnasia *as rental facilities* for exclusive "tailgate gatherings" that include reserved parking spaces (otherwise known as "**parking condos**") for the purchasers of the annual or multiyear rental or lease agreements. Fans and supporters, **both** individuals and corporations, are attracted to the availability of protected, convenient, and exclusive service in terms of having space available to host private pregame and postgame gatherings of individuals, while at the same time enjoying secure spaces for various vehicles, including cars, vans and buses.

47. The "**selling**" **of so-called luxury box seating or special reserve seating** to businesses or corporations can be implemented in any facility that enjoys **the** advantages of an attractive sporting activity in conjunction with seating arrangements that can be divided and segregated to provide an atmosphere of exclusivity. The "selling" or leasing of the seating sections to area groups and businesses can result in an additional significant annual income for the athletic program.

Game Day and Half-Time Activities

The day of an athletic contest can serve as a base of operations or a foundation for a wide variety of promotional and fund-raising activities. From the traditional tailgate party preceding the athletic contest to numerous halftime activities, the concept remains the same—to promote the sport program or a specific team and/or to generate additional funds and support. Whatever is accomplished is done to enable people to find the athletic event enjoyable and satisfying so that they will return again and again to participate and to support the sport entity. Some of the halftime or day-of-game activities used to help promote the attractiveness of the sport include:

1. **Parachutists** jumping into the stadium or onto any game field. While such an event attracts significant attention, there are several hurdles to overcome prior to actually initiating such a project. *First* is the question of legal liability; *second,* the question of obtaining permission from the appropriate authorities; *third,* the challenge of securing sufficiently skilled parachutists to actually make the jump; and *last,* the unknown factor—the weather—may or may not allow the planned jump to take place. Nothing is more embarrassing than to hype the fact that the parachutists will be taking part in the day's festivities only to find that the jumpers are blown off course and miss the landing spot altogether.

2. **Contests of skills** at halftime. In the sport of basketball, chances are sold to fans prior to each home contest. A specific number of tickets are subsequently drawn prior to halftime with the winners having an opportunity to make a basket from varying distances. Donated prizes may range from free meals at a local restaurant, to tickets to future athletic events, to automobiles, to free

Pizza Hut's half-shot contest. Over 16,000 people at this game won free pizza when this lucky spectator's half-court shot was successful. (Courtesy of University of Connecticut/photo by Bob Stowell)

trips. Of course, cash, ranging from $25 to $10,000, could also be awarded to each winner.

The same concept can be successfully used in other sports, such as ice hockey. In this sport, selected spectators attempt to shoot the puck into small targets set within the goal from the blue line. In the sport of football, the contestants attempt to kick field goals from the 5, 10, or 15 yard line.

3. **Special dress-up activities** are those promotional programs that center around a common theme and involve suggested special clothing or dress requirements by those who choose to participate. For example, in a **red freak out night** for a basketball game, the objective is to encourage those in attendance to wear outlandish RED outfits or costumes. Even faces, arms, and hands are painted. A contest is held at halftime to determine who has the most outlandish *red* costume and body paint (the school's colors being red and white). Winners are awarded prizes for the top 3 to 5 costumes or outfits, the most original, the most colorful, as well as the ugliest.

A variation of this project has anyone coming to the specific game, dressed out in an appropriate costume and taking part in the contest, receiving reduced or free admission to that game.

4. **Outside organizations, companies, or corporations competing** against one another in an athletic event prior to the school's regularly scheduled athletic contest, coupled with a $500 donation to the sport program by both companies. The challenge rests in the solicitation of the participating organizations. Once two or more organizations have indicated a willingness or

desire to compete in such an event (there could even be a series of elimination contests involving a large number of companies and organizations), the actual work involved in the implementation of the contest is minimal. Again, excellent publicity, suitable awards, coupled with a little advanced planning, can insure success if there are interested organizations willing to participate and to donate a specific sum of money for the privilege of being involved.

5. **Special announcements** made over the public address system prior to, during, and following athletic contests should never be overlooked as promotional tactics. These timely messages can play a large role in communicating with a whole host of constituencies in attendance at the contest. These announcements can be used to promote anything and everything related to the sport organization.

6. **Exhibitions, demonstrations,** or **contests** by outside schools, sport organizations, and other groups on the day of the BIG GAME and/or during periods of THE CONTEST. For example, high school band days may be scheduled on a Saturday morning and early afternoon prior to a college football game. Also, cheerleading contests among area schools prior to the BIG GAME, with the final cheerleading competition taking place during halftime. Another example would be a youth sport contest, such as the Pee Wee wrestling meet, held as part of a high school or college wrestling jamboree.

7. **Alumni or faculty contests.** Inviting alumni to return to the school to play in a preliminary game or during an extended halftime continues to be a popular event. Similarly, involving the faculty and administration at a school in a contest with students, as part of a pregame or postgame program, can reap many benefits, both in financial and public relations terms.

8. Athletic contests can also serve as the vehicle for **conducting drawings or contests.** There are numerous options available to the sport promoter in terms of such contests at an athletic event. One example is the "Dash for Cash Evenings" in which contestants are pitted against the clock in their attempt to pick up as many one-dollar bills from a large bowl as they can with only one hand. This is an excellent way to create excitement and attract the attention and interest of those in attendance.

9. **Special invitations to area groups** to attend athletic events on a full pay basis, on a free basis, or a reduced admission basis. With empty seats available, it hurts no one to give tickets away or to discount tickets to any number of charitable and noncharitable organizations and groups. Special acknowledgments of the presence of these groups sometime during the athletic contest help to publicize those individuals at the event thus highlighting the base of support for the overall program.

10. The use of **Special Days** designations **based on the group of individuals being honored or highlighted.** For example, the use of a *family day, scout day, alumni day, youth day,* or *parents' day* can be successful in attracting a specific audience to a specified athletic event and in so doing set the stage for a common theme for the day in question. Numerous promotional and

McDonald's and the Michigan Capitol Area Girl Scout Council join forces each year to sponsor the McCheer–Off, where approximately 3,000 scouts participate in poster and cheering contests. (top) Winning scout troops perform their cheers at halftime of a Michigan State University women's basketball game. (bottom) Ronald McDonald acknowledges a troop displaying its winning poster. (Courtesy of Michigan State University Relations and Sports Information Office)

fund-raising tactics (luncheons, dinners, special announcements, introduction of specific guests to those in attendance, unique halftime festivities, etc.) may be combined with the *Special Day* approach to insure that the *Special Day* is indeed special to many of those in attendance.

11. The use of a *Special Day* designation *may be based on the promotional activity itself,* for example special souvenir give-away items such as *bat night, ball night, hat night,* or *shirt night.* The number of individuals involved could include *all* in attendance, *a selected few* (for example, the first 500 in attendance), or a *small number* of individuals (1 to 10) determined via a drawing held as part of a contest. A recent study (Friedman, 1989) found that free giveaway items were most popular among those 18 to 24 years of age and those in the $20,000 to $29,000 income range.

12. Providing **fireworks** prior to a contest or at the intermission is certainly a way to attract attention, especially around the 4th of July. But the use of fireworks need not be limited to July 4th. Fireworks can be effectively used at any time of the year.

13. Special **theme nights/events** (Big Bird, Community Night, Fan Appreciation Night, Boosters Night) hold unlimited potential for the promotion of the sports activity. Such theme events can be combined with other promotional activities, such as giveaways and reduced admission prices, to increase the awareness and attractiveness of the sport activity.

14. Establishing a "**Stuff the Stadium**" or "**Stuff the Gymnasium**" contest with prizes given to groups with the largest representation. Prizes could be money, pizzas, tickets, hats, t-shirts, miniature basketballs or footballs.

    A variation of this theme could revolve around counting lifesize cardboard cutouts in addition to real people in determining the winning group. Yet another variation is to count any "stuffed animal" brought to the contest in a group's total number. Of course, a contest is held at halftime to determine the most unusual, the biggest, the heaviest, the fattest, etc., stuffed animals brought to the game with appropriate prizes to the winners. In reality, there is a potential for hundreds of stuffed animals being judged and the possibilities for publicity is almost endless.

15. Involving teachers or special boosters by extending invitations to be a **guest coach** for the week or for a specific home and/or away game(s). This would involve having the guest coach attend practices over a specific number of days. The guest(s) could also accompany the team through its regular routine on the day of the actual contest, including going into the locker room for the pregame, halftime intermission, and postgame meetings. In this way the guest coach and this person's intimate circle of friends gain a more complete understanding of the challenges of athletic participation and coaching. o

16. **Tailgate parties** and related activities can always be used at home contests to generate excitement on the day of the game for the home team, as well as providing a small, but nevertheless stable, flow of revenue through the sale of food and merchandise during the time of such gatherings. Organizing the tailgate party involves adequate publicity, setting aside a suitable area close to the game site for the tailgate participants to park their cars, as well as to

enjoy the picnic-style atmosphere. For those individuals who do not choose to bring their own food and drink, there are food concessions stationed in strategic nearby locations to cater to these individuals' needs. The sale of merchandise during this period of time prior to and following the actual game should not be overlooked.

There is even a company, Tailgater Enterprises, Inc., that markets the *Tailgate Party Book* (1985). This book includes special recipes and tips on tailgating picnicking that could be used as a gift or promotional item for fans. The cost of the book is $3.75 and can be individualized with the name of the school and/or the team logo. Sport organizations can purchase this book for resale purposes or as gifts to supporters or booster club members.

Banquets and Luncheon Activities

Kick-off luncheons or banquets have been used to generate enthusiasm and support for the upcoming sport season. The use of postseason dinners, banquets or gatherings may be used as vehicles for honoring athletes and athletic staff for their efforts, as well as thanking boosters and sponsors for their support.

In addition, these preseason and postseason activities revolving around food and beverages have the potential for serving as a means for generating additional revenue (in the form of additional contributions), for increasing the number of supporting boosters, as well as for publicizing positive facts and accomplishments to the general public. However, the use of food-centered activities or gatherings should not be exclusively associated with end-of-season team banquets.

Inviting boosters and potential contributors to a gathering at which food and beverages will be served is a timeworn, but nevertheless, successful strategy. People do not mind being told in advance that they will be asked to make a contribution when they are brought together at such an event, whether it be a breakfast, brunch, luncheon, or a dinner. In fact, if they know the general purpose of the gathering and yet still attend, it is a strong bet that they will be actual contributors unless a major gaff is committed in the process of extending the invitation or during the actual event itself.

In planning the food-oriented event, there are three essential ingredients in the successful implementation of such a gathering. These include providing an excellent speaker (pitchman), establishing a professional atmosphere, and exhibiting patience.

Having the audience salted with individuals who intend to make sizable donations on cue, and hopefully set the level for contributions at that time, is a wise move. At one college's kick-off banquet, the President stepped forth immediately following the pitchman's presentation and challenged those in the audience to meet or better his own contribution as he walked up to write a sizable check to give to the treasurer of the booster organization.

The breakfast/brunch/luncheon/dinner gathering has proven, over and over again, to be an effective way of enhancing the visibility of the sports program as well as generating sizable income. The actual *solicitation of donated* or *reduced cost food* and *beverages,* from local merchants for any athletic sponsored event involving food and beverages, is the key to enhancing the profitability of such sports sponsored events involving food and drink.

There are numerous specific fund-raising and promotional activities and strategies that revolve around the world of *food* and *beverages*. Some examples are:

1. **Traditional Fund-raising Dinners**—organized around a specific theme that dictates the decorations and the type of food served. Some of the possible themes and/or food categories from which to choose include:

American Food Night
Bar-B-Q Evening (Texas style)
Buffet Super
Chicken Fry
Chinese Banquet
Clambake
Fish Fry
German Evening (sausage and sauerkraut)
Grecian Evening
Harvest Festival
Hawaiian Luau
International Evening
Italian Evening
Kish Kebob Supper
Lobster Night
Malaysian Satay
Mexican Meal
Patio Party
Smorgasbord Supper
Spaghetti Supper
Steak Dinner
Turkey Dinner
Western Party
Wienie Roast

2. **Wine and Cheese** or **Ice Cream Socials** provide opportunities for the participants to take advantage of opportunities to sample and taste a wide variety of wine and cheese (or ice cream, in the event of an ice cream social) while being exposed to the athletic program or a pitch for additional support.
3. **Progressive Dinners** involving as many as 50 to 60 couples who purchase tickets to travel around a circuit of 5 or 6 different homes at which segments of a full-course dinner are served, smorgasbord style. The food and the use of homes are donated, the volunteer hostesses being supporters of the sports program. The *initial* stop might be cocktails and hors d'oeuvres. The *second* stop could be soups or salads. The *third* stop on the progressive dinner trail would be the main course involving vegetables and fish, meat and/or poultry. The *fourth* stopover would be fruit and cheeses, while the *fifth* home would provide donated deserts. At the *last* home, the hostesses would provide coffees (Spanish, Moca, Irish, etc.), as well as after-dinnerdrinks. The profit results from the initial sale of tickets.

Big Blue Bar-B-Que held at Old Dominion University. (Courtesy of Old Dominion University)

4. **Wine-Tasting Parties** are an inexpensive fund-raiser that can be held in the intimacy of a person's home for a small number of invited potential contributors, or a great number of tickets might be sold to the general public. Obtaining donated wine and food, as well as the site, decreases the financial outlay of the effort.

5. **Pancake breakfasts** preceding a sporting contest or planned as an isolated event can generate sizable amounts of money. The key is to secure everything from personnel working the event to the food served, the selected site, on a donated basis. If the advertising is similarly obtained without cost, all the income is profit.

6. **Adult Dinner Dances** slated for a strategic site and planned around a specific theme with appropriate decorations are excellent ways to involve spouses with the sports program. It is also a method of demonstrating to the constituencies that a sophisticated, formal, yet fun, affair can be successfully planned and implemented by a sports organization.

7. **Meet the Coaches breakfasts, luncheons, or dinners** are an excellent opportunity to use the presence and speaking skills of specific coaches to make a favorable impression upon members of the public. Most of the time the only image that the general public has of the coaches is what they see during the athletic contests or what they hear or see by the way of the media or mutual friends. The food gathering at which the coach is able to speak and answer questions is an excellent promotional event *if* the coach is skilled in speaking before groups and fielding questions. It also has the potential for

fund-raising. The objective is to put forth a positive image by the coach's presence and his or her comments.

8. **"Monday Night Football"** gatherings is an example of taking advantage of a professional sport being televised by combining a planned food gathering for backers of the local athletic program to coincide with the timing of the televised big game.

9. **Reunion of Championship Teams** at a breakfast, dinner, or luncheon function enables the sport organization to take advantage of excellent public relations potential and, by selling tickets to the event, can capture significant amounts of money for the organization.

10. **Celebrity Roasts** of individuals, either closely associated with the sport program or of individuals not associated but who are celebrities in their own right, are very popular and have the potential for wide appeal throughout the community, depending upon the celebrity being roasted.

A national survey investigation of big-time collegiate athletic departments, those with athletic programs belonging to the largest of the NCAA Divisions, revealed that the most popular single fund-raising event utilized by the NCAA division I-A athletic departments, which responded to the study, was the golf tournament. Sixty-six percent (66%) of these institutions responding to the survey used this vehicle to generate monies for their sports programs, (Sabock and Bortner, 1986).

Fund-Raising Activities in NCAA Division I Schools

In all, sixteen distinct fund-raising tactics or projects were identified as being prevalent at the big-time athletic level. The complete list of the fund-raising events most prevalent among such athletic programs, along with the percentages of respondents indicating that they utilized the projects, is provided here.

Fund-raising events	*Percentage of big-time athletic programs utilizing the event to generate additional funds*
Golf tourney	66
Social events	55
Phone-a-thons	34
Jog-a-thons	26
Mail-a-thons	17
Raffles	17
Auctions	15
Tennis tournaments	14
Basketball tournaments	6
Membership drives (booster clubs)	5
Bingo games	2
Weekend outings or excursions	2
Softball tournaments	2
Wine-tasting gatherings	2
Celebrity roasts	2
Concerts	2

From a review of this listing, it is apparent that tournaments, social events, "thons," raffles, and auctions comprise the most frequent fund-raising efforts, *in terms of special events,* at the largest collegiate athletic programs (Sabock & Bortner, 1986).

Fund-Raising Activities in Division II Colleges and Universities

Institutions belonging to the NCAA Division II were surveyed in 1990 and revealed that over 50 percent of all such schools raised less than $100,000 on an annual basis. In fact, only 25 percent were able to raise more than $300,000 each year (Marciani, 1991). The study also revealed that 94 percent of the schools studied indicated that their fund-raising efforts involved some type of a fund-raising organization, a booster club or athletic support group (ASG). Almost two-thirds of the schools (68%) had a *single* booster organization while the others had *multiple* organizations attempting to raise funds for different segments of the athletic departments. Additionally, the benefits given to athletic contributors included invitations to social events (83%), newsletters (81%), special recognition (80%), membership cards (75%), preferred parking (57%), ticket priority for basketball games (53%), press guides (51%), auto decals (43%), football ticket priority (39%), athletic apparel (37%) and so-called VIP lounge privileges (33%).

The three most popular ways of generating money for these Division II institutions were (1) face-to-face solicitation, (2) direct mail, and (3) phone solicitation. However, special projects were not neglected although there were not the number of different projects as one might expect. In fact, only two types of special fund-raising projects were utilized by more than half of the respondents to Marciani's survey. These were golf tournaments used in 80 percent of the schools and social events or gatherings which existed in 59 percent of the institutions. Other projects were in vogue in less than half of the schools. For example, phonathon (41%), raffles (38%), mail-a-thons (25%), jog-a-thons (24%), auctions (23%), tennis tournaments (16%), and basketball tournaments (15%).

This investigation also revealed that in terms of control of the fund-raising activities, over a third of the athletic directors served as the chief fund-raiser while 27 percent of the schools had given the responsibility for athletic fund-raising to an associate athletic director. Thirteen percent had hired a Director of Athletic Development. The remaining 12 percent of the institutions had all athletic fund-raising actually organized and controlled by an office other than athletics, such as the office of Development.

References

Briggs, Jr., J., & Duffy, J. (1987). *The official soccer fundraiser's guide.* North Palm Beach, Florida: Soccer Industry Council of America.

Friedman, A. (1989, March). Consumer indicates discounted tickets. *Team Marketing Report,* p. 5.

Madden, B. (1989, January). Going once, twice . . . sold. *College Athletic Management (CAM),* pp. 54–56.

Marciani, Lou. (1991, May). Mining for division II gold. *Athletic Business.* pp. 49–52.

Sabock, R. and Bortner, J. (1986, September). Fund-raising high priority in division I-A. *Athletic Business,* p. 82.

Tailgate Partybook. (1985). Redford, Michigan: Tailgater Enterprises, Inc.

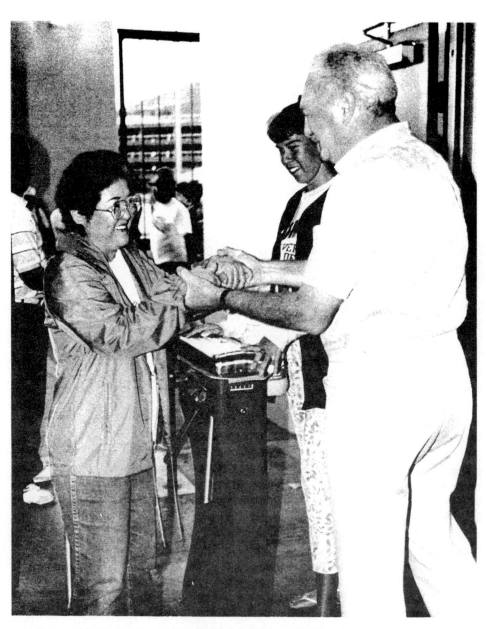

Ms. Clair Nishimura from Mililani, Hawaii, the 1,000,000th fan to enter Rainbow Stadium for a University of Hawaii baseball game, with Stan Sheriff, UH athletic director. (Courtesy of University of Hawaii Intercollegiate Athletics/photo by John Lei)

Putting Ideas and Concepts to Work in the Real World—Specific Fund-Raising Techniques

In the preceding pages of this publication, ideas, concepts, and general *principles* were presented that described the fundamental components or guidelines governing promotions and fund-raising and that formulate the basis of successful fund-raising and promotional activities. However, as indicated earlier, "talk is cheap" within the athletic world of fund-raising and promotions. If these ideas, concepts, and principles are to be more than mere words or theory, they must be put into practice. They must be adapted to meet local situations and actually implemented so that additional resources can be generated by the fund-raiser for the sports programs.

To further assist the reader toward this end, the remaining pages will be devoted to a more detailed and practical examination of successful fund-raising activities, within a wide range of broad categories. These success stories have proven to be big money producers in real life, out there on the so-called "firing line" of life, at various levels of competition.

The following examples of fund-raising strategies provide a wealth of information relating to successful fund-raising projects and promotional activities carried out at all levels of sport, from youth sports through the professional level of athletics. These examples will serve as food for thought and will provide a basis for additional ideas by the creative mind, both the neophyte as well as the veteran.

One word of warning or caution: These successful fund-raising and promotional projects outlined within this chapter may not be suitable for **exact duplication in every sports situation in the same way.** No two athletic situations are ever identical in terms of *different needs, limitations, resources, circumstances* and *goals.* Thus, it is necessary for the reader to review the following successful fund-raising and promotional activities, strategies, and tactics with an eye toward gleaning ideas and principles that may indeed be applicable in one's own circumstances in light of one's limitations and one's available resources.

Just because a school or organization is small, however, or isn't located in a densely populated area, does not mean it can't raise money or that it can't be successfully involved in a wide range of promotional activities on behalf of its sport program. Some of the success stories related in the following pages involve small athletic programs as well as some of the largest programs in the United States. One thing they all have in common is a desire to promote the sports program *and,* in many instances, to generate additional resources.

■ **Principle 127**■
In approaching the
sport fund-raising
arena, there should
be a mix of
promotional tactics,
public relations and
publicity efforts, and
fund-raising activities.

What is needed in any effort to provide the foundational support for our worth-while sport programs is a careful mix, a balance, if you will, of meaningful *fund-raising activities* and successful *promotional activities*. What is needed **in building a strong basis of constituent support** is *creativity* in terms of ideas and *"stick-to-itiveness"* in the implementation of efforts. The foundation of building strong constituent support rests upon excellent public relations efforts, coupled with an active involvement of the general public.

As stated in chapter one, regardless of what level in sports one finds oneself, re-gardless of what type of organization one is working in, there are generally accepted principles that can be adapted and made applicable to individual circumstances or situations. The key is to be able to sift through the numerous, literally thousands of ideas and to adapt, adopt, and alter them to fit particular situations with available resources, as well as limitations and restrictions.

Sport Fund-Raising Success Stories

The McCullough Quarter Back Club of the McCullough High School, in Woodlands, Texas, took advantage of the generosity of a local *restaurant* owner in planning its successful fund-raising event. Members of the booster club (parents of the football players) assumed the jobs of waiters, hosts and hostesses, and bartenders for a Sun-day evening at the restaurant called "Dave's." Each of the 16 booster members working that night had been trained by the owner for two hours the previous after-noon. On the big evening, each of the parent-workers wore their child's number to iden-tify their connection with the football program. Tips and a percentage of the total gross for the evening's activities amounted to a little over $1,700 for the quarterback club.

The University of Denver attracted 16 **corporate sponsors** to its intercollegiate athletic program. Such organizations included Adolph Coors, Pepsi-Cola, Anheuser-Busch, Mountain Bell, and United Air Lines. Each contributed a *minimum* of $5,000 to the Pioneers' athletic program on an annual basis. In return for being a corporate sponsor, a combination of program advertising, signage, variety of tickets, passes to hospitality events, special parking and designation as official sponsors of the univer-sity's athletic program are packaged for each business or corporation.

At DU, those sponsors who have joined the bandwagon enjoy the special privilege of *first right of acceptance,* in the order of priority in terms of when the company or corporation initially signed up. This *first right of acceptance* comes into play when any future promotion or fund-raising activities are contemplated by the university. In this way there is a special relationship built between the university and each sponsor-ing organization.

Another wrinkle in the corporate sponsorship program at Denver University is that there is no exclusivity agreement between the university's athletic department and the corporate sponsors. In this way the university is not locked in for any specific time period with one sponsor in terms of hindering the university from approaching another potential sponsor who might sell similar products or services to current spon-sors. Of course, the *first right of acceptance* is always there for those existing spon-sors who wish to take advantage of it.

Stanford University (California) utilized the concept of corporate sponsors by charging a $3,000 fee for fully catered tents prior to a specific football game which had significant crowd appeal. Each of the tents were large enough for 25 people to be invited by the tent's sponsor and were situated in a secluded, peaceful football practice area adjacent to the stadium. The site also provided ample and convenient private parking for the patrons.

An *all-sports auction* has been held at Southwest Missouri State University for several years for the purpose of providing for scholarship assistance. In a recent year, SMSU has grossed over $90,000 for the university's scholarship fund.

Another institution that has utilized the auction concept is Utah State University, which hosts the *Aggie Auction* involving a *formal dinner,* a *silent auction,* and a *traditional auction.* The evening's festivities are sponsored under the auspices of the Big Blue Club, in June of each year. Over 40 items are available for bid at the same time in a silent auction format. The auction begins at 6:00 P.M. and concludes at the end of the dinner hour. The items for auction are displayed in a ballroom. Each of the items has a tag attached to the item describing it and the minimum opening bid. Also, there are minimum increments specified for all successive bids. The last bid entered on the tag at the end of the dinner hour purchases the item for the bid listed.

Following the dinner hour, the main auction takes place. Here over 35 additional items are auctioned off in the more traditional manner involving a live auctioneer. Each item to be auctioned is listed in the evening's program, and spotters and runners are stationed around the room to assist those bidding. All of the diners are automatically preregistered at the accounting table by the act of having bought a dinner ticket. All accounts (purchases) are settled when the diners are ready to leave for the evening (Aggie Auction, 1985).

Boise State University (Idaho) used a slightly different approach to generate a net profit of over $170,000 dollars in 1989 for the athletic department's endowed scholarship fund. At the University a biennial schedule was deliberately planned for that athletic department's auction. The reason for this was so that the public would not become bored with the event and to allow sufficient time for the athletic staff to plan and work for the next auction. The diverse variety and high value of the donated items auctioned coupled with the philosophy that the auction provides something of value for everyone's pocketbook insures the high rate of return on investment at BSU (Schmid, 1989).

Life insurance has become the vehicle for raising future monies for the University of Florida athletic program. The university has established a gift program in which supporters take out a life insurance policy naming the Gator Boosters, Inc. (the booster support organization) as the sole beneficiary. Funds accrued through the program are earmarked for the athletic scholarship endowment. In this instance, the premiums are made payable to the booster club which, in turn, pays the insurance company that issued the policy. The minimum face value is $50,000.00 (University of Florida, 1989, p. 3).

Another institution that has taken advantage of the concept of *life insurance proceeds* is Duke University. At Duke, the cost of premiums varies but are usually under $1,500.00. "It's the next best thing to a full endowment," said Duke marketing director, Johnnie Moore. "It's something almost anyone can afford" (Innovators, 1989, p. 4).

A ticket promotion was implemented by the athletic department at Paoli Junior-Senior High School, Paoli, Indiana. The first home football game was marketed as "community night." Six local businesses (service station, radio station, grocery store, factory, a bank, and a local fast food restaurant) purchased a block of tickets for $250. These tickets were then distributed by the organizations to customers, employees, and other individuals. The high school was therefore guaranteed a minimum gate income of $1,500 plus an additional $800 worth of tickets to visitors at the gate. There were no advance sales at the school. Not only did the high school enjoy increased attendance at the game, but the revenue from concessions significantly increased as a result of more people at the football contest.

The University of Minnesota, Duluth, utilized a **unique children's promotion** for an opening football game. More than 1,000 "collector" marbles bearing the university's logo were buried in five yards of sand just inside the stadium. Youngsters were given the opportunity to "mine" the area and recover the marbles and win prizes (actual cash as well as a 10 – speed bicycle). Some 300 young people were involved and attendance at the contest exceeded 4,500. Thus, not only did the university gain greater attendance at the contest resulting in an increase in gate receipts but profits from the concessions operation increased as well (Briefly in the News, *The NCAA News*, 1988).

The University of California at Bakersfield, a NCAA Division II institution, annually hosts a *barbecue*. This event brought in some $45,000 in 1988 (Promotions Win Big at Small College, 1988, p. 42). Some 5,000 patrons walked through the turnstiles to take advantage of the excellent food and to support the total intercollegiate athletic program.

Another university that involves the *barbecue* as part of its big fund-raising event is East Carolina University in Greenville, South Carolina. The Pirates' support organization and athletic department sponsor an annual Pig Roast in conjunction with all-day carnival-type activities for the whole family. A major marketing accomplishment is the periodic involvement of big-time celebrities who are present in the day's activities courtesy of various corporate sponsors.

The traditional gambling contest, *Bingo,* is used by Bellarmine College, Louisville, Kentucky, on a weekly basis. Bingo proceeds have been responsible for making it possible for the college to spend almost a quarter of a million dollars for facilities and other aspects of the intercollegiate athletic program (personal communication, December 7, 1992).

Doughnuts and bagels have been a true boost for a Florida high school's sports program. Almost $25,000 worth of such goodies have been sold on an annual basis prior to 1988 via the marketing and selling of doughnuts and bagels prior to the start of school as well as during the school day.

Kake High School, Kake, Arkansas, supplemented its athletic coffers through the selling of *birthday calendars*. Parents of the athletes went door-to-door in the community and sold special calendars containing birthday, anniversaries, community and school events. Over $2,100 was netted through such sales. The booster club was also involved in two bingo nights each year, in which the club netted $1,000 each evening.

East Anchorage High School, Alaska, had a unique fund-raiser involving selling Christmas trees. Since such trees are typically difficult to obtain in Alaska, the Thunderbird football, wrestling, and cross-country teams secured an individual in Oregon who was entrusted to select *quality Christmas trees* for shipment to the high school.

Team members participating in the Pigskin Pig-Out festivities, East Carolina University. (Courtesy of East Carolina University Sports Information Department Cliff Hollis, photographer)

The athletes presold the trees to family, friends, and door-to-door. Incentives were given to those who sold the most trees. In the end, over 180 trees were presold, and the trees were then shipped from Oregon. Upon arrival, the athletes notified the buyers when and where the trees could be picked up. The names, mailing addresses, and phone numbers of the purchasers were retained so as to form the nucleus of the client list for subsequent sales.

The Ashland Area Boosters Club, Ashland, Maine, sponsored *Radio Disc Jockey Dances*. Minimum initial expenses were involved, thanks to volunteer chaperones and workers coupled with the free use of the gymnasium by the school board. The profits from the dances contributed by the boosters benefited the total athletic program at the Ashland Community High School.

Securing *fast food restaurants to sponsor a specific athletic event* can be most rewarding. Such was the case when Wendy's hamburger chain secured some 20,000 tickets to the Tennessee's women's home basketball game against the University of Texas. The game was not only a sell-out with 24,653 people in attendance, but more than 8,000 people were turned away at the gate. The event not only proved to be a significant money producer but a great promotional and publicity event since the game broke the national women's basketball attendance record (Milverstedt, 1988).

The *jog-a-thon* concept has been successfully used by the University of Southern California for a number of years. Pledges are solicited for running laps. A variety of prizes are donated for the participants. Sometimes money will be split with other organizations (clubs, fraternities, other teams) that have helped market and secured pledges for the *jog-a-thon.*

A *rummage sale* was conducted by the athletic department of a small northeastern college. Old uniforms, equipment, and other supplies no longer of any use to the athletic department were gathered together and sold in a giant rummage sale prior to an athletic contest. Extensive advertising, combined with scheduling the *rummage sale* on the same day as a popular athletic event, enabled the promoters to take advantage of a large audience and to make a sizable profit with very little effort.

The Ohio State University is another institution that has utilized the athletic rummage sale or garage sale concept to generate big dollars. On April 25, 1992, during the spring football game on the OSU campus, the athletic department staged a day-long athletic rummage sale where some 800 to 1,000 football, volleyball, basketball, soccer, track, and baseball uniforms the university had accumulated over the years were put on sale to the general public. The sale generated $72,000 in profit for the OSU athletic department (Cleaning house, 1992).

Coupon books, coupled with an *all-day extravaganza (carnival)*, enabled St. Cloud State University (Minnesota) to raise $20,000 for the athletic program. Over 15,000 people attended the day-long event called "Husky Showcase 88." The coupon books sold cost $10.00. Most of the coupons were good only on the day of the big event. A variety of activities were included during the day, for example, sports clinics, variety of free games testing athletic skills of those involved, giving away free prizes (donated by local merchants), a variety of different contests, etc. (St. Cloud State University, 1989).

Big-time bucks were raised by Boyertown Area Senior High School (Pennsylvania) through the concept of *mixed doubles tennis tournaments*. Alumni around the nation organized mixed doubles tennis tournaments in their respective cities. The tournaments were open to anyone who would pay a $25 entry fee, with the profits being funnelled into the school's tennis center building fund. In the initial year of the program, some 280 participants took part while the second year saw the number increase to 480 (Boyertown Area Senior High School, 1989).

An *annual pig roast* has been the vehicle used by another small college. Tickets are sold for a $50 donation, with a limit of 120 people in attendance. All food and drink are donated so that there are essentially no expenses incurred by the institution enabling some $6,000 to be put in the bank. Donated door prizes are given away during the Saturday afternoon event, which is held during the month of June.

A variation of the theme of selling something to members of the general public as well as students and student-athletes centers around the creation of a *highlight video tape of a sports season*. A high school in Ohio, with the assistance of parents, created an athletic highlight videotape at almost no cost. The parents involved in the boosters club marketed the tapes at a $7.00 profit per tape.

The advent of sophisticated videotape machines makes the creation of such a highlight production within the reach of most secondary schools. The videotape is introduced to the teams and the general public at the annual athletic banquet and is placed on sale that evening. The advantages of such a marketing tool lie more in its public relations impact perhaps than on the amount of money generated through the sale of the videotapes.

The Daniel J. Gross High School Booster Club, Omaha, Nebraska, has been most successful through two distinct, ongoing projects. The first generates over $22,000 profit through the selling of what are essentially *lottery numbers*. On Wednesdays, a drawing is for $150. There are six drawings on special days throughout the year and are for $500 in prize money. Finally, two drawings are held during the year for $1,000 each.

A second project run by the club generates approximately $1,250 monthly in profit and revolves around an *exclusive "500" club* in which members are assigned a specific number and are asked to donate $5 each month. In this way the "500" club generates $2,500 gross income. One-half of this sum is returned to the members via drawings held at the monthly booster club meetings.

A midwestern university *rents out its field house* to the state high school association for regional and sectional basketball games. Not only does the university receive money (as well as positive public relations, publicity, and exposure) from the use of its facility, but the athletic program benefits from profits from the concessions operations, from the sale of programs and program ads, and from the parking concession set up for the days of the games.

Another college in the east writes to the parents of all new students, offering the parents a special athletic ticket package for their offspring attending the college. The *discounted ticket package* is marketed as a "gift for your child entering college" and offers a substantial discount from the regular ticket prices. Parents are frequently receptive to purchasing the all-event season tickets for their youngsters who will be away from home, many for the first time in their lives. The income generated through this advance marketing and sales approach insures an early receipt of a rather large lump sum for the intercollegiate athletic program.

Another tactic that has been most successful with parents who have children in college revolves around the offer to deliver *special birthday cakes* to the children on their birthday along with a special greeting card from the parents. With approximately 60 percent to 65 percent of all college students having birthdays during the 8 to 9 months in which there are classes, there are many, many natural prospects (parents) to contact. A mass mailing is made to all parents of students in the college describing the special arrangements and providing a choice of cakes and other food items that can be purchased for their youngsters. With the cost of a cake being somewhere in the neighborhood of $4, a charge of $10 nets the program a healthy 60 percent profit.

A variation of this concept is the *final exam rescue package*. In this situation the parents are sent a letter describing special *final exam rescue packages* (food and drink) that the parents can buy and that will be delivered to their youngsters on a specific day during exam week. Naturally, a special greeting card containing individualized messages from mom and pop is included.

Another college, located in the midwest, sponsors a special *marching band day* (involving numerous area bands) on the morning and early afternoon prior to a big football game on its campus. In addition to the positive public exposure created through this activity, the school generates income through increased ticket sales to those individuals who want to see the various bands perform, as well as increased ticket sales to the football game that follows the band performances. Of course, all of the bands also take part in the half-time festivities of the football contest. Even the school's book store gets into the act by setting up a merchandise booth on the grounds of the stadium.

The concept of the *traditional golf tournament* has been utilized by a small college in midwest America for big profits. Profits are maximized through the soliciting of sponsorships for both the greens and the holes (minimum price of $100 for each green or hole). Signs are placed beside each green and hole providing advertising for the sponsors. Over $3,600 is generated through this tactic alone. Food and drinks as well as t-shirts and hats for the participants are donated as is the golf course, which leaves the entrance fee of $50 to flow right into the booster club's budget. Naturally, donated prizes are given following the dinner scheduled after the 18 holes of golf.

A one-time fund-raising event revolving around a *souvenir athletic publication* was held by a high school athletic department. Staff members in a high school, aided by boosters, designed an attractive souvenir athletic booklet that the booster organization then sold throughout the community. The large booklet featured both a written and a pictorial history of the school and its athletic teams. The publication contained advertising at a profitable rate, while not detracting significantly from the rest of the content. The ratio of advertising to the athletic/school written and pictorial information was approximately 60/40. The net profit to the athletic program was close to $10,000.

An *Octoberfest weekend* provided the means for almost $10,000 profit. The weekend activities (Friday evening and all day Saturday) were held on the college campus during Homecoming weekend. A separate admission fee was charged all participants. The *Octoberfest weekend* involved dancing, games, contests, special food, and a variety of drink available. It catered as much to the youth of the community (college students) as to the older crowd. Being held on Homecoming weekend insured that there were thousands more on campus from which to draw paying participants. Approximately 60 percent of those in attendance were college students.

The sale of *"square yards "* of a proposed football field/stadium for the newly consolidated Lincoln County High School (Fayetteville, Tennessee) generated some $79,000. Approximately 3,160 square yards were sold at $25 a square yard. The "square yards" were purchased by people for their children, for memorials, in honor of specific individuals, by class reunions, businesses, and corporations. The Lincoln County Gridiron Association utilized coupon booklets to facilitate the sale of the "square yards" and provided all purchasers with handsome documents called "deeds."

The University of Miami (Florida) baseball program under the direction of former long-time head coach Ron Fraser has enjoyed tremendous success both on the field and in generating large sums of money for the baseball team. As long ago as 1977 he initiated a $5,000 a plate dinner that was held on the infield itself of the then-new baseball facility. The dinner was catered and those in attendance were treated to strolling violinists and tuxedoed waiters during the fund-raising dinner (Success Stories, 1992).

An excellent example of creative fund-raising is the case of former Auburn football coach Pat Dye who was criticized for electing to settle for a 16–16 tie rather than going for a win against Syracuse University in the 1988 Sugar Bowl. As a result, coach Dye received some 5,000 neckties mailed to him by irate Syracuse fans. Turning a potential negative into a very big plus for his program, coach Dye had some 100 of the ties made into a quilt, signed the remaining number, and sold them all as souvenirs. The net amount generated for the Auburn University academic scholarship fund was $25,000 (Tie Dye, 1988).

Clemson University has a most successful ongoing fund-raising effort called IPTAY. This acronym stands for "I Pay Ten A Year." Today, in light of continual inflation with the American economy the IPTAY stands for "I Pay Ten Times Ten A Year." With almost 18,000 individuals contributing via athletic support group, 1991 marked the twenty-seventh consecutive year of increased donations to the Tiger athletic program. Today IPTAY is one of the most successful programs in the country, bringing in slightly less than $6 million for Clemson's athletic program (Wieberg, 1991).

A highly successful *reverse raffle* is conducted by the State University of New York College at Brockport and provides significant financial support as well as great public relations. What exactly is a *reverse raffle?* In an ordinary raffle, tickets that are pulled first are the BIG winners. In a reverse raffle, the so-called big winners are the holders of the last tickets chosen. Thus the name, *reverse raffle*. A detailed explanation of this unique approach to the raffle concept was highlighted in the March 1988 issue of *JUCO Review* and is summarized below.

The reverse raffle made its debut on the State University of New York's campus on April 2, 1984, the evening of the NCAA Division I basketball championship game between Georgetown University and the University of Houston. Since that time, over $5,000 clear profit has been generated annually for the intercollegiate athletic program via this one activity alone.

A Success Story Behind the Creation of a Reverse Raffle

The concept behind the reverse raffle is simple, but intriguing, and has proved to be most successful both in raising money and in creating positive public relations for the athletic program and the entire institution. The evening festivities consist of watching the NCAA basketball championship game on a large six-foot television screen as well as on several normal-sized TVs located throughout a large banquet room, coupled with a buffet dinner and a cash bar, on the campus of the university. A maximum of 200 tickets ($50.00 each) are sold. Purchased tickets may be split among any number of participants. A guest may accompany the ticket holder for an additional $10.00 fee.

Each $50.00 ticket assures the holder(s) of winning something during the evening activities. However, although all 200 tickets are drawn that evening, *the tickets are drawn in reverse order with the very last ticket drawn earning the grand prize of $1500.00.* The 199th and 198th tickets drawn earn $500.00 and $300.00 respectively for their owners while the 197th through the 182nd tickets drawn are each worth $100.00. The holder of the 181st through the 1st ticket pulled each receive a small gift (donated by local merchants), a remembrance of the evening (some more valuable than others with a dollar value between $1.00 and $40.00) as a token of the athletic department's appreciation for the participants taking part in the annual reverse raffle fund-raiser.

Principle 128

Don't be too proud to make improvements to already successful fund-raising projects.

Another twist that was added for the 3rd Annual reverse raffle (and retained in subsequent raffles) was a "2nd Chance Drawing." This mini-drawing was added to keep the interest of the early "winners" throughout the remainder of the evening. After the first 181 tickets are chosen— right before the money prizes are drawn— all 181 tickets are replaced into a separate bowl and one ticket from the 181 tickets is drawn for a single $100.00 prize. In essence, one ticket becomes a double winner. All in all, some $4,000 in cash is given out to the lucky patrons of the reverse raffle.

The reverse raffle is emceed by a "real life-of-the party type," who begins pulling numbers from the large bowl prior to the start of the championship game and continuing during halftime. The strategy is to pick all of the numbers except the final 19 money winners and the "2nd Chance Drawing." These money tickets are saved until after the game. This only enhances the suspense throughout the game with everyone having to wait until after the game to see which of the remaining tickets are drawn, again in reverse order, to determine the big cash winners. When the final five or six tickets are about to be drawn, the holders of these tickets begin to barter and dicker regarding the selling and buying of these tickets to and from each other. When only three or four tickets remain, the bidding becomes much more active and intense with the bigger money prizes up for grabs (and possible purchase).

All in all, the reverse raffle continues to be a huge success with some $5500.00+ remaining in the athletic support group's coffers each year, following all expenses for the evening. This fund-raising activity has been instrumental in getting the athletic support group viewed by the public as a viable organization, ready and able to accept new challenges in support of the total athletic program at the State University of New York, Brockport, New York.

The public relations benefits resulting from this success story are invaluable. The organization—Friends of Brockport Athletics (FOBA)—gains extensive exposure throughout the community as a successful organization that could produce and follow through toward the completion of important tasks. Additionally, the success of this support group (FOBA), and its professionally run programs, has a positive fallout upon and enhances the image of both the intercollegiate athletic program and the entire institution (Stier & Matejkovic, 1988).

It is essential that those athletic administrators (at any level) who are involved with the promotional and/or fund-raising aspects of sports programs remain conscious of the cost effectiveness (financial, time, effort, etc.) of their efforts and their staff's efforts. It may be far better not to become involved in fund-raising and promotion if it cannot be done in a professional fashion. This philosophy of doing it well or not doing it at all might be one that many of our athletic programs and booster clubs should consider adopting, especially in response to the present, hostile climate facing athletics in many school systems.

Similarly, there needs to be a realistic determination of exactly what role our athletic program should play in the scheme of things. Athletic programs can't be all things to all people. There are indeed real differences involving resources and limitations that exist between different school systems and athletic programs in different parts of the country, as well as in different parts of states.

Thus it is essential that individual athletic administrators recognize their position in the pecking order within the various school systems and within the hierarchy of the athletic world in light of whatever resources (financial, personnel, facilities, image, etc.) might be available or which might be mustered.

The bottom line responsibility of the private and/or public school athletic administrator is to seek to *create* ideas and concepts, to *initiate* actions, to *cultivate, titillate,* and *motivate* others as well as to *educate* constituencies so that athletic programs might *captivate* their interests and loyalties and thus *facilitate* the *solicitation* of both tangible (concrete) and intangible (moral) support. *Sometimes it seems that it does not hurt one little bit if the sport administrators in charge of fund-raising also happen to walk on water in their spare time.*

Hopefully, this publication will serve as a guidepost in terms of courses of action that might be appropriate to follow in the reader's own sport situation. The use of the **principles** and recommendations as outlined throughout this book can provide the basis for a comprehensive, successful, and systematic effort in the exciting, rewarding, and demanding world of promotions, public relations and fund-raising. **Good luck.**

Concluding Statements on Athletic Fund-Raising, Promotions, and Public Relations

References

Aggie auction. (1985). *Big Blue Club* "You Make the Difference."
Briefly in the news. (1988, September 19). *The NCAA News*, p. 16.
Boyertown area senior high school. (1989, May). *Athletic Business*, pp. 36–37.
Clearning house at Ohio State. (1992, May 13). *The NCAA News.* p. 20.
Hinz, R. (ed.). (1986, July). *Athletic Director & Coach*, pp. 1–8.
Innovators. (1989, January). *National Association of Athletic, Marketing, & Development Directors Newsletter*, pp. 1–6.
Milverstedt, F. (1988, September). *Athletic Business*, pp. 24–28.

Promotions win big at small colleges. (1988, August). *Athletic Business,* pp. 42–45.

St. Cloud State University. (1989, May). *Athletic Business,* pp. 28–30.

Schmid, S. (1989, December). BSU's big-bucks auction. *Athletic Business,* pp. 60–62.

Stier, Jr., W. and Matejkovic, E. (1988, March). A new twist to an old fund-raising tactic. *JUCO Review,* pp. 4–6.

Success Stories. (1992, March 27). *USA Today.* 1–C, 2–C.

Tie Dye. (1988, August 28). *Rochester Democrate & Chronicle.* P. 35-G.

University of Florida. (1989, March). *College Athletic Management (CAM), I* (3), 3.

Wieberg, S. (1991, October). Fund-raising arm keeps Clemson in the black. *USA TODAY.* 5-C.

Starting An Athletic Support Group

A Success Story Behind the Creation of an Athletic Support Group (Stier, 1987*)

Upon arriving at the school in the fall, one of the new athletic director's first encounters was with a group of potential athletic boosters who shared their eagerness to lend support to what previously had been a less than adequate effort at sustained athletic fund-raising. In fact, in the previous six-year period, there had been neither a concerted nor a successful effort in this area at all. There was, in fact, no viable athletic support group even in existence at this time, only the memories of two earlier attempts, which for one reason or another failed in their missions and were now only faded memories.

In examining the history of what athletic fund-raising efforts had taken place (or rather the absence of such efforts), it became evident that what was needed was an official athletic support group that was independent, but yet closely related, to the athletic department and to the institution. The entity soon to be created—the FRIENDS OF BROCKPORT ATHLETES (FOBA)—had to be broad based in its support, that is, representative of the various constituencies both inside and outside of the university and the athletic department. This broad-based support would include faculty, staff, administrators, coaches, students,

*Stier, Jr., W. (1987, October). The establishment of an effective athletic support group. *JUCO Review, Journal of the National Junior College Athletic Association*, pp. 2–4. Reprinted with permission.

general and athletic alumni/ae, and representatives from the surrounding communities.

The task, however, sounded far easier than it actually turned out to be. Challenges abounded. There had been two earlier attempts at forging such an athletic support group (or booster clubs as they were called previously). The initial attempt died an ignominious death a decade earlier. The second misguided venture toward creating such a group failed to even get off the ground as late as five years earlier under yet another different athletic administration.

With a history of two such failures very much on everyone's minds, the newly established athletic administration moved cautiously, yet boldly, ahead. *First,* attempts were made to find out why the previous two organizations failed. *Second,* previous procedural errors, as well as mistakes in judgment, were acknowledged by the athletic department and an honest effort was made to mend fences, both in terms of the general public and in terms of the general administration of the university. All constituencies were assured that the athletic program would be initiating and continuing good faith efforts to insure that the earlier mistakes and injustices—whether real or perceived—would not be repeated by either the athletic department, by the central administration of the institution, or by the athletic support organization. Assurances were made that the athletic department would attempt to begin anew with a booster organization that would seek to meet the needs of the school, the total athletic program (men and women, all sports), *and* the various constituencies, inside and outside of the institution.

The important point that the athletic department had to be sensitive to was negative feelings held by segments of the various publics. What mattered was not whether such feelings were actually justified but whether these perceptions were *thought* to be justified and true. For if so, then they were indeed true for these individuals. It mattered little whether the central administration actually did attempt to manipulate the former booster clubs as pawns or whether the institution failed to keep previous commitments. If these perceptions were held by various constituencies in the surrounding communities, then for these constituencies—whether the perceptions were correct or not—the feelings and attitudes still existed and were indeed true for those who possessed them.

On the other side of the coin were long memories still lingering in the minds of some central administrators. These administrators feared a return to what they viewed to have been an almost total runaway type of organization existing without adequate controls, guidance, and safeguards. This perception, this fear (whether justified or not) on behalf of the central administration of the institution had to be addressed from the outset. Institutional administrators were wooed and courted in such a fashion so as to clarify the true purpose of this new organization and to insure that the FOBA, its structure, purpose, and operating code were acceptable to everyone concerned.

Finally, following many months of negotiating between the initial organizing membership core of the FOBA and with key administrators, a written agreement was entered into by both the booster club's Board of Directors *and* by the school central administration. This written instrument outlined the official status of the new support organization and the relationship that it was to have to the institution and vice versa. It was upon this auspicious occasion that the real effort could commence in terms of getting the booster group off the ground and steered toward the realization of meaningful objectives and goals.

The first order of business was a membership drive that was kicked off in mid-year with a semiformal wine and cheese gathering held in a large ballroom, just prior to a big basketball game against an arch rival. As a bonus for those in attendance at the wine and cheese program, complimentary tickets were issued for the basketball game that followed. Over 300 key potential supporters received special invitations to the gathering and just over 125 actually attended. The evening festivities included a brief presentation by the new athletic director, the newly elected president of the booster club, as well as the president of the institution.

This occasion provided an opportunity for the athletic director (1) to review the successful history of athletics at the school, (2) to emphasize the need to band together if the athletic teams (both men and women) were to continue to excel in the decade to come, (3) to reveal the need to develop and sustain a broad-base support for the athletic program, (4) to provide an explanation of the benefits accompanying the various classifications of membership, and (5) to outline the immediate goals of the newly created booster organization.

The immediate goals of the booster group unveiled that evening included:

1. a reverse raffle/buffet to be held in April of each year in conjunction with the NCAA basketball championships (providing an opportunity to view the game on a large 6-foot television screen)
2. the assumption of the athletic department's annual golf outing, which would be moved from late August to late May of each year
3. the creation of the Athletic Hall of Fame during the following fall homecoming weekend (and continued in subsequent years)
4. an annual membership drive commencing each fall of subsequent years
5. a future (several years in the future) antique and craft show weekend

Following the conclusion of the formal presentations of the cheese and wine gathering, those in attendance were given an opportunity (strongly encouraged) to become CHARTER MEMBERS of the booster group.

The memberships in the booster organization were organized on various classes or levels, with each level or class costing more money but yielding more benefits to the member. The various membership plans were developed following an extensive review of how other institutions throughout the country were experiencing success within terms of similar support groups. Our philosophy was simple. If it worked at other schools, we were not in the least bit shy about adopting similar successful tactics to fit our own circumstances, available resources, and needs.

The principles underlying our membership drive were threefold: *First,* to gain members (numbers); *second,* to realize an infusion of new financial support (dollars); *Third,* to provide the membership with tangible benefits while simultaneously meeting the needs of the athletic department and the membership by providing a first rate, broad-based athletic program for women and men. The booster membership plan was designed so as to reach organizations and corporations, as well as individuals, by providing within the benefit scheme a CORPORATE PACKAGE option that would be tailored to the corporation in question.

The cheese and wine introductory meeting was a huge success with over 60 initial members signed up that first evening, including one corporate sponsor. In fact, the corporate sponsor not only purchased a corporate membership in the booster group but also made a very sizable contribution to the school's general fund through the development office. This fact helped to quell the initial fears among some administrators that the booster club would be picking up mere nickels, while interfering or hindering the development office's attempts to pick up BIG dollars.

Actually, that fear has not materialized at all. The efforts at increasing members within the booster group, coupled with the efforts to raise athletic funds through this organization, involved individuals who had not had a significant history of contributing financial support to the institution per se. Thus, the activities of the booster group have done nothing except to expand the fund-raising horizons of the institution insofar as creating additional potential and receptive donors for the total institution.

The final cog in this wheel of athletic support was a consistent and well-thought-out plan of how to spend some of the monies generated by the various activities of the support group. Nothing dampens the enthusiasm of a support group, like

the FOBA, more than the *failure to take advantage* of the opportunities to spend some of the hard-earned money on worthy and easily recognizable projects, in support of the *total* athletic program. On the other hand, good public relations highlighting how the support group constructively used the monies generated by the hard work of the membership and other supportive constituencies goes a long way toward perpetuating the positive reputation and the now successful track record of the support group.

People want, and deserve, the right to know how a support group has provided significant financial, moral, and public relations support to the athletic programs and the participants therein. With the knowledge that one's efforts have not gone in vain in terms of helping the total athletic program, the support group and other constituencies can rest assured that further involvement continues to benefit the intercollegiate athletic program by providing for a firm financial and people support base upon which may be built an even more effective and efficient athletic program.

Today, with the passage of time and with a successful track record, the support organization continues to grow in acceptance, as well as in activities. Today the booster group is viewed as an *active* entity. Success breeds success. The organization has now gained the support and allegiance of most of the constituencies originally sought and continues to court others. There is an eagerness and a willingness now to help the booster group realize its potential, rather than to merely be seen as the third in the line of mediocre or unsuccessful so-called support clubs.

With continued diligence, hard work, and support by members of the booster entity, the faculty, staff, administration of the school, and the general public(s), the future of the booster club would seem to be bright indeed. The future of this organization remains, however, in the hands of the women and men who are willing and able to take the time, to exert the effort, and to make the sacrifice for the benefit of the student-athletes, the athletic program or department, and for the institution, through the vehicle of the booster club.

Sample By-Laws Guide for Booster Clubs

Adapted from the *Official Handbook,* (1981), of the Boosters Clubs of America, North Palm Beach, Florida, pp. 22–28.

ARTICLE I—ORGANIZATION

This organization shall be a non-profit, unincorporated association, unless state laws require differently.

The name of this organization shall be:

_____

Booster Club Name

_____

School Name or Organization Name

_____

Street Address

_____

City   State   Zip Code

ARTICLE II—PURPOSE

Section 1 The booster club exists for the purpose of broadening the involvement of students, student families, and the school, through support for all female and male activities of the inter-school athletic programs. The booster club works to achieve this through active participation of as many parents as possible in booster club programs and in concentrated support for individual sports, working closely with the coaches, athletic director, activities director, and principal of the school.

1. To support, promote, and maintain a high standard of integrity and good sportsmanship in all athletic activities of high school

2. To foster and promote good will and fraternal spirit among the members.

3. To promote and encourage better attendance at all sports activities by the parents and friends of athletes, the students, and faculty of the school.

4. To promote and encourage more young men and women to become involved in athletics, either as an active participant or as a volunteer assistant such as statistician, etc.

5. To raise funds to assist all athletic programs through the school's athletic fund. The athletic director may help to create smaller booster club committees to directly support each coach's program or support a strong revenue producing program to raise the funds to assist all athletic programs and supported volunteers working for the operation of concession stands, selling of advertisements, tickets, and donations for any other legitimate purpose that the Board of Directors shall determine.

6. To assist in holding down expenses of the athletic department by volunteering services to provide people to serve as parking lot attendants, chain gang crew, admission ticket takers, timers, judges, as well as other similar activities approved and sanctioned by the athletic department.

7. Budgets are to be established at the beginning of each year. The coaches will submit to their respective committee their list of needs, prepared and approved by the

athletic director and the school principal. The committee chairperson will then present the budget requests for approval by a 2/3 majority vote of the general membership in attendance.

8. All money raised by special fund-raising projects to meet the athletic department's requests will be presented to the school administration in a manner of general agreement with the school administrator and club officers. The agreed plan is as follows:

_____

_____

_____

_____

ARTICLE III—MEMBERSHIP

Section 1 Parents and friends of all past or present student athletes, and such other sports-interested persons who desire membership shall be eligible for membership in the association.

Section 2 There will be yearly membership dues of $_____ per person for regular active members. Dues shall be payable at the beginning of each school year. Dues may be increased or decreased by the Executive Board and by a majority vote of the general membership.

Section 3 A special sustaining membership may be established for persons unable to volunteer their efforts but who can support the school athletic program through what may be a tax-free membership gift. There are three levels of contributions and memberships are to be renewed each year for non-participating supports. The three levels of contribution are as follows:

A. Gold level membership: $ _____
B. Silver level membership: $ _____
C. Bronze level membership: $ _____

Section 4 All active coaches, the Principal, the Activities Director, and the Athletic Director shall automatically be considered ex-officio members of the association. The Principal, or a representative of the Principal, shall be a member of the Executive Board of the association.

ARTICLE IV—OFFICER ELECTIONS

Section 1—Officers: Officers shall consist of a President, Vice President, Treasurer, Recording Secretary, and Corresponding Secretary. There shall be such additional officers, committee chairpersons, and other officials as the President shall appoint from time to time.

Section 2—Election of Officers: Election of officers shall take place at the meeting of the Association to be held in April of each year or as near there to as is reasonable (the election meeting). The slate of officers should be presented to the membership at the March meeting or a meeting proceeding the election meeting (the Nomination Meeting). The proposed slate of officers shall be nominated by a nominating committee, hereafter defined, and the committee may nominate more than one proposed officer for each position. The proposed nominations may be accepted by the nominating committee in their sole consideration from the floor during the Nomination Meeting or the nominating committee may generate nominations itself. The full slate or slates as nominated by the nominating committee must be accepted by the Executive Board and will be presented and voted upon during the Election Meeting.

Section 3—Nominating Committee: The nominating committee shall consist of five members; two shall be elected by the Executive Board; two shall be elected from the floor at a general meeting of the Association to be held proceeding the Nomination Meeting; and one shall be the Principal of the school.

Section 4—Term of Office: Officers shall serve for one year and not for more than two consecutive years.

Section 5—Eligibility: Only members in good standing shall hold office or vote in elections, unless this provision is waived by the Executive Board.

Section 6—Voting: Voting shall be by secret, written ballot at the Election Meeting. There shall be an election committee of three, appointed by the President of the Association on the day of the election of officers.

The duty of the election committee shall be to pass out the ballots, collect the ballots, and count them. The chairperson of that committee shall read the final account to the Association. In the event there is more than one person nominated for any one office, the winner of the majority of votes cast shall be deemed the winner of the election.

In the event there is but one nominee for any particular office, and that nominee does not receive the majority of votes cast, the Executive Board shall then appoint an eligible member to serve in that office, and hold that office until next regular election, or in the alternative, the Executive Board may determine to hold another election for that particular office. The President, with the consent of the nominating committee, may forego the secret balloting and call for election by voice vote if the President deems that the electors are clearly in favor of such a procedure.

Section 7—Installation of Officers: Installation of officers shall be at the May meeting or final meeting of the school year, at which time the new officers shall take over their duties in all matters affecting the next subsequent school year.

Section 8—Annual Meeting: The annual meeting of the Association shall be the last meeting of the school year, which ordinarily will be held in May. At the annual meeting, all annual reports shall be received and the new officers, retiring board, and the newly elected officers and new board, if organized, shall hold a joint session. At the joint session, the retiring officers and board shall transfer all books and

papers in their possession and belonging to the Association to the new administration, and otherwise advise the new administration as to the status of affairs of the Association.

ARTICLE V—DUTIES OF OFFICERS

Section 1—President: It shall be the duty of the President to preside at all regular and special meetings and all Board meetings. The President shall perform all of the duties of the office; shall appoint all committees and committee chairpersons and shall be an ex-officio member of all committees, except the nominating committee. The President shall also sign all contracts, checks and disbursements, subject however to the approval or ratification of the Executive Board. The President shall be able to disburse funds up to $ _____ with the approval of one other Board member. The President shall have regular meetings with the school Principal and the Athletic Director, as determined by the three individuals.

Section 2—Vice President: The Vice President shall act as President in the event of the President's absence, death, or incapacity and shall assume such duties for the balance of the term, unless replaced by the Board. The Vice President's line of succession shall be as designated at the time of elections.

Section 3—Recording Secretary: It shall be the duty of the Recording Secretary to keep a record of all regular and special meetings, and all Board meetings. It shall also be the duty of the Recording Secretary to maintain a procedure book, which is a record of the activities of the Association compiled into a permanent form.

Section 4—Corresponding Secretary: It shall be the duty of the Corresponding Secretary to conduct the correspondence of the Association, keep a list of the membership's current addresses, send out all notices when not hereinafter provided for, and send special letters, unless provided for in the standing rules. A sustaining membership program shall be maintained and regular reports will be given to the Treasurer.

Section 5—Treasurer: It shall be the duty of the Treasurer to receive all monies due to the Association and deposit same in a place approved by the Association. The Treasurer shall disburse the funds of the Association only for purposes approved by the Association, from time to time. The Treasurer shall present a statement of account at all regular meetings and at other times when requested to do so by the President and shall make a full, written report at the annual meeting. The accounts of the Treasurer may be audited by a committee approved by the President.

ARTICLE VI—EXECUTIVE COMMITTEE

Section 1 The Executive Committee shall consist of the elected officers.

Section 2 The duties of the Executive Committee shall be to transact emergency business in the interval between Executive Board meetings.

Section 3 The majority of the Executive Committee shall constitute a quorum.

Section 4 Meetings of the Executive Committee shall be held as needed.

ARTICLE VII—EXECUTIVE BOARD

Section 1 The Executive Board shall consist of the officers of the Association, the chairpersons of the various standing committees, and the Principal of the school or a representative appointed by the Principal. The chairpersons of the standing committees shall be selected by the officers of the Association and the Principal of the school or the Principal's representative. The members of the Executive Board shall serve until the election and qualification of their successors.

Section 2 The duties of the Executive Board shall be to:

A. Transact necessary business in the intervals between association meetings and such other business as may be referred to it by the Association.
B. Create standing committees as well as ad hoc committees.
C. Approve the plans of work of the standing committees.
D. Present a report at the regular meetings of the Association.
E. Prepare and submit to the Association for approval a budget for the fiscal year.
F. Approve any bills within the limits of the budget.

Section 3—Meetings: Regular meetings of the Executive Board shall be held monthly during the school year, the time to be determined by the board at its first meeting of the year. A majority of the Executive Board members shall constitute a quorum. Special meetings of the Executive Board may be called by the President or by a majority of the members of the board.

ARTICLE VIII—GENERAL MEETINGS

Section 1 Regular meetings of the Association shall be held on the _____ (day of month and hour) each month during the school year, unless otherwise provided by the Association or by the Executive Board, (number) _____ days notice having been given.

Section 2 Special meetings may be called by the Executive Board with (number) _____ days advance notice having been given.

Section 3 The annual meeting shall be in the month of _____.

Section 4 A quorum shall exist when _____ members are present for the transaction of business in any meeting of this association.

Section 5 QUORUMS: A quorum shall consist of not less than two-thirds of the Executive Board and not less than twenty-five members of the general membership. It is noted, however, that at times, due to other commitments of the members, it may not be possible to obtain a quorum. Under such circumstances, such actions that are taken at this meeting at which there is not a quorum shall be subject to review by a full quorum within sixty days of such action having been taken, at which time the full quorum may reverse the action taken at the meeting that failed to have a quorum.

ARTICLE IX—STANDING AND SPECIAL COMMITTEES

Section 1 The Executive Board may create such standing committees as well as ad hoc committees as it may deem necessary to promote the objectives and carry on the work of the Association. The term of each chairperson shall be one year or until the election and qualification of the person's successor.

Section 2 The chairperson of each standing committee shall present a plan of work to the Executive Board for approval. No committee work shall be undertaken without the written consent of the Executive Board.

Section 3 The power to form special committees and appoint their members rests with the Association and the Executive Board.

Section 4 The President shall be a member ex officio of all committees except the nominating committee.

ARTICLE X—PROPERTY RIGHTS

Membership in this Association shall not title or vest any of the members with any property rights or rights having monetary value of any kind whatsoever, including, but not limited to, property rights or monetary rights in the school or in the Association.

ARTICLE XI—AMENDMENT

These by-laws shall be approved by a meeting of the regularly called general membership, by a majority vote of those members eligible to vote and actually casting their vote at said meeting. The by-laws may be amended by a two-thirds vote of the members present at any regularly called meetings. Such amendments may only be recommended by the Executive Board, and shall be presented in writing and read at the regular meeting prior to the time of voting.

ARTICLE XII—RELATIONSHIP WITH THE SCHOOL ADMINISTRATORS AND ATHLETIC DEPARTMENT

The booster club shall operate in full support of the school Administrators Athletic Director and coaches. At no time shall the booster club make recommendations or become directly involved in the day to day operation of the school athletic program. The booster club serves only to support and facilitate the school athletic program and has no role in deciding the direction of policy established by the school Principal or by the Athletic Director.

Membership Plan for an Athletic Support Group

C

Friends of Brockport Athletics

BROCKPORT.
State University of New York College at Brockport

BENEFITS	Green $30	Gold $50	Century $100	Flying Eagles $150	Varsity $250	Coach's $500	University $1000
Membership Card	1	1	1	2	2	2	2
Bumper Sticker	1	1	1	2	4	6	10
Eagle "Stick On"	1	1	1	2	4	6	10
Periodic Newsletter	1	1	1	1	1	1	1
Hospitality Lounge Privilege	1	1	1	2	2	2	2
Socials		1	1	2	2	2	2
All Year Sports Pass			1	2	4	6	10
Booster Hat			1	2	4	6	10
"Eagle Pin"			1	2	4	6	10
T-shirts				1	2	4	6
Family Sports Pass (Children-18 & Younger)				yes	yes	yes	yes
Regonition Plaque (home/office)					1	1	2
Recreation Pass for Family					yes	yes	yes
Annual Recognition Plaque in Tuttle N						yes	yes
Folding Stadium Seats						2	4
Corporate Benefit Package	Contact Athletic Director						

Application Form (please print)

Name: _____ Phone _____

Address: _____ City: _____ State: _____ Zip: _____

Type of Membership Selected: _____ Date: _____

Name and Age of Children_____

Method of Payment (circle one):   check   cash   bill me

Athletic Fund-Raising Request Form

1. Name of person making request
    and assuming responsibility
    of fund-raising activities.

    _____

    Home Phone: _____

    Office Phone: _____

2. Team or organization raising funds: _____

3. Nature of FUND-RAISING ACTIVITIES (please be specific): _____

    _____

    _____

4. Amount needed to be raised: _____

5. Length or duration of solicitation/fund-raising activities: _____

    _____

6. Who will be solicited (please be specific): _____

    _____

7. Where will solicitation/fund-raising activities be conducted: _____

    _____

    _____

8. Purpose of fund-raising efforts (what will funds be spent for): _____

    _____

    _____

9. Other: _____

    _____

NOTE: **1.** No solicitation or fund-raising activities may take place without this form being filled out and written approval being given by the Director of Athletics, the Dean, and the Vice President.

2. The individual responsible for the approved fund-raising activities shall be required to provide to the Athletic Director a full, typed fiscal accounting of the fund-raising activities within three (3) weeks following the close of the fund-raising activities. This will be shared with the the Dean and Vice President.

3. All funds raised shall be placed in the special athletic income account prior to a team attempting to expend funds raised through fund-raising activities. It is necessary for the Athletic Director to sign off.

4. Approval by the Athletic Director, Dean, and Vice President may contain specific restrictions that must be strictly adhered to by the individuals attempting to raise funds. For example, specific individuals, groups, and organizations may be "unapproachable."

5. Approval by the Athletic Director, Dean, and Vice President may be removed at any time.

6. Periodic reports to the Athletic Director (by the person responsible for the fund-raising activities) are expected and appreciated (this is to keep the Athletic Director aware of the progress of various outside and inside fund-raising activities by different teams/groups, etc.).

A. _____ Approved

_____ Disapproved

_____ Approved, with the following restrictions: _____

_____

Signed: _____

Director of Intercollegiate Athletics

B. _____ Approved

_____ Disapproved

_____ Approved with the following restrictions: _____

_____

Signed: _____

Dean

C. _____ Approved

_____ Disapproved

_____ Approved with the following restrictions: _____

_____

Signed: _____

Partial Listing of Corporations, Companies, and Businesses with Matching Gift Programs

American Airlines
Anheuser-Busch Cos., Inc.
Ashland Oil, Inc.
Avon Products, Inc.
Barnet Banks, Inc.
The Black & Decker Corp.
The Boeing Co.
Bristol-Myers Squibb Co.
Caterpillar Inc.
Chrysler Corp.
The Coca-Cola Co.
Cooper Tire & Rubber Co.
Corning Inc.
Delta Air Lines, Inc.
Digital Equipment Corp.
Dow Chemical U.S.A.
The Dun & Bradstreet Corp.
Jack Eckerd Corp.
Ford Motor Co.
Ford Motor Co. of Canada, Ltd.
H.B. Fuller Co.
Gannett Foundation
General Dynamics Corp.
General Electric Canada Inc.
General Electric Co.
General Foods, Inc.
General Mills, Inc.
General Motors Corp.
The BFGoodrich Co.
The Goodyear Tire & Rubber Co.
Hallmark Cards, Inc.
Harper & Row, Publishers, Inc.
Hartford Insurance Group
H.J. Heinz Co.
Hewlett-Packard Co.
Honeywell, Inc.

Huffy Corp.
Hughes Aircraft Co.
International Business Machines Corp.
  (IBM)
Johnson & Johnson
Jostens, Inc.
K Mart Corp.
Keebler Co.
Kellogg Co.
Kraft General Foods
Libbey-Owens Ford Co.
Eli Lilly and Co.
Mack Trucks, Inc.
Marine Corp.
Marine Midland Bank, N.A.
Mattel, Inc.
McDonald's Corp.
McDonnell Douglas Corp.
McGraw-Hill, Inc.
Merrill Lynch & Co., Inc.
Milton Bradley Co.
Mobil Oil Corp.
Monsanto Co.
Montgomery Ward & Co., Inc.
Motorola, Inc.
Mutual of Omaha
Nabisco Brands, Inc.
National Gypsum Co.
National Steel Corp.
Nationwide Mutual Insurance Co.
The New Yorker Magazine, Inc.
Newsweek, Inc.
North American Philips Corp.
Northwest Airlines, Inc.
Northwestern Mutual Life Insurance
The NutraSweet Co.

Occidental Oil and Gas Corp.
Occidental Petroleum Corp.
Outboard Marine Corp.
Owens-Corning Fiberglas Corp.
Owens-Illinois, Inc.
Paramount Communications Inc.
Pennzoil Co.
PepsiCo, Inc.
Philip Morris Cos., Inc.
Phillips Petroleum Co.
The Pillsbury Co.
Pitney Bowes Inc.
Playboy Enterprises, Inc.
Polaroid Corp.
Price Waterhouse
The Procter & Gamble Co.
The Prudential Insurance Co. of
  America
R.J.R. Nabisco, Inc.
Ralston Purina Co.
Revlon, Inc.
Reynolds Metals Co.
Rockwell International Corp.
Rubbermaid Inc.
Ryder System, Inc.
Sara Lee Corp.
Charles Schwab & Co.
Shaklee Corp.
Shell Oil Co.
The Sherwin-Williams Co.
Sonoco Products Co.
Sony Corp. of America
The Southland Corp.
Southwestern Bell Corp.
Spiegel, Inc.
State Farm Insurance Cos.

Sterling Drug Inc.
Subaru of America
Sun Co., Inc.
Super Valu Stores, Inc.
Tandy Corp.
Tenneco Inc.
Texas Instruments Inc.
Time Warner Inc.
Times Mirror

Transamerica Corp.
Travelers Express Co., Inc.
Treadway Cos., Inc.
USAir
USX Corp.
Union Pacific Corp.
United Parcel Service
United States Fidelty and Guaranty
    Corp.

The Upjohn Co.
The Washington Post Co.
Wausau Insurance Cos.
Wells Fargo Bank, N.A.
Westinghouse Electric Corp.
Whirlpool Corp.
Winn-Dixie Stores, Inc.
Xerox

Partial Listing of Fund-Raising Vendors and Suppliers

Allied Costumes, 1006 W. Fairbanks Avenue, Winter Park, Florida 32789. (407) 644–9112. [Mascots]

America's Best Chocolate, Inc., 689 Myrtle Avenue, Brooklyn, New York 11205. (212) 522–4500.

American Candy Manufacturing Co., 1106 Washington Street, P.O. Box 879, Selma, Alabama 36701. (205) 875–1450.

American Knitwear & Fabric Emblem Manufacturers, Chadwick Street, Plaistow, New Hampshire 03865. (603) 382–8509.

American Products Co. P.O. Box 1355, Albany, Georgia 31702. (912) 888–6903.

Artistic Greetings, Inc., 409 William Street, Elmira, New York 14901. (607) 733–5541.

Athletic Sportswear Program, Inc. 6742 N. Manlius Road, Kirkville, New York 13082. 1–800–448–4511. NY: 1–800–962–1480.

B-Craft Fund Raising Products, 5801 65th Avenue North, Minneapolis, Minnesota 55429. (612) 537–3000; (800) 328–3057.

Bazaar & Novelty, 185 Bridgeland Avenue, Toronto, Ontario, Canada M6A 1Y7. (416) 789–9626.

Bellevue Manufacturing Co., 214 South Riverview, Bellevue, Iowa 52031.

Benchmark Products, Inc., 208 Central Avenue, Mansfield, Ohio 44905. (419) 526–9417. [Edible and non-edible items]

Best Citrus of Florida, Inc., P.O. Box 333, Ft. Pierce, Florida 33454. (305) 465–0300; (800) 327–1554.

Button King Fund Raising, 753 North 89th, Seattle, Washington 98103. (206) 784–7240. [Makers of machines for making buttons]

Canteen Corporation, The Merchandise Mart, Chicago, Illinois 60654. (312) 661–7500.

Cherrydale Farms, Inc., Quakertown Road. M.R.2., P.O. Box 40, Pennsburg, Pennsylvania 18073.

Collegiate Concepts, Inc./International Collegiate Enterprises, Inc., 7041 Owensmouth Avenue, Suite 200, Canoga Park, California 91303. (818) 887–3400. [publishers of Directory & Buyers Guide, officially licensed collegiate products]

Creative School Promotions, P.O. Box 10833, St. Paul, Minnesota 55110.

Dramatic Publishing Company, 4150 North Milwaukee Avenue, Chicago, Illinois 60641.

Gold Medal Products Co., 1825 Freeman Avenue and 2001 Dalton Avenue, Cincinnati, Ohio 45214–2089. (513) 381–1313. [Popcorn and other foods]

Kathryn Beich Candies, 334 Paseo Sonrisa, Walnut, California 91789. (714) 594–0072

Nestle-Beich, 101 S. Lumbar, Bloomington, Illinois 61701. 1–800–431–1248. [Candy]

The Nestle Co. (Fund Raising Division), 1025 Westchester Avenue, White Plains, New York 10605. (916) 682–7455 [Candy]

Old Fashioned Candies, 6210 West Cermak Road, Berwyn, Illinois (708)788–6669.

Parkway Business Promotions, 315 Fifth Avenue, N. W., New Brighton, Minnesota 55112.

Pennsylvania Dutch Funnel Cake Co., P.O. Box 35, Sewell, New Jersey 08080. (609) 486–6100.

QSP, Inc. (a subsidiary of The Reader's Digest Association, Inc.). Box 2003, Ridgefield, Connecticut 06877. (203) 438–0361 and (800) 243–9902.

Rosemary Candy Co., 352 Niagara Street, Buffalo, New York 14201. (716) 845–5466.

Sports Decals, 365 East Terra Cotta, Crystal Lake, Illinois 60014. (800) 435–6110.

Stik-ees, 1011 Camino Del Mar, Suite 264, Del Mar, California 92014. (714) 755–0088. [Maker of window decals]

Stock Popcorn Co., Inc., 304 Vine Street, Lakeview, Iowa 51450. (712) 657–8746.

Super Patch–Clark Co., 4555 S. 300 W. #100, Murray, Utah 84107. (801) 262–8829.

The Three Jacks, 618 Azalea Road. P.O. Box 91460, Mobile, Alabama 36691. [Candy and non-edible items]

Tootsie Roll Industries, 7401 S. Cicero, Chicago, Illinois 60629. (312) 581–6100.

Valerie, Inc., P.O. Box 1125, Maywood, New Jersey 07607–9953. 1–800–222–3579. New Jersey 1–800–368–1772. [Candy]

WinCraft, Inc., 1205 East Sanborn St., P.O. Box 888, Winona, Minnesota 55987.

Wisconsin Premium Cheese, Inc., 728 South Third Street, La Crosse, Wisconsin 54601. (608) 782–1622

World's Finest Chocolate, 4801 S. Lawndale, Chicago, Illinois 60602. (312) 847–4600. [candy]

Mission Statement for the Intercollegiate Athletic Department at the State University of New York, Brockport

(approved by the President's Cabinet,
April 1, 1988)

The intercollegiate athletic program offers quality competitive sport experiences to eligible students and contributes to the activities of the college designed to promote pride in the institution and a common spirit among the college community. The program focuses on the education of student athletes and thus promotes the educational mission of the college.

The program is designed to support fully the educational experiences enjoyed by the student athletes, whether competing for a national championship, a regional title, or other goals established by the coaches and teams. The program reflects the common concern for mastery and excellence in performance and on the theories which contribute to them. Accordingly, student athletes receive the support, credit, services, and instructions and facilities appropriate to the demands and values of a quality educational experience.

The athletic program offers student athletes a multitude of opportunities for participation. Competition is at the NCAA Division III level; men's and women's teams compete in the NCAA and SUNYAC and, in addition, women's teams compete and belong to the NYSWCAA. The college holds membership in the Eastern Collegiate Athletic Asso-ciation (ECAC). Competition schedules are designed which are comparable and challenging for the student athletes participating in the various sports; and the sports offered are evenly divided between women's and men's teams. Intercollegiate athletics provide a wide variety of individual and team sports during fall, winter, and spring seasons. The intercollegiate athletic program contributes to the general mission of the college by providing instruction in the disciplines, practices and principles essential to excellence in performance and by providing student athletes opportunities to demonstrate their understanding and accomplishments in public contests as representatives of SUNY College at Brockport. In its efforts to attract and retain well-motivated students, the college, through its intercollegiate athletic program, contributes to the campus an environment conducive to learning for the entire college community.

Submitted to the President on February, 1988 by:
Dr. William F. Stier, Jr.
Athletic Director
Professor of Physical Education and Sport
State University of New York, Brockport 14420

H Related Organizations—Fund-Raising Information Resources

Americal Alliance for Health, Physical Education, Recreation and Dance
1900 Association Drive
Reston, Virginia 22091
(703) 476–3400

American Association for Corporate Contributions
P.O. Box 6401
Evanston, Illinois 60204

American Association of Fundraising Councils, Inc.
500 Fifth Avenue
New York, New York 10036

American Football Coaches Association
7758 Wallace Road, Suite 1
Orlando, Florida 32819

American Sports Education Institute (A.S.E.I.)—Boosters Club of America
200 Castlewood Drive
North Palm Beach, Florida 33408
(407) 842–3600

Association of Collegiate Licensing Administrators (ACLA)
216 MSU Union
Michigan State University
East Lansing, Michigan 48824
(517) 355–3434

Athletic Fundraisers of America
P.O. Box 1611
Clemson, South Carolina 29633
803–656–2115

Athletes in Action
4790 Irvine Blvd. #105–325
Irvine, California 92714

Athletic Institute
200 N. Castlewood Drive
North Palm Beach, Florida 33408
(305) 842–3600

Athletic Congress
200 South Capitol Avenue
Suite 140
Indianapolis, Indiana 46225

Babe Ruth League, Inc.
P.O. Box 5000
1770 Brunswick Avenue
Trenton, New Jersey 08638
(609) 695–1434

Basketball Hall of Fame
1150 W. Columbus Avenue
P.O. Box 179
Springfield, Massachusetts 01101–0179

Bingo King Company
P.O. Box 2499
Littleton, Colorado 80161

Boosters Clubs of America/American Sports Education Institute
200 Castlewood Drive
North Palm Beach, Florida 33408
(407) 842–3600

Buckeye Donkey Ball Company
  c/o Jack Spicer
  P.O. Box 314
  Westerville, Ohio 43081

Champion Licensing Division
  P.O. Box 850
  Rochester, New York 14603
  (716) 385–3645

Collegiate Commissioners Association
  1111 Plaza Drive
  Schaumburg, Illinois 60173–4990

Collegiate Licensing Co.
  320 Interstate North
  Suite 102
  Atlanta, Georgia 30339
  (404) 956–0520

College Division Commissioners Association
  2013 Cummingham Drive
  Suite 241
  Hampton, Virginia 23666

College Sports Information Directors of America
  Box 114
  Texas A & I University
  Kingsville, Texas 78363

Crossland Enterprises, Inc.
  International Licensing
  1110 Eugenia Place
  Carpinteria, California 93013
  (805) 566–6600

The Council on Foundations
  1828 L. Street, N.W.
  Washington, DC 20036

Crosby Donkey Ball, Inc.
  c/o Fred Crosby
  P.O. Box 458
  Chippewa Falls, Wisconsin 54729
  800–826–7108 or 715–382–4204

Drum Corps Sights and Sounds, Inc.
  P.O. Box 8052
  Madison, Wisconsin 53708

The Fundraising Institute
  P.O. Box 365
  Ambier, Pennsylvania 19002
  215–628–8729

Fundraising Unlimited
  12861 West St. #49
  Garden Grove, California 92640
  (714) 530–2262
  (714) 537–3878

The Foundation Center
  79 Fifth Avenue, Eighth Floor
  New York, New York 10003

Gifts In Kind America
  700 North Fairfax Street
  Suite 300
  Alexandria, Virginia 22314
  (703) 836–2121

Grantsmanship Center
  P.O. Box 15072
  Los Angeles, California 90015

Great American Opportunities, Inc.
  P.O. Box 305142
  Nashville, Tennessee 37230–9969

International Olympic Committee
  Chateau de Vidy
  Ch-1007 Lausanne
  Switzerland

Licensing Corporation of America
  75 Rockfeller Plaza
  New York, New York 10019
  (212) 484–8807

Licensing Industry Merchandisers' Association
  (LIMA)
  350 Fifth Avenue, Suite 6210
  New York, New York 10118
  (212) 244–1944

Little League Baseball, Inc.
  P.O. Box 3485
  Williamsport, Pennsylvania 17701
  (717) 326–1921

Merchandising Rights Agency, LTD.
201 East 42nd Street
New York, New York 10017

MLB Properties
350 Park Avenue
New York, New York 10022
(212) 371–7800

Myers Stevens
2390 E. Orangewood Avenue
Suite 480
Anaheim, California 92806–6176.
Insurance Specialists for Booster
clubs—Coverage Packages.

National Association of Athletic Marketing, and
Development Directors
c/o Mike Palmisano
1522 High Hollow
Ann Arbor, Michigan 48103

National Association of Collegiate Directors of
Athletics (NACDA)
Director's House
1229 Smith Court
Cleveland, Ohio 44116
(216) 331–5773

National Association of Concessionaires
35 E. Wacker Drive, #1849
Chicago, Illinois 60601

National Association of Intercollegiate Athletics
1221 Baltimore Street
Kansas City, Missouri 64105
(816) 842–5050

National Association of State High School
Associations
P.O. Box 20626
Kansas City, Missouri 64195

National Christian College Athletic Association
P.O. Box 1312
Marion, Indiana
(317) 674–8401

National Collegiate Athletic Association
6201 College Blvd.
Overland Park, Kansas 66211–2422
(913) 339–1906

National Collegiate Athletic Association
P.O. Box 1906
Mission, Kansas 66201

National Conference for Athletic Fundraisers
P.O. Box 26202
Fresno, California 93729
(209) 436–0149
P.O. Box 4783
San Jose, California 95125
(408) 265–3141

National Federation of Interscholastic Coaches
Association
P.O. Box 20630
Kansas City, Missouri 64195
(816) 464–5400

National High School Athletic Coaches Association
P.O. Box 941329
Maitland, Florida 32794
(407) 628–8555

National Interscholastic Athletic Administrators
Association
P.O. Box 20626
Kansas City, Missouri 64156
(816) 464–5400

National Junior College Athletic Association
P.O. Box 7305
Colorado Springs, Colorado 80933
(719) 590–9788

National Small College Athletic Association
1884 College Heights
New Ulm, Minnesota 56073
(507) 359–9791

The National Society of Fundraising Executives
Suite 831, 1511 ''K'' Street, N.W.
Washington, DC 20005

National Sporting Goods Association
1699 Wall Street
Mt. Prospect, Illinois 60056
(312) 439–4000

Public Management Institute
358 Brannan Street
San Francisco, California 84107

Road Runners Club of America
629 S. Washington St.
Alexandria, Virginia 22314
(703) 836–0558

Royale HouseInc
P.O. Box 606
Racine, Wisconsin 53401
(800) 545–4141, extension 338.
Fund-raising bricks and tiles for walkways.

Royal Publishing, Inc.
3406 N. E. Adams Street
Peoria, Illinois 61603–9990

Samuel French Inc.
7643 Sunset Boulevard
Hollywood, California 90046

The Society for Non-Profit Organizations
6314 Odana Road, Suite 1
Madison, Wisconsin 53719

SCA Promotions
8300 Douglas Avenue, Ste. 625
Dallas, Texas 75225
(800) 527–5409
Provides bonded guarantees, funding of contingent prizes for half-time, and special sports promotions, including many types of contests, sweepstakes, and fund-raising.

Special Olympics (International Headquarters)
1350 New York Avenue, NW
Suite 500
Washington, DC 20005

Sporting Goods **Manufacturers** Association
200 Castlewood **Drive**
North Palm Beach, Florida 33408
(305) 842–4100

Sports and the Courts
P.O. Box 2836
Winston-Salem, **North** Carolina 27102
(919) 725–0583

United States Trademark Association (USTA)
6 East 45th Street
New York, New **York** 10017
(212) 986–5880

University Licensing Programs
216 MSU Union
Michigan State University
East Lansing, Michigan 48824
(517) 355–3434

The Taft Group
5130 MacArthur Boulevard
Washington, DC 20016

Tailgator Enterprises, Inc.
P.O. Box 39539
Redford, Michigan 48239
(313) 349–2717
Publishers of *Tailgate Party Books*

U.S. Olympic Committee
1750 East Boulder Street
Colorado Springs, Colorado 80909

Suggested Articles, Books, and Publications

Articles and Books

Alberti, C., Macko, G. & Witcomb, N. (1982). *Money-Makers: A systematic approach to special events fund-raising.* Ambler, PA: Whitcomb Associates.

Bayley, R. (1988). *The fund-raisers guide to successful campaigns.* New York: McGraw-Hill, Inc.

Berg, R. (1990, September). Marketing black college sports. *Athletic Business. pp. 28, 34.*

Brentling, M. & Weiss, J. (1987). *The ultimate benefit book.* Cleveland, Ohio: Octavia Press.

Brody, R. & Goodman, M. (1988). *Fund-raising events.* New York: Human Sciences Press, Inc.

Brooks, Ce. (1990, December). Sponsorship by design. *Athletic Business. pp. 58–61.*

Button, S. (1982, December). You gotta have a gimick. *Money,* pp. 171–174.

Cohen, A. (1991, May). Concessions come of age. *Athletic Business.* pp. 61–62, 64.

Cutlip, S. M., Center, A. H. & Broom, G. M. (1985). *Effective public relations.* (6th ed.). Englewood Cliffs, NJ: Prentice-Hall.

Davis, N. & Nickelsberg, B. (1988, November). Fund-raising success: Knowing why people give. Vol. 40, *Association Management,* pp. 120–129.

DeSoto, C. (1983). *For fun and funds: Creative fund raising ideas for your organization.* Parker Publishing Company.

Directory and Buyer's Guide. (1989 or latest edition). Canoga Park, CA: Collegiate Concepts, Inc./International Collegiate Enterprises, Inc.

Dunn, T. (1988). *How to shake the new money tree: Creative fund-raising for today's non-profit organizations.* New York: Penguin.

8 ways to turn yourself into a super fund-raiser. (1991, March). *Glamour,* Vol. 79, p. 43.

Ellyn, W. (1988, May-June). Dialing and dancing for dollars: Fund-raising techniques for nonprofit organizations. *Executive Female,* pp. 10–11.

Emond, L. (1987, November-December). Volunteers and funding—Rare commodities. *Management Accounting Magazine,* pp. 46–52.

Freeman, D. (1987, June). Ethical considerations in fund-raising. *Fund Raising Management,* pp. 72–77.

Ferguson, M. (ed). (1990, November). Sports marketing. *Athletic Business. pp. 18–19.*

Ferguson, M. (ed). (1990, September). Purdue retains marketing firm to check the menu. *Athletic Business. p. 22.*

Fund-raising manual. (1981). Mission, Kansas: National Collegiate Athletic Association.

Galowich, R. & Lynne, S. (1985, August). The do's & don'ts of telethons—A primer. *Fund-raising Management,* pp. 38–43.

Georgi, C. (1985). *Fund-raising grants and foundations: A comprehensive bibliography.* Littleton, Colorado: Libraries Unlimited.

Give to get. (1986, October). *Athletic Business.* p. 25.

Gleenon, M. (1986). Fund-raising in small colleges: Strategies for success. *Planning for Higher Education, 14*(3), pp. 16–29.

Goodale, T. (1987, January). Teaching volunteers the art of asking. *Fund Raising Management,* pp. 32–36.

Goodale, T. (1988, December). Cultivation of the prospect. *Fund Raising Management,* p. 74.

Gordon, A. (1967). *Techniques of successful fund-raising.* Hicksville, New York: Exposition Press.

Great fund-raising ideas. (1988, October 15). *Woman's Day,* pp. 112–115.

Greene, E. (1988, July). Fund-raising at a disco: Many colleges find success with special appeals aimed just at young alumni. *Chronicle of higher Education, 34*(43), pp. A1, 12.

Gurin, M. (1987, June). The changing capital campaign. *Fund Raising Management,* pp. 28–35.

Helitzer, M. (1992). *The dream job—Sport$ publicity, promotion & public relations.* Athens, Ohio: University Sports Press, Inc.

Hemmings, R. L. (1989, January). Creating the direct mail package. *Fund Raising Management,* pp. 38–40.

Herschell, G. L. (1989, May). How to write powerful letters. *Fund Raising Management,* pp. 36, 38, 77.

Horn, M. & Brophy, B. (1986, August 25). For alumni the checks stop here. *U.S. News and World Report,* pp. 54–55.

Hovorka, R. & Ostermeyer, E. (1989, February). Planning for your future through planned giving. *Fund Raising Management,* pp. 40–46.

How to raise funds for a good cause. (1983, May). *Sunset,* pp. 158–161.

How to raise money for worthy causes. (1987, December). *Sunset,* pp. 45–47.

Hubbard, R. (1985, June). Ham on regal. *Phi-Delta-Kappan,* pp. 717–719.

Huntsinger, J. (1985). *Fund-raising letters: A comprehensive guide to raising money by direct reponse marketing.* Richmond, VA: Emerson Publishers.

Irwin, R. (1991, January). *College Athletic Management* (CAM). *III*(1), pp. 18–22.

Kotler, p. (1984). *Marketing management: Analysis, planning and control.* Englewood Cliffs, NJ: Prentice-Hall.

Kotler, P., & Andreasen, A. R. (1987). *Strategic marketing for nonprofit organizations.* NJ: Prentice-Hall.

Kotler, P., & Fox, K. F. A. (1985). *Strategic marketing for educational institutions.* NJ: Prentice-Hall.

Kluka, D. A., and Mitchell, Carolyn B. (1990) Capturing the essence of physical education and sport programs. *JOPERD. 61*(1), pp. 36–40.

Leslie, C. (1988, September 5). Prospecting for alumni gold: America's colleges go begging in high style. *Newsweek,* pp. 66–68.

Levine, A. (1988, April 11). The hard sell behind the ivy. *U.S. News & World Report,* pp. 54–56.

Lewis, G. and Appenzeller, H. (1985). *Successful Sport Management.* Charlottesville, Virginia: The Michie Company.

Lord, J. (1984). *The raising of money—Thirty-Five essentials every trustee should know.* Cleveland, Ohio: Third Sector Press.

Luskin, B. & Warren, I. (1985, June). Strategies for generating new financial resources. *New Directors for Community Colleges,* pp. 73–85.

Marciani, L. (1991, May). Mining for division II gold. *Athletic Business.* pp. 49–52.

March, P. (1988, May). 12 mailing list "Musts" for donor appeals. *Fund Raising Management,* pp. 50–55.

Mason, B., Byrd, R., Jonas, G., Sims, W., Ecton, V. & Edley, C. (1982, May) How to raise funds for a cause. *Black Enterprise,* pp. 51–55.

Mason, J. & Paul, J. (1988). *Modern sports administration.* Englewood Cliffs, N. J.: Prentice Hall.

Moore, D. B. and Gray, D. P. (1990, January). Marketing—The blueprint for successful physical education. *JOPERD. 61*(1), pp. 23–26.

Mulford, C. (1984). *Guide to student fund-raising.* Reston, VA: Future Homemakers of America.

Naisbitt, J. (1983). *Megatrends.* NY: Warner books, Inc.

Nardone, L. (1986). *The identification and comparison of the fund-raising practices of athletic administrators in division I, II, and III institutions.* Temple University, Thesis.

NCAA Promotion Manual. (1980). Mission, Kansas: National Collegiate Athletic Association.

Nicklin, W. (1986, October). Raising money the old-fashioned way. *Folio: The Magazine for Financial Management,* pp. 246–247.

Olcott, W. (1988, May). Taking care of America: 50 years of philanthropy. *Direct Marketing,* pp. 98–101.

Parkhouse, B. (ed.). (1991). *The management of sport—Its foundation and application.* St. Louis, Missouri: Mosby Year Book.

Parks, B. and Zanger, B. (1990). *Sport and fitness management—Career & strategies and professional content.* Champaign, Il: Human Kinetics.

Plawin, P. and Spellman, L. (1988, August). The fine art of fund-raising. Volume 42, *Changing Times,* pp. 71–72.

Plinio, A. (1986, May). Business leaders take long look at fund-raising dinners. *Fund Raising Management,* pp. 86–88.

Public Relations and Promotions Guidelines. (1987). Mission, Kansas: NCAA.

Ross, D. (1985). *Fund-raising for youth.* Meriwether Publishers.

Schinner, M. (1989). Establishing a collegiate trademark licensing program: To what extent does an institution have an exclusive right to its name? *15 Journal of College and University Law,* pp. 405, 425.

Shirley, C. (1988). Another good idea to put on your fund-raising list. *Florida,* pp. 18–19.

Schnieter, P. (1978). *The art of asking: A handbook of successful fund-raising.* New York: Walker.

Schneiter, P. and Nelson, D. (1984). *The thirteen most common fund-raising mistakes.* Washington, D.C.: Taft Corporation.

Small, J. (1988, March). Is an auction in your future? *Fund-raising Management,* pp. 56–60.

Small, J. (1987, November). Benefit auctions: Raising the bid. *Association Management,* pp. 70–74.

Smith, C. (1984). *How to increase corporate giving to your organization.* San Francisco: Public Management Institute.

SportsMarket Place 1992. (1991). P.O. Box 1417, Princeton, NJ: Sportsguide, Inc.

Stephens, P. (1986, October). Universities find a new partner. *World Press Review,* p. 37.

Strazewski, L. (1987, July 27). Non-Profits learn long-term lesson. (Special Report: Direct Marketing). *Advertising Age,* pp. 51–54.

Sutton, W. A. (1987). Developing an initial marketing plan for intercollegiate athletic programs. *Journal of Sport Management. 1*(2), 146–158.

Tailgate Club—Success Guide. (1985). Deerfield, Illinois: Sports Graphics.

Takeshita, C. (1988). Wait until next year. *Athletic Trainer,* p. 60.

Toree, R. (1988). *Direct mail fund-raising: Letters that work.* Planum Press.

Tritsch, P. (1986, April). Hiring a foundation fund-raiser. *Association Management,* pp. 109–112.

USTA (1985). *USTA guide to fund-raising for community tennis associations.* Princeton, N.J.: USTA Education and Research Center.

Vanderzwaag, H. (1984). *Sport management in schools and colleges.* New York: John Wiley and Sons.

Warner, I. (1975). *The art of fund-raising.* New York: Harper and Row.

Wegs, M. (1990). Successful capital campaigns. *Athletic Director. 7*(4), pp. 22–23, 25.

Weiss, J. & Brentlinger, M. (1987). *The ultimate benefit book:How to raise $50,000–plus for your organization.* Cleveland, Ohio: Octovia.

Wilker, L. (1979). *Fund-raising,* Wisconsin: Association of College, University and Community Arts Administrators.

Woodruff, B. (1983, July-August). World's fastest fund-raisers: Savvy and sagacious support-seekers show stupendous speed of solicitation. *CASE Currents,* pp. 16–18.

Wong, G. (1986). Recent trademark law cases involving professional and intercollegiate sports. *1 Detroit College of Law Review,* pp. 87, 89.

Wong, G. M. & Barr, C. (June, 1991). Sports licensing gets a boost from Carolina case. *Athletic Business.* pp. 18–19.

Yow, D. A. (1991). The Methods of Marketing. *College Athletic Management* (CAM), *III*(4), pp. 22–26.

Publications

Athletic Administration
P.O. Box 16428
Cleveland, Ohio 44116

Athletic Management
438 West State Street
Ithaca, New York 14850

Scholastic Coach
730 Broadway
New York, New York 10003–9538

Athletic Business
1842 Hoffman **Street**
Suite 201
Madison, Wisconsin 53704

Club Industry
Sportscape, Inc.
1415 Beacon Street
C 9122
Brookline, Massachussetts 02146

Grass Roots Fund-raising Journal
P.O. Box 14754
San Francisco, California 94114

Fund-raising Management
Hoke Communications, Inc.
224 Seventh Street
Garden City, New York 11530
(516) 746–6700

Journal of Sport Management
Human Kinetics Publishers
Champaign, Illinois 61820
(217) 351–5076

JUCO Review
P.O. Box 7305
Colorado Springs, Colorado 80933
(719) 590–9788

Sporting Goods Business
1515 Broadway
New York, New York 10036
(212) 869–1300

The Sporting Goods Dealer
1212 N. Lindbergh Blvd.
St. Louis, Missouri 63166
(314) 439–4000

SportsMarketplace
Sportsguide, Inc.
P.O. Box 1417
Princeton, New Jersey 08542

Sports Marketing News
Technical Marketing Corporation
1460 Post Road East
Westport, Connecticut 06880

Sports Trend
180 Allen Rd.
Suite 300, South Building
N.E. Atlanta, Georgia 30328
(404) 252–8831

Sports Style
7 East 12th St.
New York, New York 10003
(212) 741–5976

Standard and Poor's Register of Corporations,
Directors and Executives
25 Broadway
New York, New York 10004
(212) 208–8702

Stitches Magazine
5951 S. Middlefield Rd.
Littleton, Colorado 80123
(303) 798–1274

Team Marketing Report
1147 W. Ohio
Suite 506
Chicago, Illinois 60622
(312) 829–7060

Texas Coach
P.O. Drawer 14627
Austin, Texas 78761
(517) 454–6709

Wear Magazine
P.O. Box 740995
Dallas, Texas 75374
(214) 361–2200

Examples of Team Logos